A Paralegal Primer

Second Edition

By Scott A. Hatch, J.D.
and Lisa Zimmer Hatch

The Center for Legal Studies
Golden, Colorado *Los Angeles* *Kailua-Kona, Hawaii*

Forbes
CUSTOM PUBLISHING
60 FIFTH AVE • NEW YORK, NY • 10011

For Zachary, Zoe, Alison, and Andrew Hatch and the future of law.

For information regarding Paralegal Certificate Courses, Legal Investigation Certificate Courses, Legal Secetary Certificate Courses, Victim's Advocacy Certificate Courses, Alternative Dispute Resolution Certificate Courses, and Sandardized Test Preparation Courses, please call The Center for Legal Studies at 303–526–9777 or toll free at 1–800–522–7737.

CIP Data is available
Printed in the United States of America
10 9 8 7 6 5 4 3 2 1

ISBN 0–8281–1314–9

PREFACE

This book may be used in conjunction with a course of paralegal studies or as a self-tutorial and, when coupled with *Paralegal Procedures and Practices*, is designed to quickly and efficiently train paralegals to assist their firms in initiating lawsuits, investigating facts, interviewing clients and witnesses, preparing legal documents, digesting discovery, and conducting manual and computer-assisted legal research. The book also discusses law office ethics, torts and contracts, the rules of civil procedure and evidence, and job hunting techniques. This book also assists those who embark upon *pro se* litigation.

The paralegal profession is very young, very exciting, and very intellectually stimulating, and the roles and duties of paralegals are continually evolving. Therefore, paralegals must maintain an awareness of the changing laws and ethical decisions that affect their careers. The movement to provide limited licensure for paralegals is especially exciting since it recognizes the exceptional value of paralegal services. With a firm adherence to ethics and thorough training and experience, paralegals can perform most of the pretrial duties of attorneys, except for setting fees, providing legal advice, and arguing a case before a jury, in a much more cost-efficient manner.

Acknowledgements

The authors wish to acknowledge the input of the thousands of successful paralegal students who, since 1980, have graduated from their classes at universities throughout the United States and who have contributed to the information used in preparing this book. Paralegal instructor, Kirk Hanson, and attorney and instructor, David Dougherty, have been especially helpful in providing information for this book.

TABLE OF CONTENTS

FUNDAMENTAL LEGAL TERMS

Most of the following terms will be discussed throughout this book in various contexts. General definitions are provided after each term, and paralegals should understand these definitions for use in their work. Unfamiliar Latin and other non-English terms are distinguished by italics and should be italicized or underlined when written. Dictionaries such as *Black's Law Dictionary*, *Ballentine's Legal Dictionary and Thesaurus*, and *Words and Phrases* should always be consulted when the paralegal encounters terms that are not set forth on this list.

acquittal. An acquittal is a finding of not guilty, an absolution of guilt, or a verdict of not guilty made by a jury.

action. A lawsuit brought in court is termed an action.

additur**.** This is an additional amount of money conferred by the judge to the damage award provided by the jury. The judge will tell the winning party that a new trial will be granted unless the party agrees to add an amount to the damage award. An *additur* should be distinguished from a *remittitur*, which is discussed later.

ad damnum**.** This is a statement in the complaint where the plaintiff claims the right to receive a sum of money as damages. Also known as a "prayer for relief" or "wherefore" clause, it is usually the last paragraph before the attorney's subscription.

adjourn. This means to end or postpone to a later time.

administrative agency. These agencies of the executive branch of government carry out statutes and executive orders. Paralegals may often represent clients at agency hearings under the authority of the Administrative Procedure Act, 5 U.S.C. §555 (1967).

administrative regulations. These regulations bind agencies and the public in certain areas. They consist of the rules of an administrative agency designed to explain and carry out the statutes and executive orders that govern the agency.

admissible evidence. Evidence that has been declared admissible by the judge for use in the action is admissible evidence. Admissible evidence is evidence that has been admitted for consideration regarding its truth or falsity by the judge or jury.

admission and denial. After the defendant reads the facts alleged to be true by the plaintiff in the complaint, the defendant prepares and files an answer in which he or she may decide to admit the truth of some of the facts and deny the truth of others. When in doubt, the defendant often states that he or she "is without sufficient information in which to admit or deny the allegation and therefore denies same."

admission. An out-of-court statement made by a party to the litigation that is inconsistent with the position the party is adopting in the litigation is termed an admission. An admission constitutes an exception to the hearsay rule, which has the effect of making such statements admissible. For example, Jacob sues Samantha for injuries that he sustained when the car that Samantha was driving hit him while he was crossing the street. At the time of the accident, Samantha admitted to Jacob that she sped up to beat the red stoplight and did not see him in the crosswalk. Then at trial, Samantha alleges that she had seen Jacob in the crosswalk but could not stop since her brakes failed. Samantha's prior admission to Jacob that she sped up and did not see him would be admissible hearsay as an admission by the party, who is Samantha.

adversarial hearing. A hearing where both parties are present to argue their respective positions is an adversarial hearing. This allows both sides in the controversy a chance to be heard and represents the essence of the American system of justice. The adversarial system places the burden of proving or disproving legal arguments upon the parties in the litigation process rather than on the judge.

adverse judgment. This is a judgment or decision against the party whom you and your attorney represent.

affiant. A person who swears or affirms under penalty of perjury to the truthfulness of a written statement is an affiant. An affiant is the person who signs an affidavit. Remember that courts appreciate affidavits since the parties are making representations under oath and the penalty of perjury.

affidavit. A written statement of fact that the affiant swears or affirms is true is an affidavit. Affidavits are sworn to under penalty of perjury or are affirmed by those who do not swear under oath.

affidavit of service. A written statement sworn to by the affiant that states that a party has been served with papers and stating the time and place details of the service is called an affidavit of service. This document is usually notarized and returned to the court after service has been effectuated.

affirm. To uphold or establish is to affirm.

affirmative defenses. These are new factual allegations raised by the defendant against the plaintiff that were not contained in the plaintiff's complaint. Affirmative defenses are usually contained in the defendant's answer to the plaintiff's complaint. Common examples of affirmative defenses are contributory negligence, assumption of the risk, and failure to state a claim upon which relief can be granted.

allegation. An assertion, representation, or averment is an allegation.

alternate. An alternate is an extra juror who sits with the regular jurors and who may take the place of a regular juror if one becomes incapacitated during the trial.

answer. This is the pleading filed by the defendant responding to or answering the allegations of the plaintiff's complaint. An answer may also contain defendant's affirmative defenses, cross-claims, and counterclaims.

appeal. An application to a higher court to correct or modify the judgment of a lower court is an appeal. Appellate courts are traditionally supreme courts and courts of appeals.

appeal as a matter of right. When an appeal is a matter of right, the appellate court has no discretion as to whether to hear the appeal and is thus required to review the lower court's decision, as in capital punishment cases.

appearance. A party enters an appearance when that party appears in court, whether as plaintiff or defendant, or when that party files a document called a notice of appearance. In a general appearance the party is voluntarily submitting to the court's jurisdiction, and in a special appearance the party is entering court only to object to the court's attempted exercise of jurisdiction. If a party appears in court without an attorney, the party appears *pro se*.

appellant. The party initiating the appeal is called the appellant. Traditionally, the party that lost in the trial court becomes the appellant before the appellate court.

appellate brief. An appellate brief consists of a written argument presented to the appeals court by the appellant indicating the issues on appeal and the positions of the appellant on those issues relating to the claimed errors and improprieties that occurred during the trial. Alleged trial court errors of interpretation and application of law provide the basis for the appeal.

appellate court. An appellate court is a higher court within the same judicial system as the trial court that hears the appeal from the trial court.

appellate jurisdiction. The power of a superior, appellate, court to review and modify the decision made by an inferior, trial, court is appellate jurisdiction.

appellee. The party against whom the appeal is brought is the appellee. Traditionally the party that was victorious in the trial court action is the appellee.

arbitration. The submission of a controversy to the judgment of another whose decision may then be binding on both parties is arbitration. Arbitration is one of many alternatives to litigation.

arraignment. A court proceeding in which the defendant is advised of the charges and is required to enter a plea admitting or denying the offenses is an arraignment.

arrest. The seizing of a person and the detaining of that person in custody by lawful authority constitutes an arrest of that person.

assigned counsel. The attorney appointed to represent an indigent defendant in a criminal action is an assigned counsel. Each state and county usually has indigency standards based upon a party's income, assets, and liabilities.

attorney-client privilege. Under the attorney-client privilege, a client can refuse to disclose any confidential communication made with the client's attorney that relates to legal services. Also, the attorney cannot disclose the communication without the permission of the client.

attorney of record. The attorney who has filed a notice of appearance and who is then listed in the court records is the attorney of record for a party.

attorney work product. Attorney work product is material collected and prepared for a case by counsel that is not subject to disclosure through discovery by opposing counsel. Examples of material that is generally protected by the attorney work product rule include correspondence between the attorney and client as well as interoffice legal research memos and the trial notebook.

authentication. An authentication is an attestation made by the proper officer through which the officer certifies that a record is in due form of law and that the person who certifies it is the officer appointed to do so.

bail. The property or sum of money deposited with the clerk of court to insure that the defendant will reappear in court at future designated times constitutes the defendant's bail. The bail is generally returned to the defendant if the defendant satisfies the conditions of the bail.

bar. An organization responsible for promulgating rules regarding attorneys is a bar association, such as the American Bar Association. Attorneys collectively are called the bar, and judges collectively are called the bench.

below. An inferior or lower court is the court below the appellate court.

bench. The judges collectively constitute the bench.

bench conference. A discussion between the judge and the attorneys held at the bench so that the jury cannot hear what is discussed is a bench conference. During these conferences the parties primarily discuss evidentiary issues, and the conferences are usually conducted off the record, meaning that the court reporter does not take notes of the bench conference.

best evidence rule. Under the best evidence rule, which is applied to documents introduced as evidence at trial, the original document should be produced unless it is shown to be unavailable for some reason other than the fault of the proponent of that evidence. For example, in an action for a breach of an apartment lease, the original lease must be produced so as to free this evidence from speculation of having been altered.

beyond a reasonable doubt. The degree of proof required of the state in a criminal prosecution is defined as beyond a reasonable doubt. Reasonable doubt is considered as fair doubt and not imaginable doubt and is usually measured by 100% agreement on the part of the jury.

bias. Bias is the potential for a judge, juror, or party to make unfair judgments because of prior knowledge of or involvement with a case resulting in possible preconceptions and a lack of open-mindedness.

bill of particulars. A bill of particulars is a formal motion or request made to a party requesting greater factual detail about some aspect of the pleadings. Similar to a motion for more definite statement, a bill of particulars is designed to assist the defendant in preparing an answer to the complaint.

body of the complaint. The portion of the pleading where the claims, or causes of action, of the plaintiff are presented is called the body of the complaint.

boilerplate language. Boilerplate language is too often found in legal writing and includes terms such as "wherefore," "hereinafter," and other superfluous language.

bond. A sum of money deposited with the court to assure compliance with some requirement is a bond. The premium necessary to procure a bond is usually 10%-15% of the face amount of the bond in either a criminal or civil action.

brief. A brief is most commonly a written argument presented to the court by a party in support of a motion. A trial brief consists of legal arguments submitted to the trial court, and an appellate brief is filed with the appellate court and contains arguments regarding the trial court's improper application of law.

brief of a case. A brief of a case, also known as a brief of an opinion, is a synthesis of the major elements of the case. A case brief usually includes a brief statement of the essential facts, a listing of the issues, the resolution of those issues, the holding, and the subsequent procedural history. Paralegals and law clerks frequently brief cases for their supervising attorneys.

burden of proof. The responsibility of proving something at trial is the burden of proof. Generally, the party making an allegation has the burden of proving that allegation. For instance, in a criminal case, the prosecutor has the burden of proving beyond a reasonable doubt that the accused committed the crime charged. In a civil proceeding, the plaintiff has the burden of proving by a preponderance of the evidence that the defendant caused plaintiff's harm.

business entries. A business entry is an out-of-court entry made in a business record that is compiled in the regular course of business by someone whose duty it is to make such entries. Business entries constitute admissible hearsay; examples include nurse's notes, accountant's records, and automobile maintenance records made by mechanics.

caption of pleading. The heading of the pleading is also called the caption of the pleading. It should contain the name of the court, the names of the parties, and the docket number that will be assigned by the court.

cause of action. A cause of action, also known as a claim for relief, is a legally acceptable reason for suing.

challenge for cause. A challenge for cause is a party's request to a judge that a certain prospective juror not be allowed to be a member of the jury because of specified reasons or causes such as bias. These challenges are unlimited in number as long as the party requesting the challenge is able to demonstrate to the judge that the prospective juror has knowledge of the parties to the suit, or is involved in a business which is represented in the litigation. Thus, a police officer is usually excluded from sitting on a jury in a criminal case under a challenge for cause.

challenge to the array. A challenge to the array of the jury is usually an initial challenge to the selection process and composition of the jury pool. Often when the jury pool does not reflect the ethnic composition of a community, a successful challenge to the array can be brought so that a new jury pool is summoned for duty.

charge to jury. The jury charge consists of instructions that describe the standards that the jury should apply in reaching its verdict.

charter. The law of a municipality or other local unit of government authorizing it to perform designated governmental functions is the municipality's charter.

choice of venue. Choice of venue involves deciding the fairest place for trial. An impartial venue can help in assuring due process at trial, and the defendant usually requests a change of venue if, for example, there exists too much pretrial publicity.

circumstantial evidence. This is evidence of one fact from which another fact can be inferred, and even though it can be admissible, circumstantial evidence is less persuasive than direct evidence. For instance, an automobile's fifty feet of skid marks preceding the point of its impact with a bus is circumstantial evidence of the automobile's speed based on the direct evidence of the skid marks on the road.

civil law. The legal means by which the rights and remedies of private individuals are enforced and protected is the purpose of civil law. Crime is not an issue for civil law, and the responsibility of pursuing a civil damage remedy rests with the person harmed.

civil suit. A civil action is a civil suit. This procedure enforces rights and redresses wrongs in the civil arena.

clergy-penitent privilege. A penitent can refuse to disclose any confidential communication with his/her cleric relating to spiritual counseling or consultation. Neither can disclose information without the other's consent.

clerk. An officer of the court who files pleadings, motions, orders, and judgments, issues process, and keeps the records of legal proceedings is the clerk.

closing statements or arguments. Closing arguments are the final statements made by the attorneys to summarize the evidence they think they have established and the evidence they think the other side has failed to establish.

codefendant. Codefendants are multiple defendants who are being sued in the same litigation.

collection of judgment. Effectuation and enforcement of the decision of the court is collection of the judgment, which is often the most difficult aspect of litigation.

competency. Competency is defined as legal capacity to testify and is determined by a witness' having (1) an understanding of the obligation to tell the truth, (2) an ability to communicate, and (3) a knowledge of the topic of the testimony.

complaint. The initial pleading served and filed by the plaintiff stating his or her version of the facts and law concerning the defendant's alleged wrongdoing is termed the complaint, or petition as it is called in some states, such as Texas.

concurring opinion. A judge's concurring opinion agrees with the result of the majority of the court but disagrees with the reasons the majority used to support its result.

congress. This is the legislative branch of the state and federal government whose function is to enact law.

constitution. The document that sets forth the fundamental laws which create the branches of government and identify the basic rights and obligations of citizens is a constitution. There exist fifty state constitutions and one federal constitution.

contempt. A willful disregard or disobedience toward a judge constitutes contempt.

contest. To contest is to challenge.

corporation counsel. Attorneys who exclusively represent one corporation, in-house, are corporate counsel.

corroborate. To add weight or credibility to testimony is to corroborate that testimony.

counterclaim. This is a claim or cause of action presented in the defendant's answer against the plaintiff.

criminal law. Criminal law involves an offense which harms the entire community and whose remedy is a fine or imprisonment for the offender. The responsibility of pursuing a violation of criminal law rests with the state. A person may be charged criminally and sued civilly.

cross-claim. A claim by one codefendant against another codefendant is a cross-claim.

cross-examination. During a hearing or trial, cross-examination consists of the questioning of the witness after the other side has completed direct examination. Generally, cross-examination is limited to the topics raised during the direct examination of the witness by the other side.

damages. Damages consist of money that is paid by the party found liable to compensate the harmed party. Types of damages include general/actual/compensatory, special, punitive/exemplary, nominal, consequential, and liquidated.

damage hearing. This separate hearing is sometimes held after the judge or jury has found a party liable. The hearing is limited to deciding the amount that the losing party should pay the winner and how much time the losing party has to pay the damages.

declaration against interest. An out-of-court statement made by a non-party against the interest of the non-party when he or she is no longer available for comment constitutes admissible hearsay as a declaration against interest. For instance, Joan sues Betty for the fraudulent use of Joan's credit card, but Betty introduces a signed confession from Susan, who is now dead, that Susan was the person who used Joan's credit card. Susan's statement would be admissible hearsay since it is a declaration by Susan, who is unavailable, which is against her own interest.

declaration of bodily feelings. A declaration of bodily feelings is an admissible form of hearsay in which a spontaneous declaration is made out-of-court regarding the person's present bodily condition. For instance, Zachary is called to testify that his brother told him that he had a headache during the heavy metal concert.

declaration of mental state of mind. Other admissible hearsay is a declaration of the mental state of mind, which involves an out-of-court statement about a person's present state of mind. For example, in a slip and fall trial, Robert testifies that the supermarket manager told him that she was aware of the slippery surface in the produce aisle and that "she would carpet that area in the morning."

declaration of present sense impression. Other admissible hearsay, or an exception to the hearsay rule, is declaration of present sense impression, which is an out-of-court statement detailing an event while it is being observed by the person making the statement. For instance, Joe testifies that seconds before an airplane hit power lines, Tina exclaimed to him, "The plane is flying too low!"

declaratory judgment. A court's decision which declares the rights and obligations of the parties, but does not order the parties to do or refrain from doing anything is a declaratory judgment. A declaratory judgment action does not seek damages but requests a declaration of the respective rights of the parties.

default judgment. As a result of the defendant's failure to file an answer or otherwise plead within the statutory time allowed for that purpose, which is usually twenty to thirty days, the plaintiff may request a judgment by default, which is a court order deciding the case in favor of the plaintiff.

defendant. A person or entity against whom an action is brought is called the defendant. The defendant may also be known as a respondent in a domestic or probate court action.

defense. A response made by one party to the claims or allegations of another party is a defense. The defense may be a denial of facts and may include an affirmative defense; it is usually contained in the defendant's answer.

demonstrative evidence. This is tangible evidence, evidence that can be seen or touched. Another category of evidence is testimonial or oral evidence.

deposition. This is a pretrial discovery device in which one party asks oral questions of the other party or of a witness for the other party. Depositions are usually conducted under oath outside of the courtroom and consist of questions similar to interrogatories asked of the party or witness. The person who is being questioned is called the deponent. Paralegals assist during a deposition by taking notes and by providing questions to the supervising attorney to be asked of the deponent.

digesting documents. A digest is a synthesis of a document such as a deposition or court reporter's transcript. Paralegals frequently digest depositions by summarizing the most important elements of the deponent's testimony for the purpose of quick reference and review by the supervising attorney.

directed verdict. A directed verdict is an order entered by the trial court judge in favor of the party requesting the verdict because the opposing party has failed to establish a *prima facie* cause of action or an adequate defense. The defendant may request a directed verdict after plaintiff has rested his case, and the plaintiff may request a directed verdict after defendant has completed her defense.

direct evidence. Direct evidence is evidence that tends to establish a fact without the need for an inference and is preferred over indirect, or circumstantial, evidence.

direct examination. The attorney who calls the witness to the stand usually conducts the direct examination of that witness, which is then followed by the cross-examination of that witness by the adverse party. After cross-examination, the attorney may conduct redirect examination of that same witness.

discovery. Discovery consists of pretrial devices that can be used by one party to obtain evidence and information from the other party to prepare for trial, prevent surprise, and facilitate settlement. The most common kinds of discovery are interrogatories, depositions, request for admissions, request for production of documents, and request for mental or physical examinations.

dismissal with prejudice. A dismissal with prejudice to refiling is an adjudication on the merits of the case which bars the right to bring a subsequent action on the same claim. A dismissal with prejudice can only be appealed to a higher court.

dismissal without prejudice. A dismissal without prejudice to refiling consists of a dismissal of a case based on a procedural error. The case can be filed again so long as the procedural error is corrected in the amended action.

dissenting opinion. This opinion disagrees with the decision of the majority of the appellate court.

diversity of citizenship. This is a basis for the federal court to hear a case. The parties to the litigation must be from different states, and the amount of money involved in the suit must exceed a statutory minimum, which changes frequently and is currently $75,000.

docket. The court's calendar of pending cases is called the docket. The docket is usually posted outside of the courtroom and specifies the names and kinds of cases that are being heard in that courtroom on that day.

doctor-patient privilege. The doctor-patient privilege is one of many evidentiary privileges in which a patient can refuse to disclose any confidential communication made to his or her doctor that relates to medical care. The information cannot be disclosed without the consent of both parties.

domicile. A physical presence in a state with the intent to reside there permanently constitutes a domicile.

draft. To draft is to write. Paralegals draft letters, pleadings, discovery, motions, and briefs for their supervising attorneys to proof and sign.

due process. Due process of law is the evaluation of a case based upon the judgment of a disinterested objective party. Due process is a fundamental constitutional right which necessitates that the judicial system accords parties notice and opportunity to be heard and to defend themselves.

dying declaration. A dying declaration is admissible hearsay consisting of an out-of-court statement concerning the causes and circumstances of death when made by a person whose death is imminent.

elements. The components of a cause of action or claim for relief are its elements.

eminent domain. The power of the state to take possession of private property for public use without the consent of the property owner is called eminent domain. In these cases, such as when property is taken for utility easements or new highways, the state must provide reasonable compensation to the property owner.

en banc. When all of the judges on an appellate court decide a case, that decision is rendered *en banc*, as opposed to by a panel of judges, which usually consists of only three of the judges.

equal protection. Equal protection is the Fourteenth Amendment right which states that no person should be denied the same protection of law enjoyed by others.

escheat. When a person dies without a will (intestate) or when there is no other person who is competent to inherit, the state may take possession of that person's estate under its escheat powers.

estate. Estate refers to all property that is left by a decedent from which any obligations or debts of the decedent must be paid. It also may refer to the surviving representatives of the deceased.

evidence. This consists of written or unwritten proof of the allegations at issue between the parties to a lawsuit.

exhibit, trial. Items of tangible evidence that are to be or have been offered to the court and jury for inspection and consideration are trial exhibits. Paralegals frequently prepare and mark exhibits for trial. Plaintiff's exhibits are traditionally marked with numbers whereas defense exhibits are marked with letters.

***ex parte* hearing**. A hearing where only one party to the action is present is an *ex parte* hearing. A temporary restraining order (TRO) is heard *ex parte*. To *ex parte* a judge is to talk to a judge about a case without the other side's presence, which is unethical.

expert witness. A person who has been qualified as an expert and who then will be allowed (through his/her answers to questions) to assist the jury in understanding complicated and technical subjects which are not generally within the jury's understanding is an expert witness.

failure to state a cause of action. As a common affirmative defense or response to plaintiff's complaint, defendants frequently allege that the plaintiff has failed to allege sufficient facts to constitute a cause of action against defendant. Even if the plaintiff were to prove all of the facts alleged in the complaint, those facts would not establish a cause of action entitling plaintiff to recover against the defendant.

Federal Rules of Civil Procedure. Rules governing the manner in which civil cases are brought in and progress through the federal courts constitute the Federal Rules of Civil Procedure (F.R.C.P.).

felony. These are crimes punishable by a sentence of one year or more and by a fine exceeding $1000.00. Felons are usually required to serve their time in the state penitentiary as opposed to a county jail.

filed (in court). Paralegals frequently present documents to the clerk of the court which means that these documents have been filed with the court. If the court clerk's office is closed, paralegals may then attempt to file the documents with the judge or the judge's clerk.

forum. The court or judicial tribunal can also be called the forum.

forum non conveniens. Even if the venue of the court is proper, that court may be an inconvenient forum within which to litigate the action. Thus, if it appears that for the convenience of the litigants and witnesses and in the interest of justice the action should be heard in another forum, the court may act on its own, or may grant a litigant's motion to change venue on the basis of *forum non conveniens*.

foundation for evidence. Foundation for evidence must be established by the party seeking to admit the evidence into court. To lay a proper foundation for evidence, that party must establish a legal reason for the evidence, which is usually done by the attorney's asking questions of the witness on direct examination.

garnishment. A garnishment is a method of executing a judgment through which part of the judgment-debtor's salary is automatically turned over to the court. The court then gives the money to the judgment-creditor until the judgment is satisfied. Garnishments may be 25% of one's net monthly take-home pay to satisfy many judgments and as high as 65% for child support arrearages.

general verdict. A general verdict is a jury's verdict which simply states which party has prevailed and what amount should be paid to the winning party, if any.

general verdict with interrogatories. This verdict is the similar to the general verdict but includes the jury's answers to a series of specific factual questions concerning important aspects of the case.

good time. Time deducted from a sentence for good behavior while incarcerated is good time and is often calculated differently for state and federal convictions.

grand jury. This group of persons, traditionally not fewer than 12 nor more than 23, upon hearing the evidence for the prosecution in each proposed bill of indictment, must decide whether a sufficient case is established on which to hold the accused for trial. If it feels that sufficient evidence has been presented, it will return a "true bill" or "bill of indictment" confirming that it is satisfied with the truth of the accusations presented by the prosecutor. The prosecutor may then file the complaint and make arrests as warranted. Evidence from a grand jury investigation is usually not admissible in the subsequent court proceeding.

hearing. A hearing is a proceeding, usually formal but sometimes informal, in which the judge or hearing officer examines some aspect of a dispute and renders a decision or determination.

hearsay. Hearsay is a statement which is not based upon personal observation but on what has been said or written by someone else who is not in the courtroom. It is inadmissible unless it can be shown to fall within one of the hearsay exceptions.

impanel. To select, swear in and seat is to impanel, such as impanelling a jury.

impeach a witness. To impeach a witness is to discredit that witness by introducing evidence that the testimony of the witness is not credible.

in camera. A discussion or meeting held in the judge's chambers is said to be held *in camera* and is usually held off the record.

indictment. A formal charge by a grand jury accusing the defendant of a crime is an indictment.

indigent. One who is destitute of property or means of comfortable subsistence is indigent and may be entitled to taxpayer supported defense in felony charges.

information and belief. When a party qualifies a statement made in a pleading as believed to be true from available information that party has pled on the basis of information and belief. This phrasing protects a plaintiff who is not absolutely certain of truth of the allegations in the complaint.

in issue. Also known as at issue or in question, this refers to the factual or legal points of contention between parties.

initial appearance. The initial appearance for a defendant accused of a felony is a court proceeding during which the judge advises the defendant of the charges against him/her and of his/her rights, decides on bail and other conditions of release, and sets the date for the preliminary hearing.

***in personam* jurisdiction**. A court's jurisdiction over a person is *in personam* jurisdiction.

***in rem* jurisdiction**. A court's jurisdiction over property or a controversy is *in rem* jurisdiction.

intent. Intent is probably the most important word in law. It refers to a "determination of the mind" of a party which is usually determined by the jury and is very difficult to establish. "Reasonable" and "foreseeable" are other important words which similarly defy universal definition.

interlocutory appeal. An appeal to a higher court made during the progress of a case requesting temporary relief rather than a final judgment is an interlocutory appeal. This appeal usually takes the form of a motion made to a higher court requesting a review of the action, or inaction, of the trial court. For example, when a defense's motion to suppress evidence obtained during a search of the defendant is granted by the trial court, the prosecution often appeals the trial court's granting of that motion. An interlocutory appeal is requested before final judgment.

interrogatories. Interrogatories are discovery techniques that consist of written questions submitted by one party to the other party. The answers to interrogatories are usually provided under oath.

introduce (into evidence). To introduce into evidence is to place evidence before the court so that it will become part of the record for consideration by the judge and jury.

issues on appeal. The claimed errors of law committed by the trial court provide the only basis for the issues on appeal. The appellate court does not retry the case and no witnesses are called. The appellate court examines the record and determines whether errors of law were committed by the trial judge.

joint and several liability. Responsibility together and individually constitutes joint and several liability.

judgment. Judgment is the court's final decision, which resolves the dispute and determines the respective rights and obligations of the parties.

judgment creditor. The party that wins the judgment award is the judgment creditor.

judgment debtor. The losing party who owes the judgment is the judgment debtor.

judgment *non obstante verdicto*. A judgment *non obstante verdicto*, or judgment *n.o.v.*, is a judgment ordered by the court in favor of the plaintiff that is contrary to the jury's decision in favor of the defendant. This is also known as a judgment notwithstanding the verdict, since the court's decision opposes the verdict reached by the jury and in effect overrules the jury.

judgment on the merits. A judgment on the merits of a case is the preferred form of judgment since it is based on the legal rights of the parties as distinguished from mere matters of practice, procedure, and jurisdiction.

judicial branch. The judicial branch of government interprets laws created by the legislative and executive branches of government.

jurisdiction. Jurisdiction is a court's power to hear a case and decide the outcome.

jury. The group of citizens who will decide the issues or questions of fact at the trial is the jury. Members of the jury are summoned from sources such as motor vehicle registration lists, driver's license lists, voter registration lists, and property ownership lists. Most juries consist of either six or twelve jurors.

jury instructions. Guidelines and law given by the judge to the jury which the jury uses in deciding issues of fact at trial constitute jury instructions. Paralegals can be very instrumental in preparing jury instructions, which become the jury charge when they are read to the jury by the judge.

jury panel. These are the group of citizens who have been summoned to jury duty.

leading question. This is a question asked of a party or witness which suggests the desired answer, assumes to prove a fact that has not been proved, or embodies a material fact and implies its admission by a simple negative or affirmative answer. "Isn't it true that you bought drugs with the money that you stole?" is an example of a leading question which, if objected to, would be inadmissible in court.

legislative branch. The branch of government whose purpose is to create law is the legislative branch. Congress is the legislative branch of government.

liable. To be liable is to be responsible or accountable in law or equity.

lis pendens. A notice of *lis pendens* is filed in the public records to prevent any transaction which would thwart the purpose of the pending lawsuit. For example, in a quiet title action, where title to real property is being contested, the party who is not listed as the owner in the public records might file a *lis pendens* to prevent the sale of that property before resolving the quiet title action.

litigation. Litigation is an action or lawsuit.

magistrate. A magistrate is a judicial officer who has limited jurisdiction in criminal and civil matters, such as a justice of the peace or federal magistrate.

majority opinion. The majority opinion, often conveyed in written form, is the decision of the majority of the members of the appellate court.

mandate of court. A court's mandate most commonly consists of a command or order from a superior court to an inferior court.

marital communications privilege. This privilege can prevent one spouse from disclosing confidential communications made to the other spouse during their marriage. One spouse can also prevent the other spouse from making such disclosures and both spouses must agree to the disclosure for it to be admissible.

misdemeanor. This is any crime or offense not amounting to a felony or petty offense. Misdemeanors are crimes generally punishable by a sentence of less than one year and a fine of less than one thousand dollars. Misdemeanants also serve their sentences in the county jail as opposed to the state penitentiary.

motion. A request made to a court is a motion.

motion for a new trial. This motion requests that the judge set aside the judgment and order a new trial on the basis that the trial was improper or unfair due to specified prejudicial errors that occurred during the trial.

motion for summary judgment. This is a pretrial request by a party that a decision on an issue be made on the basis of the pleadings and discovery without having to go through a trial. A party requesting summary judgment tries to convince the judge that no issues of material fact exist between the parties and thus a decision should be rendered by the judge without the necessity of jury consideration.

motion *in limine*. A motion *in limine* is a pretrial motion made to the court for the purpose of excluding potentially prejudicial evidence at the subsequent trial. Gruesome photographs are often excluded in response to this motion, or black and white photos may be substituted for color photos.

motion to dismiss. A motion to dismiss is a request by a party to end a case without a trial.

motion to suppress. A motion to suppress is a party's written or oral application to the court requesting the suppression of particular evidence.

movant. The person or entity who requests relief from the court or administrative tribunal, usually through oral or written motions, is the movant.

move into evidence. To request that the court declare that specified items be admissible as evidence is to move those items into evidence.

***nolle prosequi*.** This is a statement by the plaintiff or prosecutor of an unwillingness to further prosecute a case, resulting in a dismissal of some or all of the allegations.

notice of appeal. A notice of appeal is the document announcing an intention to appeal, which is filed with the appellate court and served on the opposing party.

***nolo contendere*.** This is a no contest plea. It has the effect of a guilty plea and allows the judge to sentence the defendant as though he or she pled guilty. A defendant is sometimes counseled to plead no contest to a criminal accusation so that this could not be used as an admission of liability in a related civil suit.

***nunc pro tunc*.** When a court allows the entry of an order, judgment, or other act to have retroactive effect, that court is said to have acted *nunc pro tunc*, or "now for then."

objection to evidence. When a party objects to evidence, that party is challenging the admissibility of the evidence that the other side is trying to introduce.

opening statement. An opening statement is presented by each side to the judge and jury, which outlines the facts and the positions of each party to the litigation.

opinion of the court. This is an explanation by the court as to why it reached a certain decision. Opinions are often collected in official and unofficial reporters.

opinion evidence. Opinion evidence is evidence that a witness believes or infers to be true regarding facts in dispute. An opinion is an inference from a fact and is generally not admissible. Opinion evidence should be distinguished from personal knowledge of the facts, which would more likely be admissible.

opinion of the attorney general. This is an opinion provided by the attorney general to governmental officials on legal issues such as the interpretation of a statute or new legislation. These opinions are primary authority, which is often published.

parol evidence rule. Parol evidence is oral evidence. According to this rule of evidence, oral representations made prior to a written agreement must be integrated into that agreement to be admissible and enforceable.

peremptory challenge. This is usually the final challenge made in the jury selection process. It is exercised by each litigant, and no cause or reason need be provided for the dismissal of a potential juror. These challenges are sometimes limited to three per side.

personal recognizance. One who is criminally accused may apply for a personal recognizance bond, which consists of a sworn promise to return to court at designated times without having to post cash or collateral bail. Various criteria are considered by the probation department in granting personal recognizance bonds, including the accused's prior criminal record, family and job contacts in the community, and the crime alleged to have been committed.

personal service. Personal service consists of service of process upon an individual, or the designated agent of an individual or corporation, by delivering, or attempting to deliver, a copy of the summons and complaint to that individual or agent. A subpoena should also be served in this manner.

petition. To make a formal request for action from the court, similar to a motion, is to petition the court. A petition in some states, such as Texas, is a complaint.

physical evidence. Physical evidence is evidence that can be seen or touched.

plaintiff. The one bringing a suit is the plaintiff, sometimes known as a petitioner in domestic or probate actions.

plea bargaining. The process whereby the accused and the prosecutor negotiate a mutually satisfactory disposition of the case is plea bargaining. The defendant usually agrees to plead guilty to a lesser charge in return for the state's willingness to drop the more serious charge.

plead. To plead in criminal cases is to formally admit or deny the charges made by the prosecutor.

pleadings. The initial documents filed in a lawsuit which state the positions of the parties pertaining to the causes of action and the respective defenses are the pleadings. The most common pleadings are complaints, answers, replies, third-party complaints, cross-claims, and counterclaims.

poll the jury. To question each juror individually in open court as to whether he or she agrees with the verdict announced by the jury foreman is to poll the jury.

prayer for relief. A prayer for relief is a request contained in the complaint or petition which asks for the relief to which the plaintiff thinks he or she is entitled. Common wording after this request are the words "and such other and further relief as to the court may seem just and proper." This enables the court to grant whatever relief it feels is appropriate in addition to that which was specifically requested. This is also known as a "wherefore" or "*ad damnum* clause."

preliminary hearing. In criminal law, this hearing is a means of determining the question of whether probable cause for the arrest of a person existed. It is held shortly after arrest and before trial, and the prosecution must produce enough evidence to satisfy the judge that the defendant committed the crimes as charged.

preponderance of the evidence. This is the standard of proof that must be established to win a civil case. This standard is met when a party's evidence indicates that "more likely than not" the fact is as the party alleges it to be. A majority of the jurors must agree for a plaintiff to prevail in a civil action.

presumption. A presumption is an inference regarding the truth or falsity of any proposition of fact. A presumption may also indicate the weight given to evidence.

pretrial conference. A pretrial conference is held between the judge, or magistrate, and the attorneys to prepare the case for trial. At this conference the presiding judge sometimes tries to encourage the parties to settle part or all of their dispute.

***prima facie* case**. A case sufficient on its face that is supported by the requisite minimum evidence and free of palpable defects is a *prima facie* case. This must exist for a party to prevail under any cause of action.

privilege. A privilege in the law of evidence is the right to refuse to testify or the right to prevent someone else from testifying on a matter.

privilege against self-incrimination. The privilege against self-incrimination holds that an accused cannot be forced to testify in a criminal proceeding or to answer incriminating questions that directly or indirectly connect the accused to the commission of a crime.

probable cause. Probable cause is a reasonable basis to believe that the defendant has committed a wrong or is guilty of the crime charged.

probation. Probation is an alternative to imprisonment whereby a defendant found guilty of a crime upon a verdict or plea is released by the court subject to the conditions imposed by the court and under the supervision of a probation officer.

procedural law. The rules setting forth the steps required to conduct a lawsuit constitute procedural law. It is distinguishable from substantive law, which governs the rights and duties of the parties.

process. Process is defined as a summons and complaint.

proof. The evidence offered to confirm or refute a fact or an issue is proof. In civil cases it is defined as a preponderance of the evidence and in criminal cases as beyond a reasonable doubt.

pro se. When a party appears in an action without representation by an attorney, that party appears *pro se.*

prosecute. When the government, through the attorney general or district attorney, files criminal charges, the government has begun to prosecute the accused.

qualify a witness. Before testifying in court, witnesses often must be qualified to testify. The court must be convinced through a demonstration of background and experience that the witness has expertise to testify in a particular area.

quasi in rem **jurisdiction.** This jurisdiction is a court's power to resolve a personal claim against the defendant with the judgment being satisfied out of property or assets that the defendant owns within the state.

quasi-judicial. When an agency is acting similar to a court, it is acting quasi-judicially.

recidivist. A person who makes a trade of crime, who is a habitual criminal, is a recidivist.

record. The official collection of all the trial pleadings, exhibits, orders, and word-for-word testimony that took place during the trial comprises the record of the court. The trial court record must be ordered and prepared as a prerequisite to prosecution of the appeal.

redirect examination. Redirect examination takes place after questioning the witness on cross-examination. The attorney who conducted the direct examination conducts the redirect examination.

relevant. Something which tends to prove or disprove a fact in issue is declared relevant by the court and is admissible for consideration by the judge and jury.

remand. To remand is to send back to an inferior court for further consideration.

remittitur. *Remittitur* is the procedural process by which the verdict of a jury is diminished by subtraction. The judge tells the winning party that a new trial will be granted unless this party agrees to decrease the damage award reached by the jury.

reply. A reply is a defensive pleading which may be filed by the plaintiff in response to new allegations raised by defendant in defendant's answer. An appellant may file a reply brief which responds to new matters set forth in the appellee's answer brief.

request for admissions. Request for admissions are discovery techniques consisting of written statements of facts which are submitted to an adverse party and which that party is required to admit or deny.

request for physical or mental examination. This is a form of discovery that requires court approval unless the parties agree, or stipulate, to this discovery. A defendant usually wishes to conduct a physical or mental examination of the plaintiff in an effort to verify the damages and injuries complained of by the plaintiff.

request for production and inspection of documents. This is a discovery devise asking a party to produce at a specified time and place documents or other things in the possession or control of that party.

res gestae. *Res gestae* is an evidentiary term applying to exceptions to the hearsay rule involving statements which are made closely connected to or concurrently with the happening of a transaction or occurrence.

res judicata. This is the legal doctrine that a judgment on the merits will prevent the same parties from re-litigating the same cause of action since the parties have already had their day in court and the controversy has already been judicially decided. It is similar to the doctrine of double jeopardy in a criminal case.

respondent. The party against whom a petitioner brings a case is called the respondent.

restitution. The restoration of property or a right to the person who has been unjustly deprived constitutes restitution. Restitution is often a condition of sentencing in a criminal case.

retainer. A contract between an attorney and client stating the nature of the services to be rendered and the cost of those services is the retainer agreement.

review, appellate. A judicial reconsideration of the proceedings of a court or other body is an appellate review. The appellate court examines or reviews the record of a lower court concentrating on the errors of law that may have been made by the lower court.

rule on witnesses. This rule requires that all witnesses be removed from the courtroom until it is time for their individual testimony to prevent them from hearing others' testimonies. Either party may invoke this rule.

rules of court. Laws governing practice before a particular court and the procedures to be followed in litigation before that court constitute the rules of court. Paralegals should be aware of the nuances in practice and procedure among the various federal and state court systems in which they practice.

satisfy. To satisfy is to comply with a legal obligation. A release and discharge of an obligation is the satisfaction of that obligation.

sentence. The punishment ordered by the court to be assessed upon a person convicted of a crime is a sentence.

serve. To present legal papers to a party notifying that party of a lawsuit constitutes service of those papers.

service of process. The delivery of a summons and complaint to a defendant ordering that defendant to answer the allegations made by the plaintiff constitutes service of process. Service of process is a prerequisite to the court's acquisition of personal jurisdiction or power over the defendant.

set for trial. To schedule a date on which a trial is to begin is to set the case for trial.

settlement. A settlement is a compromise achieved by the adverse parties in a civil suit before the final judgment in which they agree on their respective rights and obligations and thus eliminate the necessity of a trial. Statistics indicate that ninety percent of civil actions are settled prior to trial, and paralegals can be instrumental in the preparation of settlement demands that are used to achieve a settlement.

special verdict. A special verdict is a form of verdict that requests that the jury answer specific factual questions in addition to rendering its verdict for plaintiff or defendant.

spontaneous declaration. Spontaneous declaration is an exception to the hearsay rule and consists of an out-of-court statement or utterance made spontaneously during or immediately after an exciting event by the observer of the event. This admissible hearsay is also called an excited utterance.

standard of proof. The standard of proof is a statement of how convincing the evidence must be in order for a party to comply with his or her burden of proof. In criminal cases the standard of proof is "beyond a reasonable doubt" and in civil cases it is "by a preponderance of the evidence".

stare decisis. *Stare decisis* is one of the most important doctrines in law and means that a court is obliged to stand by decided cases and to follow the precedent set by those cases. As long as the facts and issues presented and decided in prior cases are substantially similar to the case being considered by an inferior court, the inferior court must apply that prior precedent in resolving its case.

state a cause of action. To state a cause of action is to include all of the relevant facts and law in the complaint so that if those matters are successfully proved at trial, the plaintiff would be entitled to win.

statute of limitations. The statute of limitations is the law establishing the period of time within which a complaint must be filed. If it is not timely filed, the suit will be barred.

stay execution of the judgment. This delays enforcement of the court's judgment.

stipulated. A fact agreed upon by the parties is said to be stipulated. A stipulation of fact will not be contested or disputed so that no evidence need be presented concerning the truth or falsity of that fact at trial.

subpoena. A writ issued under authority of a court to compel the appearance of a witness at a judicial proceeding is called a subpoena. Generally, a subpoena must be served personally and cannot be served by substitute service on a person not named in the subpoena.

subpoena *duces tecum*. This is a writ issued under authority of a court to compel the appearance of a person at a judicial proceeding and to command that person to bring specified documents with him or her. Its primary objective is to order that person to produce documents at a deposition, hearing, or trial so that those documents can be reviewed.

subject matter jurisdiction. A court's power to hear the type of case being presented is the court's subject matter jurisdiction. A bankruptcy court would not have subject matter jurisdiction over a child custody case, for example.

subscription. The signature of the attorney who prepared the complaint and who represents the plaintiff is the subscription. If a plaintiff prepares a complaint and acts as his/her own attorney, the plaintiff signs "pro se."

substantive law. Substantive law is the positive law that creates, defines and regulates the rights and duties of the parties and that may give rise to a cause of action. It represents the non-procedural rights and duties imposed by law.

substitute service. Substitute service is service of process upon the designated agent of the party, usually a defendant. Paralegals often consult the secretary of state's office to ascertain the name and address of the registered agents for the corporations against which their offices are filing actions.

summons. A summons is a formal notice from the court ordering the defendant to appear in court or to answer a complaint in lieu of appearing.

Supremacy Clause. The Supremacy Clause is the popular title for Article 6 of the United States Constitution. It states that federal laws have precedence over state and local laws.

sustain. To support, approve, or grant is to sustain an action or motion.

take under advisement. When a court takes a matter under advisement, that court is delaying its ruling on the matter, usually a motion, until a later time.

tangible evidence. This is physical or demonstrative evidence, evidence that can be seen or touched.

testimonial evidence. This is oral evidence that can be heard and considered by a judge and jury.

third party complaint. This pleading is filed by the defendant against a new, third party and alleges that the third party is or may be liable for all or part of the damages that the plaintiff attributes to the defendant.

tickler system. A tickler system is a common filing system that allows the secretary and paralegal to alert the attorney of approaching deadlines. Tickler systems are important for keeping the law office staff abreast of court dates, filing deadlines, and other important dates.

tortfeasor. A tortfeasor is the wrongdoer, the person who committed the tort.

transcript. A transcript is the written record of proceedings, the verbatim transcription of everything that was said on the record during the hearing or trial.

trial court. The court where the trial is held is the trial court. Trial courts are generally the only forums which allow for a trial by jury.

trial *de novo*. A trial *de novo* is a totally new fact finding hearing.

United States Court of Appeals. The United States Court of Appeals is an appellate court of limited jurisdiction. The jurisdiction is limited to appeals from the United States District Court.

United States District Court. This is the federal trial court where the litigants are entitled to a trial by jury. This court's jurisdiction is limited to cases in which the U.S. is a party, there is a federal question at issue, or diversity of citizenship exists between two or more of the parties and at least $75,000.00 is at stake.

United States Supreme Court. This is the court of last resort. It is the nation's highest court and selects certain appeals referred to it from the United States Court of Appeals and state supreme courts. It also has original jurisdiction in cases involving ambassadors, public ministers, and consuls, and those in which a state is a party. There is a chief justice and eight associate justices on the United States Supreme Court.

venue. Venue is the place of trial. An impartial venue is critical to a fair trial.

verdict. The final decision of the jury is called the verdict.

verification of pleadings. A verification is an affidavit that is submitted with a pleading and signed by the party on whose behalf the pleading was prepared. The affiant swears that he or she has read the pleading and that it is true to the best of his or her knowledge, information, and belief. A verification is much more likely to be filed with a complaint for breach of contract, where the facts are relatively certain, than with a complaint for negligence where the facts are less certain. Furthermore, attorneys who may be skeptical of their clients' allegations will often request that their clients verify their complaints to protect themselves if the complaint is later proven to be frivolous.

***voir dire*.** *Voir dire* is the jury selection process. It is the examination of prospective jurors by the attorneys and the court. *Voir dire* may also refer to the examination of the qualifications of a prospective witness prior to allowing that witness to testify.

warrant. This is an order from a judicial officer authorizing the arrest of an individual or the search of property.

writ. There are many forms of writs; each is a written order from a court.

writ of *certiorari*. A writ of *certiorari* is an order by an appellate court concerning the review or re-examination of the actions of a lower court. If the writ is denied, the higher court refuses to hear the appeal and in effect the lower court's decision stands unaffected.

CHAPTER 1: INTRODUCTION TO THE LEGAL PROCESS FOR PARALEGALS

The study and practice of paralegalism is exciting because the law reflects society's changing modes of conduct. The law is flexible and evolves as society changes. Despite its flexibility, however, the law has specific theoretical and historical origins, and before studying paralegalism, students should understand the theoretical and historical context within which the American legal system has evolved.

THE EVOLUTION OF THE AMERICAN LEGAL SYSTEM

Law has two main interpretations: one is based on the concept of natural law and the other is a secular interpretation. The more ancient of the two interpretations is Aristotle's theory of cosmic or natural law. Aristotle believed that there was a law inherent in the universe that was more important than the laws made by men and women. In contrast, the more recent secular, or common law, theory holds that law develops from the history of a nation and that legal experts only interpret the historical drift of a nation.

American jurisprudence has been derived primarily from English legal traditions, which began with the Norman Conquest of 1066. One of these traditions, common law, is judge-made law and is based on the traditions, customs, business usages, and moral standards of the people. The common law courts recognize, affirm, and enforce these customs and usages by awarding money damages to the wronged party.

The principle of equity is another legal tradition that originated in England. In contrast to common law, equity rights wrongs by granting the wrongdoer an injunction or specific performance. In England, the courts of equity are vested with the responsibility of affording relief in matters where the common law court is powerless. The foundation of the court of equity is a moral standard rather than a judicial precedent, and its overriding principle is that of fairness. Whereas the court of equity enforces obligations, the common law court awards money damages.

The English common law and equity systems crossed the Atlantic Ocean with the colonists and were adopted by America after the revolution. However, the court of equity was merged with the common law courts so that today most American trial courts can administer both monetary and equitable remedies.

For Discussion The following are definitions of law as stated by individuals from various backgrounds and various time periods. Examine each definition, decide whether the speaker holds to a natural or secular view of law, and explain the reason for your choice.

1. "By "particular" law I mean that which an individual community lays down for itself;. . . and by "universal" law I mean the law of nature. For there is a natural and universal notion of right and wrong, one which all men instinctively apprehend. . . .
   - Aristotle, *Rhetoric* 1373b (Cooper trans. 1932), p. 73.
2. "There is in fact a true law - namely, right reason - which is in accordance with nature, applies to all men, and is unchangeable and eternal. By its commands this law summons men to the performance of their duties; by its prohibitions it restrains them from doing wrong. Its commands and prohibitions

always influence good men, but are without effect upon the bad. To invalidate this law by human legislation is never morally right, nor is it permissible ever to restrict its operation, and to annul it wholly is impossible. Neither the senate nor the people can absolve us from our obligation to obey this law, and it requires no. . . (great lawyer) to expound and interpret it. It will not lay down one rule at Rome and another at Athens, nor will it be one rule today and another tomorrow. But there will be one law, eternal and unchangeable, binding at all times upon all peoples; and there will be, as it were, one common master and ruler of men, namely God, who is the author of this law, its interpreter and its sponsor. The man who will not obey it will abandon his better self, and, in denying the true nature of a man, will thereby suffer the severest of penalties, though he has escaped all the other consequences which men call punishment."
- Cicero, *On the Commonwealth* (Sabine and Smith trans. 1950), pp. 215-16.

3. "[Law is]. . . a rule of civil conduct prescribed by the supreme power in a state, commanding what is right, and prohibiting what is wrong."
- Blackstone, *Commentaries* (1847), p. 44.

4. "When there is such a degree of probability as to lead to a reasonable assurance that a given conclusion ought to be and will be embodied in a judgment, we speak of that conclusion as the law."
- Cardozo, *The Growth of the Law* (1924), p. 33.

5. "Reason is the life of the law, nay, the common law itself is nothing else but reason. . . . The law is the perfection of reason."
- Coke, *First Institute* (1826), p. 1.

6. "The life of the law has not been logic; it has been experience."
- Holmes, *The Common Law* (1881), p. 1

7. "Law is not a brooding omnipresence in the sky, but a flexible instrument of social order, dependent on the political values of the society which it purports to regulate. . . ."
- Friedmann, *Law in a Changing Society* (1959), p. xiii.

8. "This doing of something about disputes, this doing of it reasonably, is the business of the law. And the people who have the doing in charge, whether they be judges or sheriffs or clerks or jailers or lawyers, are officials of the law. What these officials do about disputes is, to my mind, the law itself."
- Llewellyn, *The Bramble Bush* (1930), p. 3.

9. "Law . . . is nothing else than an ordinance of reason for the common good, made by him who has care of the community, and promulgated."
-St. Thomas Aquinas, *Treatise on Law*, Question 90, Article 4 (1964), pp 10-11.

10. "Law is a system (or order) of social relationships which corresponds to the interests of the dominant class and is safeguarded by the organized force of that class."
- Stuchka, in *Soviet Legal Philosophy* (Babb translation 1951), p. 20.

THE IMPORTANCE OF PRECEDENCE

Law is relatively easy to study and understand since most of the issues of law presented in court everyday have been decided in previous trials. The American system of justice is based upon the doctrine of *stare decisis,* which means that past precedent largely determines the outcome of future cases. As long as there is a sufficient similarity between the facts and issues of a precedent case and those of the present case, and as long as the court that rendered the decision in the precedent case is within the same system as and higher than the present court, the present court is bound to use the decision of the precedent case as authority in rendering its decision.

Stare decisis provides paralegals, attorneys, and judges with security, certainty, and predictability in researching the law. The paralegal's goal is to find the most applicable case precedent, integrate that authority into a memorandum of law, and present that memo to the supervising attorney, who should then argue the applicability of that particular *stare decisis* to the court.

The vast majority of cases that paralegals research are based upon facts and issues that have already been decided. The public policy has already been set. However, as society's modes of conduct change, so do laws. Thus, there are times when there is very little or no *stare decisis* for a case because of the uniqueness of that case's facts and issues. For example, in the early 1950's, the law in seventeen states and the District of Columbia allowed segregation in school facilities. Among the precedent cases interpreted to permit segregation was *Plessy v. Ferguson*, 163 U.S. 537, 16 S.Ct. 1138, 41 L.Ed.256 (1896), in which the United States Supreme Court upheld a Louisiana statute that provided that "separate but equal" accommodations in railroad cars was constitutional. The *stare decisis* at that time favored segregation, and there was no precedent favoring school integration.

When Thurgood Marshall and the National Association for the Advancement of Colored People argued to the Supreme Court in 1952 that the separate but equal doctrine was unconstitutional, they had very little precedent support and had to rely on sociological and psychological data to advance the cause of integration. On May 17, 1954, the United States Supreme Court rendered its decision in the watershed case of *Brown v. Board of Education*, 347 U.S. 483, 74 S.Ct. 686, 98 L.Ed. 873 (1954), where the Court held unanimously that the separate but equal doctrine had no place in public education and that separate educational facilities were inherently unequal.

So, although the vast majority of cases are rooted in *stare decisis*, a few occasions arise when precedent is nonexistent. These cases of first impression are often resolved on the basis of non-legal traditions and consequently form the foundation for future precedent.

For Discussion Name landmark cases, like *Brown v. Board of Education*, that recently have set precedent for evolving societal norms.

THE AMERICAN JUDICIAL SYSTEM

An understanding of government structure is essential to an understanding of the legal process. The United States operates under three branches of government: the executive, the legislative, and the judicial branches. Each one of these branches has its own function.

The legislative branch, which is comprised of the house and the senate, creates statutory law. The bicameral legislature must pass a bill through both the house and senate and then send it to be signed by the executive branch, the president on the federal level or the governor on the state level. Once it is signed, the bill becomes law.

In addition to signing bills into law, the executive branch enforces the laws. The executive branch oversees the multitude of administrative agencies that are empowered to enforce the laws that are created by the legislature. The phrase alphabet soup is still commonly used to describe the administrative agencies (e.g., HUD, EPA, DEA). These agencies also create the law in certain instances. Often the statute which empowers these agencies to enforce the laws also enables the agencies to regulate the public with respect to the statutes passed by the legislature. For example, the IRS was created to implement the tax code. If Larry has a problem with his federal income taxes, he contacts the IRS. Larry can enter the court system only after the IRS makes an administrative determination about Larry's problem.

The court system stems from the third branch of government, the judicial branch. The duty of the judicial branch is to interpret the laws which are created and enforced by the other two branches of government. Since paralegals deal with the judicial branch more than the other two branches, they should be very familiar with the structure of the United States court system.

The Federal Judicial System

The United States employs a unique blend of federal and state court systems. Each is a separate entity, but they work together to form the case law on which attorneys and paralegals rely to develop their cases.

The federal court system is comprised of three levels of adjudication: the courts of original jurisdiction, the courts of appellate jurisdiction, and the courts of last resort. The federal courts of original jurisdiction are the United States District Courts. These courts are geographically situated throughout the country, in Washington, D.C., and in the territories of the Northern Mariana Islands, Puerto Rico, Guam, and the Virgin Islands. These courts have a large amount of casework because they are the courts in which almost all federal litigation begins. Federal litigation that does not commence in the United States District Courts originates in the specialized courts with original jurisdiction: the United States Court of International Trade, the United States Tax Court, the United States Bankruptcy Court, and the United States Claims Court. The United States Supreme Court also has original jurisdiction in all cases involving ambassadors, consuls, and public ministers and all cases in which a state is a party.

Cases beginning in the United States District Court or the specialized courts are appealed to the United States Court of Appeals. The Court of Appeals is comprised of thirteen units of jurisdiction called circuits. Circuits 1 through 11 are numbered and regionally arranged; the other two circuits are the D.C. Circuit and the Federal Circuit, both located in the nation's capitol. The first appeal from the United States District Court is heard at the circuit court level. Each circuit hears appeals that originate within the geographic confines of its borders. Appeals from the United States Claims Court or the Court of International Trade are most commonly heard by the Federal Circuit Court. However, appeals originating in the United States Tax Court are heard by the circuit court that has jurisdiction over the party involved in the suit. For example, if Alice lives in Colorado, her appeal from the United States Tax Court will be heard in the 10th Circuit Court of Appeals.

In the United States, the court of last resort is the United States Supreme Court. The Court provides final review on appeal of any case emanating from the Courts of Appeals. The Supreme Court also may review decisions that are appealed from each state's supreme court. The United States Supreme Court has a somewhat temperamental view of what cases it will choose to hear, however, and not every case will be heard. The Court selects the cases it wants to hear from the circuit courts or state supreme courts. Historically, the court has levied a great amount of discretion in deciding which cases to hear. Sometimes, the cases are taken because the justices desire to rule on a controversial issue, or the United States Supreme Court will reconcile conflicting decisions from among differing jurisdictions.

The State Judicial System

In some states, the court structure mirrors that of the federal system. There are courts with original jurisdiction, appellate courts, and courts of last resort. However, in many states, there is only one level of appeals. In those states, the trial court decision is appealed to the highest court in the state. Then, an appeal from the highest court in the state may be heard by the United States Supreme Court. Table 1 is a diagram of the federal and state judicial systems.

For Discussion Name the federal district and circuit in which your region is located.

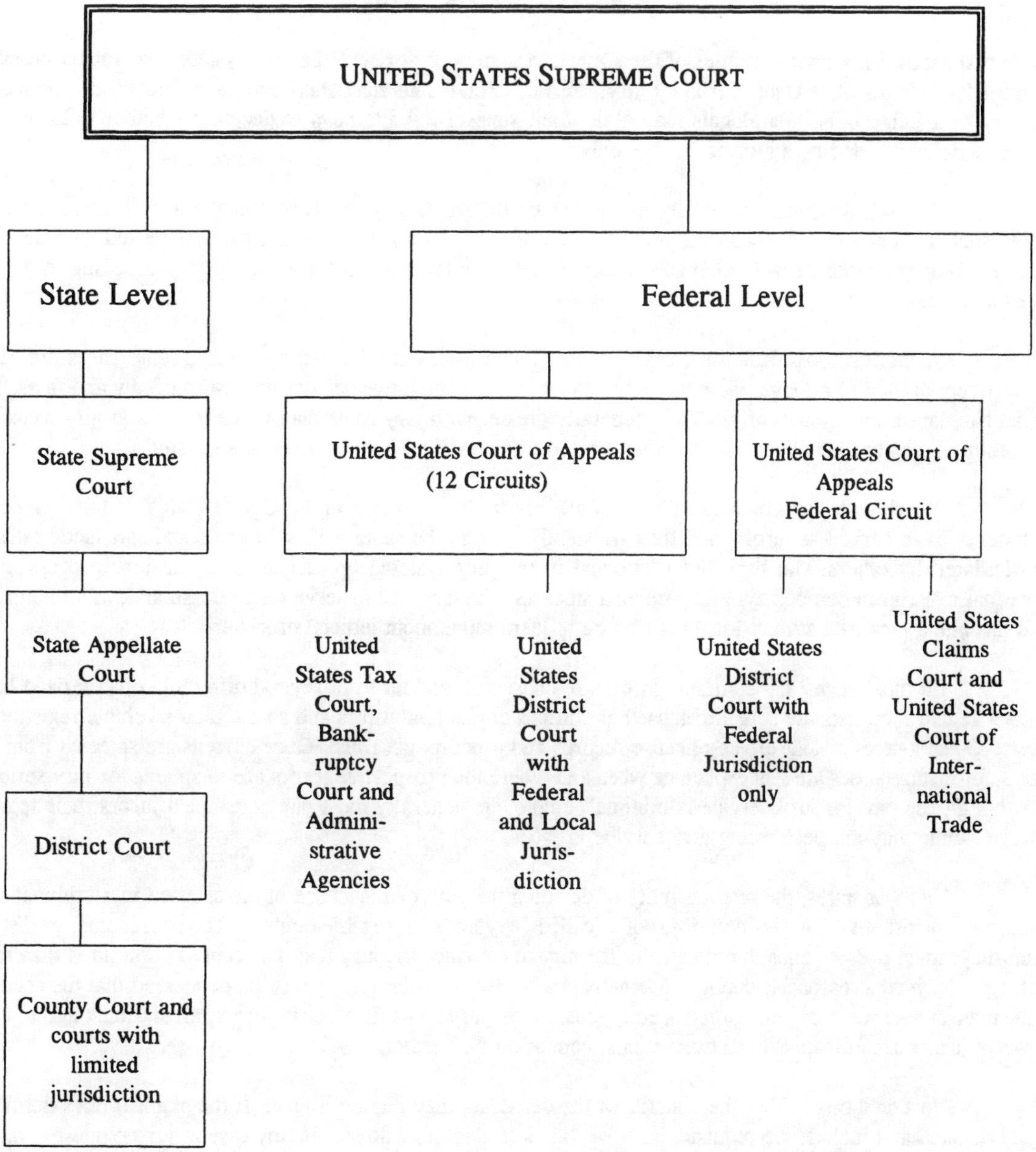

Table 1: Federal and State Judicial Systems

THE AMERICAN JURY SYSTEM

One of the most important attributes of the American system of justice is the jury system. Persons accused of crimes have an absolute right to trial by jury. Parties to civil suits may choose to have their cases decided by a jury or a judge only. Paralegals may assist their supervising attorneys in deciding whether to have their clients' cases decided by a jury or a judge only.

At trial, the functions of jury and judge are different. A judge is responsible for deciding issues of law, such as how a statute should be properly interpreted. A jury, on the other hand, is vested with the duty of deciding questions of fact, such as whether a party to a lawsuit acted reasonably in proceeding through a yellow caution light.

Although most trial court cases in the United States are decided by a jury, some cases are more effectively argued to a judge without a jury. In these cases the judge decides the issues of 'aw and fact. The trial backlog in our system of justice is generally greater with jury trials than judge trials, and jury trials are much more costly to conduct. These costs are most often assessed to the loser in a lawsuit.

Worldwide, approximately 95% of all jury trials take place in the United States. Many paralegal students have served as jurors, and they frequently express the same feeling of pride and satisfaction that is articulated by others who have been involved in the jury system. Participating in the jury process is an unequaled lesson in democracy, and paralegal students who have yet to serve on a jury should, at a minimum, sit through a jury trial at their local courthouse to learn more about judicial procedure.

In most states and counties, jurors are chosen at random from several different computerized lists. Voter registration lists are sometimes used as sources of potential jurors and so are motor vehicle registration lists. Other sources include driver's license records and property tax rolls. Once citizens are selected from the lists, juror summonses are sent explaining when and where the prospective jurors are to appear for jury service. Although the pay for jury service is minimal, employers generally must pay empaneled jurors their regular wages while they are performing jury service.

In most states, the responsibility of deciding the guilt or innocence of the accused in a criminal trial must be unanimous. This burden of proof is called "beyond a reasonable doubt". The prosecutor, or district attorney, must present enough evidence to the jury to convince the jury that the accused committed the crime charged "beyond a reasonable doubt." Mathematically, 100% of the jurors must be persuaded that the accused committed the crime charged. Consequently, since most jury trials involve six jurors, all six must agree, or if twelve jurors are empaneled, all twelve must concur on the verdict.

In a civil case, either the plaintiff or the defendant may request a jury. If the plaintiff does not file a jury demand and include the requisite jury fee, the defendant may do so. In any case, a jury request is rarely granted if it is not made before, or shortly after, the close of pleadings. In other words, a jury demand usually must be filed no later than ten days after the service of the last pleading. As always, paralegals should consult their state and local rules of court to ascertain the last day allowable for the filing of a jury demand. In practice, though, attorneys representing plaintiffs usually request a jury at the time of filing the complaint, and defense attorneys will demand a jury with the filing of the answer if the plaintiff has not previously requested a jury.

Attorneys and their paralegals often corroborate on the decision to try a civil case to a jury. Rarely, if ever, would a criminally accused individual be desirous of arguing a case to a judge only. However, civil cases involving complex legal issues may be more appropriately tried before a judge without a jury since the jurors may have difficulty understanding the complex legal terminology and issues. The tactical decision of whether to argue a civil action to a jury is among the more important decisions to be made in the litigation process.

For Discussion The following three hypotheticals will test a paralegal's understanding of the jury system. Read each of the case scenarios and answer the questions at the end.

1. Recently, six astronauts from the United States were launched from Kennedy Space Center on a thirty day mission to explore Mars. On the thirtieth day, after the space explorers had gathered all of the information that they were sent to collect, they began their return to earth. On their return, however, a meteor brushed so closely to their rocket that all communications with mission control at the Kennedy Space Center were lost and the rocket was forced off of its path and into an orbit of Mars.

   Space center scientists back on earth were stymied as to how to rescue the forlorn astronauts. As the scientists pondered the rescue plans, the six astronauts were quickly running out of provisions. On the fortieth day in space, the six astronauts had depleted all of their food. At that point, the astronauts reasoned that the only way that they could further sustain themselves was to kill and consume one of their members.

   Thus, on that same day, five of the six astronauts decided to draw straws to decide who would be eaten. The one astronaut who refused to participate, Alvin Pack, was a vegetarian who felt that if they waited another few days, they would be rescued. The other five astronauts decided that when it was Mr. Pack's turn to draw a straw, another astronaut would choose for him.

   The straw drawn for Mr. Pack happened to be the shortest straw, and Mr. Pack was summarily put to death and consumed by each of the other five astronauts. On the very next day after they ate Mr. Pack, the five surviving space explorers were rescued by another rocket which removed them from their orbit of Mars and returned them to earth.

   After recuperating from malnutrition at a hospital, the five astronauts were charged with homicide for the death of Alvin Pack under a statute which provides that "[a]nyone who knowingly or willfully takes the life of another shall be punished by life imprisonment or death."

   As paralegal for a criminal defense firm, you have been called upon to help decide whether this case should be tried and defended to a judge only or to a jury. Your office represents one of the defendant astronauts.

   a. How do you think a jury would decide this case? Why?

   b. Would the case be decided differently if it were tried by a judge only? Explain.

   c. Would a judge or jury be more likely to acquit your office's client?

2. Mary O'Brien was recently shopping at Ace's Grocery Store. While she was in the produce section of the store, she slipped and fell on a grape which, approximately thirty minutes earlier, Irwin Mitchell had dropped from his hand as he was grazing through the store. As a result of Ms. O'Brien's slip and fall, she sustained a broken ankle and much embarrassment.

   Ace's has refused to reimburse Mary for her medical bills, and all efforts to amicably resolve the dispute between Mary and Ace's have failed. As a paralegal working for the firm that represents

Mary, you have been asked to assist in deciding whether a jury should be demanded in the proposed lawsuit against Ace's Grocery Store.

a. Should a jury be demanded in this case? Why or why not?

b. Would the case be decided differently if it were tried by a judge only? Explain.

3. On January 1st, a building owner, Sally Marfield, contracted with a tenant, Drew Lippon, for the lease of Ms. Marfield's building beginning on March 1st. At the same time, Ms. Marfield contracted with Western Renovators, Inc., to renovate the building. The contract between Ms. Marfield and Western Renovators, Inc., specified that all renovations were to be completed no later than February 1st.

The lease agreement between Ms. Marfield and Mr. Lippon contained a clause providing that if the building were not ready for occupancy by March 1st, Ms. Marfield would pay the costs incident to storing all of Mr. Lippon's business inventory until such time that Ms. Marfield's building would be ready. As of March 1st, Western Renovators, Inc., had not completed the agreed upon renovations, which prompted Ms. Marfield to file a lawsuit against the renovation company seeking to recover not only the rental value of the building during the period of delay but also the amount that she had been obliged to pay Mr. Lippon for storing his inventory. As a paralegal working for the law firm that Ms. Marfield has retained, you have been asked to assist in deciding whether a jury should be requested in the anticipated lawsuit filed against Western Renovators, Inc.

a. Should a jury be demanded in this case? Why or why not?

b. If the contract between Ms. Marfield and Western Renovators, Inc., contained more conditions, and if Mr. Lippon was one of 30 potential tenants affected, would your answer to the previous question change? Explain.

THE LITIGATION PROCESS

In practice it is very rare for cases to be argued to a judge only, even though trials before a judge without the jury may save time and money. Settling cases before a trial takes place saves even more time and money, and therefore most cases are negotiated outside of the courtroom. Whether a case is settled out-of-court or is tried in the courtroom, the paralegal is directly involved in the process.

The Three General Areas of Law

There are generally three areas of law in which paralegals may work: civil, criminal, and administrative. Criminal actions involve injustices against the "people of the state" that are filed by the state or federal government or both against an individual alleged to have committed a crime. As in the case of assault and battery, there may be an overlap between the criminal and civil justice systems so that a person can be charged criminally and sued civilly. Administrative law involves the agencies of the executive branch of government and is bound by the Administrative Procedure Act. Administrative law practices challenge the massive bureaucracies which govern such important matters as social services, worker's compensation, and unemployment benefits.

The discussion of the litigation process in this section concentrates on the prosecution of a civil case. Civil litigation provides the majority of court activity and the concomitant work for paralegals, and therefore most paralegals will work in firms that practice primarily civil law. Civil lawsuits seek the reimbursement of monetary damages incident to or equitable relief for harm caused to an individual or group. The great bulk of cases in our trial courts today are civil and traditionally involve an individual, business, or governmental agency that is seeking relief from another individual, business or governmental agency. These cases are based upon tort (in Latin, *ex delicto*) and contract law (*ex contractu*) and include products liability actions, personal injury suits, probate actions, and domestic relations.

The two most popular remedies available for the complainant, or plaintiff, are a suit in equity and a suit for money damages. Equitable relief suits, which usually are not tried before a jury, do not generally involve a request for or a reward of money damages. Equity suits petition the courts for an injunction or specific performance. An injunction is a request to the court that a wrong be prevented or discontinued. Injunctions are commonly sought by environmental groups to prevent the development of forests and wetlands; they are also common in divorces where one party desires to restrain the other party from disposing of marital assets or leaving the state with a child of the marriage.

Specific performance suits request the court to compel the performance of a contract to sell real estate or unique personal property. If a request for specific performance is granted, parties can be forced to transfer real property according to the terms of the sales agreement. Similarly, parties can be ordered by the court to transfer items of personal property, such as a one-of-a-kind Babe Ruth baseball card, pursuant to the terms of the parties' agreement.

The vast majority of civil actions do not involve a request for equitable relief; rather they demand money damages. These breach of contract and tort actions are based upon our Anglo-Saxon common law, or judge-made law, system of justice. Each cause of action requires the establishment of actual damages caused by the defendant, or tortfeasor, to the plaintiff. These causes of action, or claims for relief, are discussed more thoroughly in chapter two.

Beginning the Lawsuit

A person, group of people, or business entity that feels harmed by another usually consults with an attorney in an effort to resolve the dispute and obtain equitable relief or money damages. The attorney, and often her paralegal, conducts an extensive interview to ascertain the underlying facts and circumstances of the problem. The attorney and her staff interview witnesses and perform legal research to decide whether the prospective client has a cause of action.

If the attorney decides that the prospective client has a legitimate cause of action against the wrongdoer, the attorney and client will commence the attorney-client relationship by executing the retainer agreement. Once this retainer is executed, the plaintiff becomes a client of the firm and all privileges and obligations pertinent to that relationship accrue.

Retainer Agreements

The form of the retainer agreement is largely dependent upon the cause of action. If the cause of action is for breach of contract, which includes divorce cases, or a criminal law action, the attorney will request that the retainer stipulate that she be paid hourly, perhaps $150 an hour for her services and $50 an hour for her paralegal's services. If the cause of action is determined to be a tort and the client appears to have a strong case, the attorney may request that the retainer be a contingent fee agreement.

There is much legitimacy in the statement that contingent fee agreements are the poor person's "key to the courthouse" since the client is only obligated to the attorney for costs and does not owe the attorney anything if there is not a settlement favorable to her client. Attorneys frequently work harder under a contingency arrangement since they realize that unless they win, their efforts will not be compensated. A typical contingent fee agreement provides for the attorney to recover 33% and the client 67% of the net settlement if the case is resolved before trial, and, because this agreement provides the attorney with a greater percentage of the settlement if the case goes to trial, approximately 90% of all civil cases are settled before trial. Few clients appreciate their attorneys' receiving a greater share of their awards than they do, especially when the clients are the ones who have sustained the loss and suffering. If the case is not settled before trial, perhaps because settlement negotiations have broken down or the client has refused the settlement offer, the attorney may receive 40%, or sometimes even 50%, of a trial verdict. Contingent fee agreements are negotiable, and plaintiffs with strong cases are often successful in increasing their percentage share of the settlement relative to their retained counsel.

Demand Letters

Once the attorney-client relationship has been established, the plaintiff, through a demand letter prepared by her attorney, notifies the defendant of the damages she has sustained as a result of the defendant's negligence. The demand letter specifies a time period in which the defendant must answer the plaintiff's allegations and requests a specific restitution. If the defendant does not answer the demand letter within the specified time period or if the defendant refuses to offer the requested amount of damages, the parties then prepare for trial.

Preparation For Trial

The plaintiff and defendant, through their respective attorneys, prepare for trial by gathering as many of the facts bearing upon the case as possible. Before the plaintiff initiates litigation, the attorney and her paralegal must select the proper court in which to file the case. Therefore, proper jurisdiction must be established first.

Jurisdiction

Jurisdiction determines what type of court can hear a case. A court has no authority to render a judgment in any case unless it has jurisdiction over the person or property involved, and a case may be dismissed if it is filed in an improper court. For instance, bankruptcy matters can be tried only in the United States Bankruptcy Court, and matters that involve parties who reside in different states are generally tried in the United States District Court.

Types of Jurisdiction Courts have jurisdiction over people and their property or they have jurisdiction over particular matters. There are three types of jurisdiction that a court may have over the parties involved in a case: *in personam* jurisdiction, *in rem* jurisdiction, and *quasi in rem* jurisdiction.

If a court exercises *in personam* jurisdiction, it has the authority to determine the rights or duties of the parties involved in the dispute. The court also has the power to bind the parties personally to a settlement agreement or other court remedy. A court has *in personam* jurisdiction if it meets at least one of the following qualifications:

1. The defendant resides in the county in which the court has jurisdiction.

2. The defendant is present in the county in which the court has jurisdiction. The defendant must be personally served with proper process while in the confines of the county.

3. The defendant and the plaintiff consent to a specific jurisdiction. The defendant's consent is key in this qualification.

4. A nonresident defendant must have "sufficient minimum contacts" with the state. This requirement would be met if the defendant transacted business within the state.

Under *in personam* jurisdiction, the defendant must be served with proper and timely notice of the impending action. The counsel for the plaintiff has the responsibility of serving the defendant while the defendant is present in the county or when the defendant can be contacted to consent to jurisdiction. Generally the notice of the impending action cannot take on a form other than personal service and cannot be made by publication.

In the present court system, a state court obviously has *in personam* jurisdiction over resident defendants. This jurisdiction is not so obvious where the plaintiff is suing a nonresident defendant. The United States Supreme Court has ruled that a nonresident defendant must have "sufficient minimum contacts" with the state for its courts to have *in personam* jurisdiction. This requirement is based upon the due process clause of the constitution. The Supreme Court has declared that it is unfair for a nonresident defendant to be forced to litigate a case in a distant court where the defendant has few or no contacts with that state.

What constitutes "sufficient minimum contacts" is a fact-based analysis for the courts to determine. Obviously, if a nonresident defendant is doing business in the state and those activities result in a lawsuit, the courts have *in personam* jurisdiction over that defendant, but *in personam* jurisdiction is not clear in cases where the defendant has fewer contacts with the state. As guidance, many states have enacted long-arm statutes that specify under what conditions a court will have *in personam* jurisdiction over a nonresident defendant.

All *in rem* jurisdiction actions are local rather than transitory. *In rem* jurisdiction is a court's power over a defendant's property or status. Ownership of property within a state is "sufficient minimum contact" for a court to have *in rem* jurisdiction and make an adjudication regarding that property. For example, the court may determine the rightful owner of a property, force a sale of a property, or foreclose on a property located within its jurisdictional boundaries.

Quasi in rem jurisdiction is exercised rarely and usually only in cases where a court is "grasping at straws" to obtain jurisdiction. A court may have jurisdiction over a party to an action if that party owns some property, such as real property or municipal bonds, within its confines even if that property is not involved in the dispute, as long as a judgment can be satisfied by that property.

Jurisdictional Requirements Jurisdiction is also determined by subject matter of the case. In general, cases may originate at the state or federal level. Jurisdiction at the federal level is determined by specific requirements. Courts with specific jurisdiction include the United State Bankruptcy Court, the United States Tax Court, the United States Court of International Trade, and the United States Claims Court. To originate in the United States District Court, a case must meet one of the following requirements:

1. The United States is a party to the case.

2. The case involves a matter arising under the United States Constitution, such as civil rights matters.

3. The case involves a diversity of citizenship, which means the controversy is between citizens of different states or between a United States citizen and a foreign national. There must be complete diversity and the damage claim must exceed $75,000.00.

The jurisdictional requirements at the state level are determined by state statute. Determining factors include the amount of monetary damages sought and the type of matter that is being heard. In most states, matters asking for damages exceeding $10,000.00 originate in the trial court. There are also courts with specific jurisdiction like water courts and family law courts.

An understanding of the types of jurisdiction and the jurisdictional requirements provides paralegals with the information necessary to determine the proper court for their clients' cases. Once proper jurisdiction is determined, paralegals must choose the trial's venue, which means location.

Venue

Generally the venue for the trial is chosen for the convenience of the defendant; venue plays an important role in allowing defendants to receive an impartial jury and a fair trial. The bases for determining the venue of each dispute are as follows:

1. Residence of one of the parties. Statutes commonly allow for the action to be brought in the county where the defendant resides.

2. Defendant's place of doing business. Corporations are often sued in courts in the county or district where they do business.

3. Site of the subject matter. A trial involving a dispute over real property, for example, must be held in the county where the property is located.

4. Site of the cause of action. Some actions may be brought where the cause of the dispute occurred. For example, an assault case that occurred in Los Angeles County involving a defendant who resided in Orange County, might be heard in either the Los Angeles County Court or the Orange County Court, depending on the consent of the defendant.

5. Where the venue rules allow a choice of venue, the plaintiff usually gets to make that choice. For example, if the defendant resides in Orange County and the cause of action arose in Riverside County, the plaintiff usually has the right to decide whether to bring the lawsuit in Orange or Riverside County.

Venue may be changed to another county or district upon application or by agreement. It is the defendant who usually requests a change of venue. Where wide publicity has been given to a case before trial, a change of venue is sometimes sought in an effort to secure jurors who have not formed an opinion about the case or to provide a neutral forum not charged with local bias. Venue also may be changed to serve the convenience of witnesses. A change of venue may also be granted through a party's claim that the judge hearing the case has a conflict of interest that would prevent that judge from being completely unbiased during the trial. This motion is traditionally called a motion to recuse.

Carefully following the rules of jurisdiction and venue results in a faster end to a case. Whether that means establishing a quick court date in the proper court or forcing the opposing counsel to negotiate an agreement, a well-organized office that knows and applies the correct rules of law will be able to settle cases more quickly than an unorganized office.

Initial Pleadings and Motions

If initial attempts to negotiate are unsuccessful, the plaintiff initiates the cause of action by serving the defendant with a summons and complaint. In some states, a complaint is termed a petition, and a summons is called a citation.

Complaint The complaint is a pleading that states the facts of the plaintiff's action against the defendant and sets forth the damages, judgment, or other relief sought. The complaint must contain enough information to state a claim upon which relief may be granted for the plaintiff. The defendant may begin his or her defense by filing one or more of the following pleadings and motions.

Answer In response to a complaint, the defendant usually files a pleading called an answer that either admits or denies each of the allegations in the plaintiff's complaint or admits all and pleads an excuse. The defendant's answer may also contain affirmative defenses which the defendant argues will serve to diminish or mitigate his liabilities to plaintiff. Some common examples of affirmative defenses are: accord and satisfaction, arbitration and award, assumption of the risk, contributory negligence, discharge in bankruptcy, duress, estoppel, failure of consideration, failure to mitigate damages, fraud, illegality, injury by fellow servant, laches, license, payment, release, *res judicata*, statute of frauds, statute of limitations, and waiver. A defendant may also include in his answer a cross-claim against a codefendant or a counterclaim against the plaintiff or both.

Counterclaim A counterclaim is typically filed by the defendant as part of his answer to the complaint. The counterclaim consists of a cause of action that requests relief or damages for the defendant against the plaintiff. A plaintiff usually files a reply to the new allegations raised in the counterclaim in the same manner that a defendant files an answer to the complaint.

Cross-claim A cross-claim may be alleged by one defendant against a codefendant concerning matters raised by plaintiff in his complaint. The primary purpose of a cross-claim is to establish affirmative relief against the codefendant or plaintiff, or both, on the part of the defendant who submits the cross-claim.

Motion to Quash Service of Summons This motion questions whether the defendant has been properly served with process, which is defined as summons and complaint.

Motion to Strike A motion to strike asks the court to eliminate allegations in the plaintiff's complaint or petition that the defendant deems to be irrelevant, prejudicial, or otherwise improper. If the court agrees with the defendant, the court may order such matter to be deleted from the complaint.

Motion For A More Definite Statement This motion requests that the court require the plaintiff to set forth the facts of his complaint more specifically, or to describe his injury or damages in greater detail so that the defendant can answer the complaint more precisely. This motion is similar to a motion for a bill of particulars, which is also designed to assist the defendant in preparing his answer to the complaint by providing him with more detailed information regarding the plaintiff's cause of action.

Motion To Dismiss. A motion to dismiss requests that a plaintiff's complaint be dismissed on the grounds that it does not state a *prima facie* case against the defendant even if, for the purpose of the motion, the defendant admits that all of the facts alleged by the plaintiff are true. A motion to dismiss in some states is termed a demurrer. A defendant generally desires that the plaintiff's complaint be dismissed "with prejudice" so that it cannot be filed again in the same court. The plaintiff can only appeal this dismissal to a higher court. The plaintiff, on the other hand, does not want his complaint to be dismissed, but if there is a defect with the pleading, the plaintiff will more readily accept a dismissal "without prejudice" since the plaintiff need only amend the error noted by the defendant and refile the complaint with the same court.

Reply Another pleading is the reply. The plaintiff files a reply in response to new assertions raised in defendant's answer to the plaintiff's complaint.

Discovery

After the filing and service of the last pleading allowed by court rules, the parties begin discovery which is conducted during the pretrial stage of litigation. Even though some states allow discovery to be served concurrently with the initial pleading, most of the time discovery is served after filing the last pleading. Thus, in most cases, after an answer, a reply, or motion to dismiss has been filed, paralegals assist their supervising attorneys in the process of discovery. Discovery assumes two very similar forms: oral and written. Oral discovery consists of depositions, and written discovery consists of interrogatories, request for admissions, request for production of documents, and request for mental or physical examinations. Either party to a lawsuit may request discovery in an effort to ascertain the facts necessary to prepare for trial, prevent surprises at trial, and, ideally, settle the action. Without a court order, written discovery can only be served upon parties to the lawsuit, whereas both parties and non-parties can be deposed.

Since paralegals create many of the questions for written discovery, and since so much of written discovery is easily stored in the law office's computers, this relatively inexpensive discovery is usually undertaken prior to administering more expensive depositions. Unless limited by court rule or statute, most supervising attorneys will request their staffs to prepare a massive amount of discovery. Once the law office receives the answers to written discovery, the party who answered that discovery may be deposed in an effort to clarify responses and resolve questions. Even though answers to both oral and written discovery are provided under oath, the deposition responses are spontaneous and thus may be more helpful. Some attorneys will conduct depositions rather that written discovery at the close of pleadings in an effort to achieve the most accurate information possible. Written discovery would then follow the deposition testimony.

Requirements for Taking Depositions A deposition is an out-of-court statement given under oath by a witness of or party to an action. Under the statutes and rules in most states, either party in a civil action may take the deposition of the other party or of any witness. To be effective, a notice to take deposition must be served upon the deponent accompanied by a subpoena and check for mileage and witness fees.

Depositions are frequently necessary to preserve the testimony of important witnesses who cannot appear in court or who reside in other states or countries. These witnesses may be friendly, neutral, or even hostile toward your office's client. Their deposition testimony assists in determining the nature of the evidence that they would testify to if subpoenaed as witnesses in the trial. The deposition may take the form of answers to written questions or of oral examination followed by cross-examination. A deposition is not a public record and is not available to the press until it is made so by court order. A deposition is usually sealed in an envelope until trial.

It is very difficult for a state to compel the presence at a civil trial of a witness who resides outside of that state. Therefore, often a deposition of these witnesses will suffice. When the testimony of such a witness is sought, the party seeking the testimony applies to the court in which the case is pending for the issuance of an out-of-state commission, commonly called letters rogatory, which empowers an official or attorney in the jurisdiction where the witness is residing to take the witness's deposition and forward it to the court in which the action is pending. In some states, the issuance of an out-of-state commission is unnecessary; paralegals should always consult their local court rules.

If a witness is absent from the jurisdiction or is unable to attend the trial in person, her deposition may be read into evidence. If a person who has given a deposition also appears as a witness at the trial, his deposition may be used to attack his credibility if his oral testimony at the trial is inconsistent with that contained in the deposition.

Requirements for Written Discovery Either party may submit to the other party written discovery questions, in a document called interrogatories, which must be answered under oath. Unlike depositions, written discovery is not routinely filed with the court unless ordered by the court.

Other discovery documents include request for production of documents, which require adverse parties to produce books, records and documents for inspection; request for admissions, which require the adverse party to admit to or deny the genuineness of statements and documents; and request for a physical or mental examinations, which require the adverse party to submit to a physical or mental examination. If the other party does not provide responses to discovery, a party may file a motion to compel. Since an underlying purpose of discovery is to uncover all relevant evidence and to promote settlement of the case, the courts liberally construe and apply discovery techniques. Therefore a party will more than likely be required to provide the information required by the discovery process, even though that same information may not necessarily be admissible at the ensuing trial.

Pretrial Conferences

After each of the parties finishes conducting discovery and the case is determined to be "at issue", many courts then set the case for a pretrial hearing or pretrial conference. Generally the attorneys appear at this hearing without their clients. In the presence of a judge, the attorneys seek to agree on undisputed facts and issues called stipulations. These stipulations may include such matters as the time and location of an accident, the use of pictures, maps, or sketches at trial, and other matters, including points of law.

The objective of the pretrial hearing is to shorten the actual trial time without infringing upon the rights of either party. Pretrial procedure frequently results in the settlement of the case without a trial, and case settlement is actually a primary purpose of the pretrial conference. If the case does not settle, the court assigns a specific trial date for the case.

Trial Stage

After the parties set a date for trial, the case takes on a new light. The attorneys and their paralegals prepare trial notebooks containing pleadings, digested depositions and other discovery information, motions, exhibits, trial briefs, and any other information that may be pertinent to the trial. Organization of these trial notebooks differs with each attorney, and attorneys will provide paralegals with careful instructions on how to prepare these devices.

On the first day of the trial the parties engage in *voir dire*, which is the process of selecting the jury. During *voir dire* the attorneys question potential jurors to determine whether there is any reason for the attorneys to exclude any of them. In most trials, the attorney has a certain number of exclusions that can be made for no reason. These are called peremptory challenges. *Voir dire* is practically used to exclude any jurors that may appear to be harmful to a party's case and is necessary to assure a fair and impartial jury.

After the jury is selected, the attorneys make their opening statements. The plaintiff speaks first. In the opening statements, the attorneys lay out the facts and points of law regarding the case. It is very important in the opening statements that the attorneys include only what they can prove because the jury will notice if there is a lack of evidence to prove any point, and if the jury does not notice the lack of evidence, the opposing attorney will be certain to point out any inconsistencies during the closing statements.

After the defendant's opening statement, the introduction of evidence begins. Again, the plaintiff's side goes first. Evidence consists of exhibits of information and the testimonies of witnesses. The party that calls the witness asks the first set of questions. Then, the opposing counsel has the opportunity to cross-examine the witness. After cross-examination, the first party is allowed to redirect the examination of the witness. When all of the witnesses for one party have testified, the opposing counsel brings her witnesses to the stand and the process is repeated.

The evidence is next entered into the record, and the parties make their closing statements. The plaintiff presents the closing arguments first. The plaintiff's attorney may request an additional amount of time after the defendant's closing statement so he can speak last as well. It may seem inequitable for one party to speak first and last. However, the plaintiff usually has the burden of proof, and is therefore allowed to initiate and finalize the closing arguments.

Once the closing arguments are finished, the judge administers instructions to the jury. The attorneys usually propose these instructions to the judge for his or her approval. After receiving the instructions, the jury recesses to deliberate. Deliberation may take as long as is necessary for the jury to reach a decision. When deliberations are finished, the verdict is entered and the judgment is rendered.

Post Trial Procedures

After the judgment is rendered, two procedures remain. If monetary damages have been awarded, the winning party must collect the judgment. Garnishment of wages and attachment of assets are two means of collecting a judgment from a uncooperative defendant. Collection of the judgment in full finalizes the dispute.

Some cases go on to the appellate stage. A party who wishes to appeal the original court's decision must file a motion for a new trial within the prescribed amount of time in order for the appeal to be heard. Procedural rules in the appellate stage differ from those in the trial stage. The notice of appeal is filed with the trial court and the appellate court, and the appellant files an opening brief with the appellate court that the appellee answers with a response or answer brief. The issues on appeal must be based on the trial court's errors. No new evidence is admitted, except under very restrictive situations. If the court deems necessary, the attorneys may present oral arguments to the court. These arguments are short, usually 15 - 30 minutes in length. Based on each party's written and oral argument, the appellate court renders its decision to affirm, modify, or dismiss the lower court's rulings, and the dispute is finalized, unless it is appealed to the state supreme court or United States Supreme Court.

For Discussion Discuss the following questions as they apply to the hypothetical case involving Stephen Taylor.

Your supervising attorney represents the family of Stephen Taylor, who died as a result of ingesting an over-the-counter allergy medication purchased at Gidget's Pharmacy in Bakersfield, California, and produced by Pseudo Pharmaceuticals, Inc, of Indianapolis, Indiana. A criminal investigation revealed that Sarah Alexander, a disgruntled Pseudo Pharmaceuticals employee, had attempted to discredit the company's reputation by lacing several bottles of allergy medication with cyanide. Two other individuals, unrelated to Taylor, died as a result of ingesting the cyanide laced medication. Taylor's family wishes to bring a wrongful death suit against the responsible parties.

1. What would be the general differences between a civil suit filed against Alexander by Taylor's estate and a criminal suit filed against her by the district attorney's office?

2. What sort of fee agreement will your supervising attorney and Taylor's family likely enter into?
3. How would jurisdiction and venue be determined for the civil case against Alexander and Pseudo Pharmaceuticals?
4. What initial pleading and motions are likely to be drafted by your office?
5. What parties should be named as defendants in the complaint filed by your office?
6. What initial pleadings and motions are likely to filed by the defendants?
7. What appropriate questions should be included in discovery performed by your office?
8. What characteristics of the jurors would your office likely look for during *voir dire*?
9. What evidence and witnesses would be most helpful to your office's client during trial?

CONCLUSION

This first chapter has introduced the paralegal to the foundation of the United States legal system, its primary characteristics, and the process by which a suit is tried. The next chapter provides the paralegal with information about the substantive law of torts and contracts and examines the specific rules governing civil procedure.

CHAPTER 2: TORTS, CONTRACTS, AND THE RULES OF CIVIL PROCEDURE FOR PARALEGALS

As previously stated, most paralegals work in the area of civil law. Much of civil law deals with the substantive law of torts and contracts. To work successfully in the area of civil law, a paralegal must be familiar with torts and contracts and must have a working knowledge of the rules of civil procedure. The following chapter highlights the important points of all three areas.

INTRODUCTION TO TORT LAW

A tort is a "civil wrong other than a breach of contract, for which the court will provide a remedy in the form of an action for damages." William Prosser, *Law of Torts* 2 (5th ed. 1984). The tort system gives us our civil laws. These laws govern wrongs done to other people and their property. It is the tort system that allows for the compensation of those wrongs. Paralegals are extensively involved in the prosecution and defense of tort actions.

The tort system is comprised of six general areas: intentional torts, quasi-intentional torts, negligent torts, strict liability, products liability, and nuisance. This section provides a brief overview of each of these areas and the component elements within each area.

Intentional Torts

The one distinctive element of intentional torts is the intent of the actor, or tortfeasor. Each intentional tort requires that the actor who commits the tort has an intent to do whatever injury is protected by the tort. The actor must be certain, or substantially certain, that his or her actions will have a detrimental effect upon the person or property to which the action is directed. There are two separate categories of intentional torts: intentional harm to the person and intentional harm to property.

Intentional Harm to the Person

The first group of intentional torts involves injuries to the person. These torts include assault, battery, false imprisonment, and intentional infliction of emotional distress. In each of these torts, the person who is injured by another's act can bring a lawsuit to determine if a wrong has been caused and to provide compensation for that wrong. For example, when a person strikes another, the underlying tort is called battery. By proving the elements that constitute battery, trial attorneys can receive a verdict for injured parties in a court of law and damages can be awarded to the injured parties in an attempt to make them as whole as they were before the battery. Each of the four torts discussed in this section varies according to what type of harm they are designed to guard against.

Assault Assault actions are brought to protect individuals from threat of harm or offensive contact. An assault occurs whenever the tortfeasor places the plaintiff in imminent fear for his or her well-being, such as when the tortfeasor takes a stick, brandishes it over the head of the plaintiff, and shouts, "Your money or your life!" The tortfeasor does not need to strike the plaintiff in order for the tort of assault to occur.

Battery A battery action is brought to protect the plaintiff who is actually hit with the stick in the above scenario. Battery is the wrongful touching of another person, and because assault and battery often occur in the same action, they are usually alleged together in a complaint.

False Imprisonment If a tortfeasor unreasonably detains a plaintiff against his or her will for an undue length of time, the plaintiff can bring a false imprisonment action. This tort can be brought by people who have been held hostage, by people who have been detained by the police without just cause, or by anyone who can prove that the tortfeasor detained them in an injurious manner. Injuries in a false imprisonment action may be both physical and emotional.

Intentional Infliction of Emotional Distress The fourth intentional tort covers actions that force a plaintiff to experience a particularly gruesome event. The tort can also be alleged by victims who have been unfortunate enough to see their loved ones suffer injury or death at the hands of another. For instance, if during a football game someone were to knowingly trample a dog that was the home team's mascot in plain view of the team's fan, this person may be found liable for intentional infliction of emotional distress.

These four intentional tort actions are brought against those who intentionally injure other people. There are similar tort actions that provide for the protection of property.

Injury to Property

Torts involving injury to property include trespass to land, trespass to chattels, and conversion. These torts are concerned with protecting a person's property from the willful destruction by others or protecting a person from the inability to use his or her own property to its full enjoyment.

Trespass to Land This tort covers the unauthorized entry on or use of land. If a tortfeasor enters upon land that is not his or her own, the owner of the land may bring a trespass to land action. Even if the tortfeasor merely drops some debris on the land, the owner has a right to bring an action.

Trespass to Chattels The same sort of tort applies to personal property that applies to land. The trespass to chattels tort covers the property owner's exclusive use of his property. The only difference between trespass to land and trespass to chattels is that while land covers only real estate, chattels include all other physical property.

Conversion The tort of conversion pertains to an exercise of dominion and control over chattel in a manner that is adverse to the rightful owner's interest in the chattel. It provides the owner of stolen or converted property with the means to recover that property or with damages equal to the fair market value of the chattel at the time of the conversion.

Intentional torts pertain exclusively to actions that are executed deliberately. Over time, however, the tort system has evolved to cover not only intentional harm but also harmful situations that may be unintentional. These unintentional torts form a general category of wrongs that are tested by the standard of negligence.

Quasi-Intentional Torts

Quasi-intentional torts include defamation, invasion of privacy, intentional misrepresentation, and wrongful institution of legal proceedings. The protection that these tort actions offers is rapidly increasing in popularity.

Defamation

To establish a *prima facie* case for defamation, the plaintiff must prove that the defendant used language that harmed his or her reputation. This defamatory language must have been communicated to a third party either through written means or broadcast (libel) or through injurious spoken comments (slander). A defendant may defend a defamation action by proving that the injurious comments were actually true or, if aimed at a public figure, were made non-maliciously and in jest.

Invasion of Right to Privacy

An invasion of privacy occurs when a defendant uses a plaintiff's name or picture, without the plaintiff's consent, for the defendant's commercial advantage, unreasonably pries into the plaintiff's private affairs, or unreasonably publicly discloses the plaintiff's private matters. The main defense to right of privacy torts is that the defendant had the plaintiff's consent.

Intentional Misrepresentation

Intentional misrepresentation torts allege that the defendant has committed fraud against or deceived the plaintiff. To establish a *prima facie* case, the plaintiff must prove that the defendant falsely represented himself or herself, that the defendant knew that the representation was false, that the defendant intended the plaintiff to act in a predisposed manner because he or she was relying on the defendant's representation, and that damage resulted as a result of this reliance.

Wrongful Institution of Legal Proceedings

These torts cover the wrongful prosecution of a defendant in criminal cases and the wrongful suing of a defendant in a civil action. To establish a *prima facie* case for malicious prosecution, the plaintiff must prove that there was a criminal proceeding against the plaintiff that was decided in favor of the plaintiff, that there existed a lack of probable cause for the proceedings, that the purpose of bringing the criminal proceedings against the plaintiff was one other than to serve justice, and that the plaintiff suffered damages. The plaintiff alleging wrongful institution of civil proceedings must prove the same elements as those in malicious prosecution except that the prior case was tried civilly rather that criminally. Abuse of process may be alleged by a plaintiff in either a criminal or civil case to prove that the case was brought about to serve a purpose other than to serve justice. For instance, if a person is wrongly accused of and tried for a crime solely because the accuser wants to injure the reputation of the accused, the accuser would be liable to the accused for damages due to abuse of process.

Negligent Torts

Negligent torts are the most common and the most varied torts in our civil law system. An example of a negligent tort is personal injury, where a defendant's negligence results in injury to the plaintiff.

Necessary Elements for Proving a Negligent Tort

To prove a negligent tort, the trial attorney must prove duty, breach, proximate cause, and damages. Paralegals assist in the development of each of these four elements of the *prima facie* case for negligence. If the court or the jury finds that the attorney has proven each of these four elements, then damages can be awarded to the wronged party.

Duty The element of duty is based on the belief that each person owes a duty to others to refrain from hurting them. For example, John owes a duty to Mary to refrain from hitting her while driving his car. Duty is often judged by the "reasonable person" standard. Society would consider John's hitting Mary with his car unreasonable, and John has a duty to act reasonably. Therefore, he is negligent in hitting Mary. The jury determines the "reasonable person" standard if the case goes to trial.

Breach of Duty When John hits Mary with the car, he is said to have breached the duty of care he owed to Mary. Breach of duty is the second element that requires proof in a negligence action. In order to prove breach, the attorney must prove that either the instrument that caused the injury was within the exclusive control or possession of the tortfeasor (*res ipsa loquitur*) or the actor violated a statute or ordinance (negligence *per se*). Proving either *res ipsa loquitur* or negligence *per se* usually results in proving that the defendant did breach a duty. If John violated a statute when he hit Mary with his car, it would be fairly easy to prove that he breached his duty to Mary. Once the plaintiff proves a breach of duty, her attorney progresses to proving proximate cause, which is usually the most difficult element to prove.

Proximate Cause In proving proximate cause, the attorney must prove not only that the defendant actually caused the injury, but also that the defendant was the cause in fact of the injury. The attorney through the assistance of the paralegal must show that the injury was foreseeable and that there were no other causes of the injury. In the example, Mary's attorney must prove that "but for" John's actions, the accident never would have happened. The attorney must also prove that the accident happened without any superseding causes, such as an earthquake's forcing John's car to hit Mary. Next, Mary's attorney must prove that the result of the accident was foreseeable and that there were no intervening events that caused the accident, such as another car's hitting Mary.

Damages If the defendant's negligence is found to be the proximate cause of the plaintiff's injuries, the defendant is liable for paying damages to the plaintiff. The plaintiff establishes damages by introducing evidence that indicates pecuniary damages (e.g., hospital bills and car repair receipts), non-pecuniary damages (e.g., pain and suffering), and other categories of damages, including punitive damages and consequential damages. In every case, the plaintiff has the duty to take reasonable steps to mitigate any damages. Also, the defendant may prove that the plaintiff was partially responsible for the damages sustained. Under the comparative negligence theory, which is included within the statutes of a majority of states, the amount of the plaintiff's damages may be reduced by the percentage of negligence that the jury attributes to the plaintiff.

To be successful, the plaintiff in a negligence action must establish each of the four elements of the *prima facie* case. Paralegals are instrumental in defining the facts that are vital to establishing and proving their offices' clients' cases.

Defenses to a Negligent Tort

The defendant who is alleged to have committed a negligent tort may respond with several defenses. These defenses include contributory or comparative negligence and the concepts of joint and vicarious liability.

Contributory and Comparative Negligence Damages may be diminished or may not be awarded if it can be shown that the injured party contributed to the accident. If Mary was not wearing a seat belt at the time of the accident with John, she could be found to be contributorily negligent. John, therefore, might not have to pay damages, or the amount of damages for which he is responsible might be limited.

The modern trend is to move away from the strict standard of contributory negligence and move toward a standard of comparative negligence. Under the doctrine of comparative negligence, the judge or jury examines each party's negligence and decreases the damage award by the percentage of negligence that was caused by the plaintiff. In Mary's case, if she were found to be 30% at fault, and John was found to be 70%

at fault, the damages for which John would be responsible would be decreased by 30%. The specific elements of this rule depend on the law of the state where the action is tried.

Joint and Vicarious Liability Actions for negligence can be further complicated by the concepts of joint tortfeasors and vicarious liability. If two people are acting together to produce the harm, both may be held liable for the injury; even if the two tortfeasors perform different deeds but the responsibility for the resulting injury is inseparable, they still may be held jointly liable. The issue of joint liability may become especially important in cases involving numerous defendants.

Courts have commonly held defendants jointly and severally liable in cases where the plaintiff was injured by defective drugs or environmental hazards. For example, a plaintiff suffered brain damage from taking a particular tranquilizer over a period of ten years. The tranquilizer was manufactured by at least five different companies. At trial, the parties were unable to establish which company manufactured the drugs ingested by the plaintiff, so the court ruled that all five defendants were jointly and severally liable. Therefore, if one or more of the defendants were unable to pay its share of the judgment, the codefendants would be responsible for the insolvent defendant's share.

The concept of vicarious liability relates to the liability one has for another's actions. If John were to hit Mary while delivering a pizza for his employer, his employer may be held liable for the injuries that Mary sustained. In this case, Mary would bring an action against both John and the pizza company. Vicarious liability does not just apply to employer/employee relationships; it also applies to parent/child relationships and owner/user relationships.

Strict Liability

Strict liability offenses make up a category of torts that do not require a demonstration of fault as do negligent torts. To prove that a defendant is strictly liable, the plaintiff must establish that the defendant had an absolute duty to make conditions safe, the defendant breached that duty, and the breach of the duty was the actual and proximate cause of the injury to the plaintiff.

The owner of dangerous or wild animals is strictly liable for any injuries caused by the animals as long as the injured persons did not knowingly and voluntarily place themselves in harm's way. For example, many state statutes and municipal ordinances hold an owner strictly liable for injuries caused by domestic animals, such as dogs and cats, sometimes even in cases where the animals have no known vicious propensities.

Individuals who carry on ultrahazardous activities are strictly liable for any resulting injuries to potential plaintiffs. Activities are considered ultrahazardous if there is a substantial risk of serious harm no matter how much care the defendant exercises. For example, bungee jumping and blasting with dynamite are considered to be ultrahazardous activities. A defendant engaged in these activities will be held strictly liable for any resulting injuries.

Products Liability

There are several causes of action used to find defendants liable for injuries caused by manufactured products. Many of these causes of action, such as intentional torts, negligence, breach of warranty, and strict liability, have already been discussed. The easiest claim to prove is strict liability because no demonstration of fault is required. Rather, a plaintiff must show that a product is defective and unreasonably dangerous. Many products liability cases are brought through class action suits because many people are affected by the product in a similar manner. One or several affected individuals represent the entire group. Recent cases have involved exploding gas tanks on cars and trucks, certain cancer causing drugs, and contraceptive devices such as the IUD.

Nuisance

Nuisance actions are brought when a defendant interferes with another's reasonable use and enjoyment of property. There are three categories of nuisances: public, private, and mixed. A public nuisance is harm done to the general community. The community as a whole has a right to seek legal redress for the community's injuries. A private nuisance is a harm effected upon a specific individual. The individual has a right to hold the defendant liable for his or her private injuries. A mixed nuisance is a combination of both public and private nuisances. For a nuisance to be mixed, a public nuisance must occur in which an individual suffers a different injury from that sustained by the community.

An example of a public nuisance would be a chemical plant emitting substantial amounts of pollution into the air surrounding a town. If the same chemical company disposed of its toxic waste on a private individual's land, there would be a private nuisance and the landowner would have the right to sue the chemical company to prevent further dumping and pay for any cleanup costs. If Mary, a resident of the affected community, had an acute case of asthma or was allergic to the chemical particles emitted by the company, there would be a mixed nuisance.

In nuisance actions, the court can award money damages, injunctive relief, or both. When awarding money, the court determines a figure that would provide restitution for those who were injured. Injunctive relief allows the court to prevent the injuring party from causing further damages. This relief assists in controlling companies from polluting the air or land and also allows for a free market resolution of damages. In the example above, the community could have the plant shut down or force it to pay for pollution control devices on its emissions.

As the criminal law system protects society from harmful individuals, the tort system provides restitution for individuals harmed by others and protects individuals from future harm. The criminal law system vindicates the public at large while the tort system protects individual interests from wrongdoers. The tort system is a method of engineering social change. Without the continual evolution of tort litigation, the justice system would be confined to past traditions. Paralegals play a major role in developing their office's tort cases and, in turn, influencing changes in society.

For Discussion Describe what type of tort or torts each of the following hypotheticals demonstrates.

1. Micki forgot to leave her five barrels of household trash on the street to be picked up by the waste removal company. Her neighbor, Angela, had three acres of land adjacent to Micki's yard. Micki chose to dump her trash on the far end of Angela's acreage. One of Angela's favorite horses became seriously ill as a result of consuming items contained in Micki's trash.
2. Mitch and a group of his friends approached Michelle from behind as she was walking along a trail that bordered a steep precipice. As the group neared Michelle, Mitch yelled out, "You'd better move over or we'll push you over!" Startled, Michelle slipped, fell on a large rock in the middle of the path, and broke her collar bone.
3. Terry, in a hurry to reach work on time, drove through a red light and hit Mark. Mark suffered a broken back and was hospitalized for four weeks.
4. Lucy told Geoff that she would represent him in his case against Tom. Geoff claims that Lucy suggested that she was a bar certified attorney. After losing his case, Geoff learned that Lucy never finished her third year of law school and never passed the state bar exam.
5. Ed, realizing that he could no longer manage his ranch alone due to his failing health, asked Peter, his best friend's son, to give up his job in the city to manage the ranch and care for Ed. Ed told Peter that if he granted Ed's request, the ranch would be Peter's upon Ed's death. Peter moved to the ranch and assisted Ed. After Ed's death, Ed's nephew, George, moved into the ranch telling Peter that

although he realized that his uncle had intended for Peter to own the ranch, George felt the ranch should remain in the family and therefore intended to possess the property.

6. Sandra had to undergo psychiatric treatment after she witnessed the shooting and maiming of her brother by Hal.
7. At a company Christmas party after having been spurned by Robert and after consuming several alcoholic beverages, Jill shouted, "Robert has been embezzling company funds for years." Jill's remark was overheard by the company president, and although the validity of the claim was never proved, Robert was demoted from his position of head accountant to the lower paying position of staff accountant.
8. As she was driving along the interstate, Tina was stopped by a police officer who said she appeared to have been weaving. The officer required that Tina take a breath test to show blood alcohol content, so he drove her to the police station. Although Tina passed the breath test, the police officer locked her in a holding cell for two hours.

The Substantive Law of Contracts

Contract law is another area of civil law with which paralegals should be familiar. A contract is an agreement between competent parties to do or abstain from doing some act in exchange for something of value. In legal terms, a contract is bargained for consideration. Attorneys and their paralegals are involved in both the drafting of contracts and the litigation that results when a contract has not been honored.

The Elements of a Valid Contract

To be valid, a contract must include an offer, an acceptance of that offer, a mutual manifestation of assent to be bound by the offer and acceptance, and consideration. If a contract is missing any of these elements, it is not valid. The following brief explanation of the elements of a contract will help paralegals better understand the law of contracts.

Offer

An offer initiates a contract. The offer may be phrased as, "I will give you $500.00 in return for two video cassette recorders," or it may be simply phrased as, "Here is $500.00," when the intention is that the $500.00 is being traded for two video cassette recorders. Making an offer is fairly simple, and it is therefore easy to enter into a contract. A valid offer essentially requires that the offering party intend that his or her proposal be legally binding and that the proposal be complete.

Acceptance

A valid acceptance of an offer necessitates on the part of the acceptor an intent to be bound by the terms of the offer, an unconditional manifestation that the acceptor intends to be bound to the offer's terms, and a mutual agreement of the parties. If John says that he will give Sam $500.00 for two video cassette recorders and Sam agrees to John's offer, Sam's agreement to the offer is an acceptance. If Sam accepts the valid offer and Sam indicates that his acceptance of the offer's terms is unconditional, Sam and John have formed a contract.

Manifestation of Assent

Essential to any offer or any acceptance must be the belief and intent of both parties that they actually are bound to the terms of the contract. This is called the manifestation of assent to be bound. It is difficult to accurately understand a person's thoughts and intentions at the time of a contract's formation, but both parties' actions should reasonably manifest that they intend to be bound by the terms of the contract. From Sam and John's behavior at the formation of the contract it was apparent that they desired to be bound by their agreement. However, if Sam shrugged and stated, "I do not think that we should be doing this," the manifestation of assent would fall short of being fulfilled as would the acceptance of the offer.

Consideration

The final prerequisite of a valid contract is consideration. There must be an exchange of something of value. One party cannot merely give the other party the offered item. This would constitute a gift rather than a contract. Consideration may consist of an item of value, such as money, a legal detriment, such as forbearance, or a legal benefit, such as a monetary loan. Under Sam's and John's agreement, the $500.00 and the video cassette recorders are the contract's consideration.

Types of Contract Litigation

Paralegals assist in the prosecution and defense of lawsuits that are brought under the law of contracts. There are three primary contract actions. These are breach of contract, bad faith, and breach of fiduciary duty.

Breach of Contract

Breach of contract results when there is a failure by one of the parties to fulfill written or oral commitments. This is the most common action under contract law. If two parties entered into a valid contract and one party did not fulfill the terms of that contract, the result is a breach of contract. The party who did not receive fulfillment of the agreement may bring an action against the party who failed to fulfill the agreement.

Bad Faith

Entering into an agreement with no intention of fulfilling the terms of the agreement constitutes bad faith. Bad faith is usually remedied through the court's compelling the party who entered into the agreement in bad faith to pay the other party the amount that he or she may have lost due to the other's bad faith. That amount may be the total cost the injured party incurred, or the total profit the injured party lost, depending on the situation. Many states allow recovery for bad faith against insurance companies that do not properly pay benefits to the insured or who otherwise act in bad faith toward the insured.

Breach of Fiduciary Duty

Failing to act in the best interest of a party when there exists an obligation to do so may bring about an action for breach of fiduciary duty. This breach often occurs when one is making investments for others. Stockbrokers, bankers, and other investors owe their customers a fiduciary duty to invest their money safely and act in their best interests. If an investor breaches this duty, the aggrieved party may seek remedy from him or her through contract litigation.

For Discussion Provide specific factual examples of each of the following types of contract litigation: breach of contract, bad faith, and breach of fiduciary duty.

THE FEDERAL RULES OF CIVIL PROCEDURE

The previous sections of this chapter have provided an overview of some of the possible civil litigation actions. To assist in the successful litigation of any civil case, paralegals must be very familiar with the rules of civil procedure. The rules governing civil procedure were adopted to create uniformity within the court system.

Until the modern Federal Rules of Civil Procedure were accepted, the court system often produced diverse procedural results. Under the current rules, every suit brought before any tribunal in the United States is on equal footing with any other suit. The rules eliminate bias in the court system by establishing a pattern of procedure that must be followed and implementing sanctions for breaches of proper procedure.

Although the rules of civil procedure for the majority of states closely mirror the federal rules, each state has its own set of procedural rules, and paralegals should consult their states' codes. The following discussion of the Federal Rules of Civil Procedure, or F.R.C.P., highlights thirteen rules with which paralegals should be familiar.

The Commencement of an Action, Rule 3

Filing a complaint (in some states it is called a petition) with the court commences a civil action. The first regulated step in the legal process requires that a complaint or petition initiate the civil lawsuit.

Service of Process, Rule 4

Rule 4 of F.R.C.P. covers the requirements for service of process. Failure to adhere to these rules may result in the premature termination of a lawsuit. The requirements are quite involved, and although the following discussion covers their key points, paralegals should make an effort to understand all of the requirements in their entirety. When parties file their complaints with the court, they must serve the defendant with proper process. Process consists of the service of a summons and a complaint. The summons must contain the name of the court, the names or designations of the parties to the action, the county in which it is brought, the time when the defendant must appear to answer the allegations in the complaint, and a statement of the specific penalties for not responding.

Usually, the summons is served with a copy of the complaint. However, when such service is not made, a copy of the complaint must be filed with the court and served upon the defendant within ten days of service of the summons. If the complaint is not filed within that period of time, the case will be judged without prejudice and dismissed.

Generally, any person who has reached the age of majority and who is not a party to the action may serve the summons on the defending party. However, some states stipulate that the sheriff must serve process. Law office employees may serve process, but usually the preferred agent is an independent paralegal or investigator who specializes in process serving. In criminal cases, the local sheriff or constable traditionally serves the defendant with the summons.

There are also rules governing the actual delivery of the summons. Substitute service may be made for natural persons over the age of eighteen. A natural person is a non-corporate citizen of the United States. The summons may be left at their domiciles with family members who are over the age of eighteen, or it may be left at their place of employment with a secretary, bookkeeper, stenographer, or chief clerk. The summons may also be left with a duly appointed agent of the defendant.

Process for natural persons who are between thirteen years and eighteen years may be served on the parties, their mothers, fathers, or legal guardians, their appointed agents, or their employers. Process for persons under the age of thirteen must be served on their parents or legal guardians.

Computation of Time Limits, Rule 6

F.R.C.P. regulates the computation of time limits for filing documents with the court. In general, time begins to accrue the day after the event, act, or default occurs. For example, if a plaintiff has a two-year statute of limitations within which to serve and file a complaint against a defendant doctor, the plaintiff must serve and file the complaint within two years of the day after she discovered she had been harmed due to the doctor's malpractice.

If the last day of the regulated period falls on a Saturday, Sunday, or legal holiday, the time period will actually run out on the next business day. Therefore, no time period may run out on a weekend or legal holiday. If the time period includes less than seven days, the intermittent Saturdays, Sundays, and holidays are not included in the computation of time. If the time period is greater than six days, the computation includes weekends and holidays.

General Rules Regarding Pleadings and Motions, Rules 8, 11, and 12

Because cases are initiated with a summons and a complaint, paralegals should know the rules regarding pleadings. The most important types of pleadings include complaints, counterclaims, cross-claims, third party claims, answers, and replies.

In general, all pleadings must be simple, concise, and direct. In addition to containing a proper caption and subscription, each pleading must include the pleading party's address, must be signed by the attorney who is representing the pleading party, and must include the attorney's current registration number, address, and phone number.

Claims for relief, which are included in complaints, counterclaims, cross-claims, and third party claims, must contain, at a minimum, the following: a short and plain statement of jurisdiction, a short and plain statement showing that the pleader is entitled to relief, and a demand for judgment for the relief to which one is entitled.

According to F.R.C.P. 12, "[a] defendant shall file his answer within twenty days after the service of the summons on him, or if a copy of the complaint is not served with the summons,. . . within thirty days." The answer must assert all affirmative defenses which apply to the complaint. Affirmative defenses include the following: accord and satisfaction, arbitration and reward, assumption of risk, contributory negligence, discharge in bankruptcy, duress, estoppel, failure of consideration, fraud, illegality, injury by fellow servant, laches, license, payment, release, *res judicata*, statute of limitations, statute of frauds, and waiver. Answers must contain a defense to each claim asserted in the complaint being answered, an admission to or denial of each claim, or a response that acts as a denial by indicating that one is without knowledge or information sufficient to form a belief as to the truth of the claim. Any claim in the complaint that is not specifically denied is deemed to have been admitted. Therefore, an answer must be prepared with much care.

Every defense to a claim for relief should be made within a pleading with the exception of the following six defenses, which may be made by motion, such as a motion to dismiss:

1. lack of jurisdiction over the subject matter,
2. lack of jurisdiction over the person,
3. insufficiency of process,
4. insufficiency of service of process,
5. failure to state a claim upon which relief can be granted, and
6. failure to join a party under Rule 19.

These six defenses name the sanctions for not following the preceding rules governing pleadings. A defense must be made through motions or pleadings within specific time periods or the defense will be waived. Defenses 2, 3, and 4 must be made by motion before the case continues. Defenses 5 and 6 may be made in any pleading or in any amended pleading or at the trial on the merits of the case. The defense of lack of jurisdiction over the subject matter is never waived and therefore can be brought at any time in the proceedings.

Rule 12 regarding defenses is a very involved rule, but knowledge of its components is essential for the effective practice of law. Paralegals should take the time to memorize it.

General Provisions Governing Discovery, Rule 26

Rule 26 begins the section of discovery rules. Discovery will be discussed in greater detail later in this book; therefore, this examination of discovery rules will focus on the methods of obtaining discovery and the sanctions imposed for improper discovery methods rather than describe each of the discovery tools.

Any non-privileged information that is relevant to the subject matter of the pending action is obtainable through discovery. The methods of discovery include depositions upon oral or written examination, written interrogatories, production of documents or permission to enter upon land or other property for inspection purposes, physical and mental examinations, and requests for admissions.

Unless there is a court ruling to the contrary, there is no limit to the frequency or extent of discovery methods that a party might use. A request for discoverable information may be made at any time up until the time of trial, or shortly before trial as stipulated in a pretrial order, or, if the case is pending appeal, up until the time of appeal. Under special circumstances, the court may order discovery procedures during the trial or appeal. A party must respond to the discovery requests with truthful responses, usually made under oath. Failure to respond truthfully will result in sanctions, as will a failure to reasonably supplement any responses to any discovery requests.

Depositions Before Action or Pending Appeal, Rule 27

According to Rule 27, notice must be given before a deposition may proceed. Once notice is given and a place and time are set for the deposition, the party calling the deposition must meet certain requirements. There must be a person present who is authorized to administer oaths to swear in the deponent. There must also be a way to record the testimony given in the deposition. Most commonly, a court reporter or stenographer transcribes the deposition. Recently, the courts have allowed depositions to be taped and later produced in written form.

Depositions upon Oral Examination, Rule 30

According to Rule 30, no deposition may be taken before the expiration of thirty days after the service of the original summons without leave, or permission, of the court. When a deposition has been taken and fully transcribed, the paralegal often sends a copy to each deponent who then has thirty days to make any changes to the transcription, sign it, and return a signed copy to the officer of the court.

Interrogatories to Parties, Rule 33

Interrogatories are used liberally in the discovery process. Each interrogatory must be answered separately and fully in writing under oath unless the party objects to the question, in which case the objection stands in place of the answer until the court can rule on the objection. Generally, answers to interrogatories must be served on the party initiating the discovery within 30 days of service of the interrogatories.

Request for Admissions, Rule 36

A request for admissions is served by one party on the other and requests that party admit to the truthfulness of a fact, an opinion, or a relevant document. The answer again must be set forth separately, and must be made in good faith as to its truthfulness. If no answer is returned within thirty days of service of the request for admissions, the item is deemed admitted. The court may use any admission during the trial to ascertain the truth of a matter in dispute. It is very essential, therefore, to timely answer all requests for admissions.

Sanctions for Failure to Make Discovery, Rule 37

A party may file a motion to compel discovery if the other party fails to answer discovery or provides evasive or incomplete answers. The costs of the motion may be assessed to the party who failed to comply with the discovery requests. If that party does not follow the court order compelling discovery, Rule 37 provides the following remedies:

1. contempt of court charges may be executed against the unresponsive individuals or their attorneys,
2. expenses of the discovery may be taxed to the unresponsive party, and
3. the court may order that the unresponsive party be refused any opportunity to oppose the designated claims or defenses sought in discovery.

Paralegals must make sure that their office is strictly following the rules of discovery. Not only does noncompliance jeopardize a client's case, but the client or attorney, or both, may be held in contempt of court and be sanctioned through fine, incarceration, or both.

Summary Judgment, Rule 56

Summary judgment is a pretrial motion that is filed when there is no dispute regarding the material facts of the case. The motion requests the court to reach a decision on the basis of the pleadings alone, without going through a trial. A motion for summary judgment may be aimed at dismissing one or some of the causes of action or may attempt to dismiss the entire complaint. Affidavits provide strong support for or against this motion.

The preceding section comprised an overview of the Federal Rules of Civil Procedure. The F.R.C.P. was established to provide for a uniform and equitable system of dispute resolution. Compliance with these rules is essential to the successful practice of law in the federal court system. Each state has similar rules to which paralegals must adhere. Note that these rules regard civil procedure and that there are also rules governing criminal procedure with which paralegals who work in criminal law should be familiar.

For Discussion Discuss the ways in which your state's rules of civil procedure differ from the federal rules of civil procedure.

CONCLUSION

This chapter has provided an overview of the substantive law of torts and contracts and a summary of the rules of civil procedure. The discussion of the rules of civil procedure highlighted the procedural requirements for many court documents. The next chapter more specifically discusses how to properly prepare the most common court documents.

CHAPTER 3: DOCUMENT PREPARATION FOR PARALEGALS

Paralegals should be familiar with all of the types of documents that are relevant to the practice of law. This chapter discusses important legal documents in rough chronological order as they are prepared in the course of litigation, from the demand letter to the appellate brief.

TYPES OF LEGAL DOCUMENTS

For the purpose of highlighting the important types of legal documents, marked in bold letters, it is assumed that a prospective client, Robert Scott, has just slipped and fallen on the vinyl tile surface in the produce aisle of Sam's Supermarket. As a result of the fall, Mr. Scott suffers a broken hip. Mr. Scott knows of a particular law office's reputation for integrity and competency, so he calls and briefly discusses his case with the attorney, Mary Cortez.

Preliminary Documents

Ms. Cortez suggests that Mr. Scott arrange an appointment with her paralegal and asks the paralegal to prepare an **intake memorandum** based on the initial client interview. The **intake memo** summarizes background information about Mr. Scott, details the facts of the slip and fall, and proposes the action that Mr. Scott would like the law office to take on his behalf; an **intake memorandum** is just one of the many **memoranda of law** that paralegals may prepare. After submitting this **intake memo** to Ms. Cortez, the paralegal calls Mr. Scott to tell him that Ms. Cortez has offered to represent him in a slip and fall action against the supermarket under a **contingent fee agreement**.

After reading and agreeing to the terms of representation, Mr. Scott and Ms. Cortez execute the **contingent fee agreement** and the attorney-client relationship commences. A typical **contingent fee agreement** stipulates that if the case is settled before trial, the client will keep 67% of the settlement proceeds after costs are deducted, and the attorney will keep the remaining 33%. If the case does not settle before trial, a typical **contingent fee agreement** provides that the attorney will retain 40%, or even 50%, of the award as a result of a favorable trial court decision. The contingency percentages are negotiable so that given a strong case with clear-cut liability, the attorney may agree to retain less than 33%. Defendants in tort cases and both parties in non-tort cases, such as contracts and divorces, usually execute **retainer agreements** with their attorneys. **Retainer agreements** provide for a certain sum of money to be paid up front as a retainer and specify an hourly fee for services which are usually billed monthly.

Once the attorney-client relationship has been established, Ms. Cortez should attempt to resolve the dispute without litigation. In fact, even though the number of lawsuits is increasing every year, civil litigation should be the last resort for the resolution of disputes. All efforts at settling cases without litigation, including mediation and arbitration, should be attempted, and paralegals should inform their supervising attorneys of the various alternatives to litigation that exist within the local community.

The initial effort to resolve litigation involves making Sam's Supermarket aware of the damages Mr. Scott has sustained as a result of Sam's Supermarket's negligence, so the paralegal prepares a **demand letter**. This **demand letter** notifies Sam's Supermarket of the circumstances underlying the damages that Mr. Scott has sustained and provides Sam's Supermarket the opportunity to settle the dispute for a specific amount of money to avoid litigation. **Demand letters** usually allow the defendant thirty days to respond before litigation is initiated. After Ms. Cortez proofs and signs the letter, it is sent to Sam's Supermarket.

Pleadings

Disputes are not often resolved through the use of a demand letter, so once the response time period provided in the demand letter expires and it appears to Ms. Cortez that the matter will not be resolved without litigation, the paralegal drafts a **complaint** to be served on Sam's Supermarket and filed with the court. The **complaint** presents the *prima facie* case against Sam's Supermarket and requests damages or other relief. The **complaint** should be served with a **summons**, which is a document issued by the court explaining that Sam's Supermarket has been sued and that it has a certain time limit in which to respond to Mr. Scott's allegations. The paralegal merely fills in the blanks in the **summons** with the necessary information. A sample summons is set forth in Figure 4.

In Mr. Scott's case, the paralegal would prepare a **complaint** alleging negligence on the supermarket's part and requesting damages to compensate for Mr. Scott's medical bills, lost wages, and pain and suffering. The paralegal would also prepare the **summons** and, upon Ms. Cortez's approval, arrange that both the **summons** and **complaint** be served upon the supermarket or its designated agent.

Within twenty to thirty days of service of process, depending upon the state rules of civil procedure, Sam's Supermarket would prepare an **answer** to the complaint in which each of Mr. Scott's allegations would be admitted or denied. The **answer** may also include affirmative defenses. For instance, Sam's Supermarket might allege that Mr. Scott was contributorily negligent because he was running at the time of the slip and fall.

Sam's Supermarket may also assert a **counterclaim** against Mr. Scott for damages that the supermarket sustained because Mr. Scott overturned the store's lobster tank as he was falling. If there are multiple defendants, for instance Mr. Scott may have sued the independent cleaning company that maintains the floors at Sam's Supermarket, Sam's Supermarket may file a **cross-claim** against the cleaning company. In many states, once the defendant files the **answer** to the complaint, the plaintiff may then file a **reply** to the answer. A **reply** responds to the new matters or allegations that may have been brought up in defendant's **answer**.

Another pleading which may be served and filed is the **third party complaint**. Through a **third party complaint**, the defendant may bring a new party, or parties, into the litigation who were not listed in the original **complaint** and who may be liable to the plaintiff for some or all of the damages alleged by plaintiff. Sam's Supermarket might also desire to file a **third party complaint** against the manufacturer of the vinyl floor tile alleging that this tile should have prevented slip and falls and was therefore defectively designed and manufactured. The tile manufacturer would become a third party defendant and would have to file an **answer** to the third party complaint filed by the supermarket.

Motions

A motion is a legal document that requests the court to take specific action or order that one or more of the parties takes some action. Although a **motion to dismiss** may be filed by the defendant in response to the receipt of a complaint, the majority of motions are filed during and after discovery.

If a party has been improperly served with process, that party may file a **motion to quash service of summons** or a **motion to quash the return of the service of summons.** A **motion for change of venue** may be filed by the defendant if that party feels that a fair trial cannot be conducted in the court or county in which the suit was filed. A **motion to recuse** may be filed if one of the parties feels that the appointed judge is biased and should be disqualified from presiding over the case.

A **motion for more definite statement** may be filed by a defendant in response to a complaint that lacks sufficient clarity or specificity for the defendant to answer the allegations in the complaint. A **motion to strike** may be filed by either party requesting that the court delete part or all of the allegations in a pleading, especially if those allegations are scandalous or indecent. A **motion to file an amended pleading** may be filed by a party desiring to add or subtract a party to the litigation or otherwise change some aspect of a pleading on file. A **motion for enlargement of time** is a commonly filed request that the court grant additional time for one of the parties to take some action or file a notice, motion, or brief.

The party who feels a discovery document contains irrelevant questions may file a **motion for a protective order** where the court is requested to rule on whether that party must respond to all or some of the discovery. If a party does not timely respond to discovery, or provides incomplete or evasive answers, the opposing party may file a **motion to compel** the answers to discovery.

Another pretrial motion is a **motion *in limine*** in which either party requests that the court limit the introduction to the jury of a specified piece of evidence, usually because that evidence is irrelevant or too gruesome. A **motion for summary judgment** requests that, because there is allegedly no dispute as to material facts between the parties to an action, the court reach a decision on causes of action in the complaint on the basis of the pleadings alone without conducting an entire trial.

During trial, either party may file a **motion for directed verdict** requesting the court to enter a verdict in favor of the party making the motion. The defendant may request a directed verdict after plaintiff has rested her case, and the plaintiff may request a directed verdict after the defendant has completed his defense.

After the court or jury has rendered a decision, either side may request a **motion for new trial** asking the judge to set aside the verdict or judgment and grant a new trial to the parties. Similarly, a **motion to alter or amend judgment** requests that the judge change, modify, or otherwise vary the judgment rendered. A **motion for a judgment notwithstanding the verdict** may be requested of the Court asking it to set aside the jury's verdict that was, as a matter of law, allegedly incorrectly rendered.

When filing each motion, the paralegal should consult the pertinent local court rules, which usually mandate that, in addition to filing each motion, the party files a **notice to set** the hearing on the motion, a **notice of hearing** on the motion, a **memorandum of law** or **brief** in support of the motion, and a proposed **order.** Prior to filing these documents with the court and sending them to the opposing party, the paralegal should have the supervising attorney critique and sign each document.

Discovery

Generally, after the last pleading is filed, the discovery stage of litigation commences. During discovery, each party seeks information from the other in an effort to learn as much about the other party's position as possible, prevent surprises at trial, and settle the case prior to trial. Each side can serve upon the other **interrogatories, request for admissions, request for production of documents,** and **request for a physical or mental examination. Interrogatories** are written questions that require written answers to be provided under oath. **Request for admissions** are requests that a party admit to the truthfulness of a fact or opinion or verify the genuineness of a document. A **request for production of documents** is a request that one party be allowed to inspect or duplicate documents or other materials that are relevant to the subject matter of the litigation; parties may also request permission to enter land for the purpose of inspecting it. A **request for a physical or mental examination** is a request for a party to submit to a physical or mental examination to determine the legitimacy and extent of the physical or mental injuries claimed by that party. A **deposition** is another common form of discovery requiring a witness or party to provide oral testimony under oath in a location outside of a courtroom.

In the supermarket slip and fall scenario, both parties would submit **interrogatories** and **request for admissions** to each other in an effort to determine background information, insurance coverage, and facts underlying the occurrence. A **request for production of documents** would also be appropriate to gather documentation regarding the earnings of both parties, possible existing insurance policies, and other information relevant to the action. Finally, Sam's Supermarket would serve a request for physical examination upon Mr. Scott requiring him to be examined by the supermarket's physician to assess the severity of his broken hip.

Trial and Post-Trial Documents

As trial nears, the paralegal is instrumental in the preparation and filing of **pretrial statements**. A **pretrial statement** is a lengthy document outlining the manner in which each party plans to proceed up to and during trial. The contents of the **pretrial statement** are products of the pretrial conference. Once it becomes likely that the case will go to trial, the paralegal assists in the preparation of the **trial brief**, a document that states the legal issues of the case and establishes the validity of the party's position on each issue. The paralegal will also assist in the selection and preparation of **jury instructions**, which are given to the judge to be read to the jury after closing statements and before deliberation.

After trial, paralegals assist in the preparation of documents which assist in the collection of judgment, such as **writs of execution**, **garnishment**, and **attachment**. If a party loses the case, the paralegal may prepare and file a **notice of appeal**, a **designation of record on appeal**, and an **appellate brief**, which presents the reasons that the party thinks the trial court erred. The party that was victorious in the trial court responds to the **appellate brief** with an **answer brief**, to which the other party may respond with a **reply brief**.

TECHNIQUES OF DOCUMENT DRAFTING

The preceding discussion highlighted the most important and common types of legal writing with which paralegals should be familiar. In preparation for the drafting of each of these documents, paralegals should first consult their law firm's form books or document files for samples. Once paralegals have input a document into their offices' form file databases, they should place a hard copy of that document into the document files for future reference. Through the explanations and the use of sample documents, this section conveys the techniques paralegals employ for drafting specific documents. For the purposes of demonstrating variety, the sample documents in this chapter are either formatted according to Colorado rules or California rules, both of which are similar to the federal rules. Paralegals should consult their state's rules to ascertain the precise formats that their states require.

The Format of a Demand Letter

Many rules, even whole books, have been written about proper ways to format a letter. Some paralegals need to follow a strict structure to be satisfied that they are doing the work right, and there is plenty of material in bookstores and libraries to fill this need. For most, however, following some simple rules, using good judgment, and having pride in appearance will suffice. With the advent of computerized word processing, the paralegal has the luxury of previewing and manipulating the format of the letter for the best appearance.

Paralegals should keep the following basics in mind:

(1) Very short letters should have wide left and right margins (usually 1.75"). A few extra spaces should be placed before and after the date line, and the body of the letter (address through signature line) should be positioned at the page's "optical center," which is slightly above the exact center of the page.

(2) Medium length one-page letters should have margins of 1.25 to 1.5 inches and a little less space before the date line.

(3) Longer one-page letters should receive 1" margins left and right. The date line should be two spaces below the letterhead, and the address line should begin two spaces below the date line.

(4) Often, the body of a letter fits nicely on one page, but a second page is necessary for the signature block. To avoid making an orphan of the signature block, the paralegal should make the margins wider, thus forcing some of the text (preferably a full paragraph) to the second page.

(5) If the letterhead is centered, the date should be centered also, each paragraph should be indented, and the signature block should begin at the center point of the page.

(6) If the letterhead is block style with the main body flush with one of the margins, the letter should be formatted in block style, that is, the date aligned with one of the margins, paragraphs begun flush left, and signature block placed on the left margin.

(7) In a business letter a colon should always come after the salutation line even with a first name only, e.g., *Dear Ms. Jones:* or *Dear Al:*.

(8) The first page should not be numbered, but the second and succeeding pages of any letter should be numbered. The style and placement of the page number is optional, but should be consistent as a matter of office procedure.

(9) The complimentary close should begin with a capital letter, and end with a comma, e.g., *Very truly yours,*.

(10) The two most often used styles of signature blocks are these:

Very truly yours,	Yours truly,
Jonathan L. Severts	Jonathan L. Severts
Severts & Murray, P.C	Attorney at Law

(11) The last feature of a letter, following the signature block, is the block which shows who the writer and the typist of the letter are, *JLS:ss*, the

designation of enclosures, and the names of to whom copies of the letter have been sent. This information is placed after the signature line flush with the left margin. An example of the block on a letter that accompanies enclosures would appear as follows:

JLS:ss
Enclosures

The preceding features of letter format are demonstrated in Figure 1 on the sample demand letter for Robert Scott's case. A demand letter should include the facts surrounding the incident for which the plaintiff is demanding settlement, a settlement proposal of either a specific dollar amount or specific action, and a time period within which the defendant must respond.

The Complaint

The format of a complaint, in some states called a petition, varies from state to state, but all complaints should include a caption, text, and a subscription, or signature block. Because a complaint is personally served on the defendant, it does not include a certificate of mailing, but a complaint may include a verification.

The Caption

The caption states the court in which the action is filed, the case number, the name of the document, and the names of the parties to the action. The caption is usually separated from the text of the complaint by a line. It is critical that paralegals check the case number, court name, division or courtroom number, and parties' names to make sure that they are proper in all respects.

The Text

The text of a complaint must include the following elements in the form of numbered paragraphs in the order that they are listed:

1. an opening paragraph,
2. a statement of jurisdiction and venue,
3. the plaintiff's general allegations, which include the specific elements of the offense and the resulting damages, and
4. a prayer for relief.

Opening Paragraph The opening statement introduces the complaint and explains its purpose. The legal community is slowly changing its format to include clearer, more precise language that omits unnecessary legalese. Old expressions such as "whereas" and "wherefor" are discouraged. Even the time honored introductory phrase, "Comes now the Defendant, by and through his attorney...," is giving way to the more straightforward, "The Defendant, by his attorney...."

Statement of Jurisdiction of the Parties and Statement of Venue The first numbered paragraph of the text usually states the facts on which the plaintiff has relied to determine the jurisdiction of and venue for the action. For example, if the plaintiff is suing in a federal district court and is relying on diversity of citizenship to give the court jurisdiction, the opening paragraph of the complaint will allege the plaintiff is a citizen of one state, that the defendant is a citizen of another state, and that the amount in controversy exceeds $75,000. This statement may be nothing more than an assertion of the names and addresses of the plaintiff and the defendant.

Mary Cortez
Attorney at Law

511 South Grape
Denver, CO 80203

(303) 526-9777 • FAX (303) 526-5415

January 5, 199_

Richard A. Johnson
Peak Insurance Company
444 North Broadway
Denver, CO 80202

RE: DEMAND FOR SETTLEMENT
Your insured: Sam's Supermarket, Inc.

Dear Mr. Johnson:

Sam Campbell, agent for Sam's Supermarket, Inc., has informed our office that Peak Insurance Company provides coverage for Sam's Supermarket. This office has been retained by Robert Scott to pursue his remedies for negligence against Peak Insurance Company in the Denver County District Court. On December 27, 199_, Mr. Scott slipped and fell in the produce aisle of Sam's Supermarket causing severe injuries to his legs and spine and resulting in a broken left hip. It is Mr. Scott's contention that Sam's Supermarket improperly and negligently maintained the produce aisle at the time of Mr. Scott's injury.

Mr. Scott has had to undergo surgical operations and physical therapy and has lost the equivalent of two months of wages. His condition will require future physical therapy and time off from work.

This letter serves as a demand for settlement in the amount of Two Hundred and Fifty Thousand Dollars ($250,000.00) to be paid by certified funds, no later than February 15, 199_. This settlement amount and any future correspondence should be sent directly to the undersigned.

I trust that you will give this matter your most serious attention and will assist in avoiding attorney's fees and court costs by accepting this settlement proposal. Please have your attorneys contact my office if you should have any questions.

Most Sincerely,

Mary Cortez
MCC:bl

Figure 1: Sample Demand Letter

General Allegations The body of the complaint asserts in numbered paragraphs statements that present the case in a logical and sequential order. There exists a variation of opinion on how much detail is required in alleging the facts on which the plaintiff bases his recovery. The Federal Rules of Civil Procedure and most state rules require very little factual detail. Many of the specific facts are usually fleshed out during the discovery process. In a negligence action, it is usually sufficient to allege that on a certain date, at a described place, the plaintiff slipped and fell on the floor of the defendant's business, and as a result the plaintiff's hip was crushed, requiring him to seek medical help and miss work, which resulted in expenses of a specified amount. Each paragraph should be constructed as succinctly as possible. A good rule of thumb for paralegals to follow is to include only one allegation per paragraph.

Prayer for Relief The complaint concludes with a prayer for relief or *ad damnum* clause, which is a short summary of the plaintiff's request. This may vary from the simple, "Wherefore, the plaintiff demands judgment against the defendant in the sum of Two Hundred Fifty Thousand Dollars ($250,000.00) with interest, attorney's fees and costs" to a request consisting of several pages. The prayer for relief may also be worded, "The plaintiff demands judgment against the defendant in an amount to be determined at the time of trial, including interest, attorney's fees, and costs."

The Subscription

The subscription is the attorney's signature block. It must contain the attorney's name, registration number, mailing address, and phone number. Many states also require that the plaintiff's name and address be set forth opposite the subscription.

In Robert Scott's case, Sam's Supermarket has failed to respond to the demand letter by the designated date, so Mary Cortez's paralegal drafts the complaint as shown in Figures 2 and 3.

DISTRICT COURT, CITY AND COUNTY OF DENVER, STATE OF COLORADO
Case No. ____________ Courtroom ____________

COMPLAINT

ROBERT SCOTT,

Plaintiff,

v.

SAM'S SUPERMARKET, INC.,

Defendant,

The plaintiff, Robert Scott, by and through his attorney of record, Mary Cortez, for his Complaint against Defendant alleges as follows:

1. Plaintiff is a citizen of Colorado, residing at 444 Bishop's Lane, Denver, Colorado, 80211. The action occurred in the state of Colorado, county of Denver.

2. Defendant is incorporated to do business in the state of Colorado, with the principal place of business located at 150 North Alameda, Denver, Colorado, 80213, and the defendant's registered agent is Sam Campbell, who can be served at that address.

3. On December 27, 199_, the plaintiff was shopping for groceries in the defendant's store when he lost his balance and slipped and fell in the produce aisle of the store, suffering the injuries and damages described below.

4. Plaintiff's loss of balance, fall, and resultant injuries were caused by the negligent and careless conduct of defendant in owning, operating, and maintaining the floors and premises of the grocery store.

5. Defendant owed a duty to the plaintiff to operate and maintain a safe premises, and the defendant breached this duty, which resulted in the injuries and damages described below.

6. As a direct and proximate result of the negligence of the defendant, the plaintiff suffered severe and permanent injuries to his left leg and hip, including a broken left hip and injuries to other parts of his body, which resulted in the plaintiff's being under medical care up to the time of filing this complaint and for an indeterminate amount of time in the future.

Figure 2: Sample Complaint

7. As a further direct and proximate result of the defendant's negligence, the plaintiff suffered shock and has suffered extreme physical and mental pain since December 27, 199_, up to the time of filing this complaint, and he will suffer physical and mental pain, suffering, and humiliation for the rest of his life.

8. As a further direct and proximate result of the defendant's negligence, the plaintiff has suffered loss of earnings and impairment of his earning capacity from and after December 27, 199_, and will suffer loss of earnings and impairment of his earning capacity for the rest of his life.

9. As a further direct and proximate result of the defendant's negligence, the plaintiff is unable to perform normal family recreational and business activities and will be unable to live a full, useful, and enjoyable life for the remainder of his life.

10. As a further direct and proximate result of defendant's negligence, plaintiff has been forced to incur significant expenses for doctors, physical therapists, and other medical expenses, the reasonable value of which exceeds Twenty-Five Hundred Dollars ($2500.00); the plaintiff will be forced to expend sums of money in the future for hospital and medical treatment; and the plaintiff will incur additional medical expenses in an amount not now determinable for the remainder of his life.

11. As a further direct and proximate cause of defendant's negligence, the plaintiff has become nervous and irritable and has become permanently disabled for the rest of his life.

WHEREFORE, the plaintiff prays for judgment against defendant in an amount to be proven at the time of trial, including medical bills, lost wages, pain and suffering, costs expended in filing this suit, interest from the date of the commencement of this action, expert witness fees, paralegal's fees, attorney's fees, and for such other and further relief as to this Court may seem just and proper.

THE PLAINTIFF DEMANDS THAT THIS ACTION BE TRIED TO A JURY.

Plaintiff's Address:
444 Bishop's Lane
Denver, CO 80211

Mary Cortez, Registration #1212
Attorney for Plaintiff
511 South Grape
Denver, CO 80203
(303) 526-9777

2

Figure 3: Sample Complaint - Page 2

DISTRICT COURT, ______________ COUNTY ________________, COLORADO
CASE NO. ____________________ Div/CtRm _____

SUMMONS

Plaintiff Defendant

The People of the State of Colorado
To the Defendant(s) named above:

You are summoned and required to file with the clerk of this court an answer or other response to the attached complaint within twenty (20) days after this summons is served on you in the State of Colorado, or within thirty (30) days after this summons is served on you outside the State of Colorado.

If you fail to file your answer or other response to the complaint in writing within the applicable time period, judgment by default may be entered against you by the court for the relief demanded in the complaint, without any further notice to you.

The following documents are also served with this summons:

Date: ____________________ ______________________________________
Signature of Attorney for Plaintiff or Clerk/Deputy Clerk of Court
If signed by attorney, type: Name, address, tel. #, reg. # below.

This summons is issued pursuant to Rule 4, CRCP, as amended.
A copy of the complaint must be served with this summons.

RETURN OF SERVICE

State of ______________________ County of ______________________
I declare under oath that I served this summons and a copy of the complaint in this case on ______________
______________________________ in ____________ County ____________,
on ______________________________ (Date) at ______________ (Time) at the following location:
____,

☐ by handing it to a person identified to me as the defendant.
☐ by leaving it with the defendant who refused service.
☐ by leaving it with ______________________ designated to receive service for the defendant.

☐ I am over the age of 18 years and am not interested in nor a party to this case.
☐ I attempted to serve the defendant on ____________ occasions but have not been able to locate the defendant.
Return to the plaintiff is made on ______________________ (Date).

Subscribed and sworn to before me this ____________ day of ____________________, 19 ________ in
____________________ County of ____________________, State of ____________________.

______________________________ ______________________________
Notary Public* Signature Date

as ☐ Private process server
☐ Sheriff, ______________________________ County
Service $ ________________
Mileage $ ________________

*Notary should include address and expiration date of commission.

No. 195CA. Rev. 3-87. SUMMONS IN CIVIL ACTION

Bradford Publishing, 1743 Wazee St., Denver, CO 80202 — (303) 292-2500 — 10-95

Figure 4: Sample Summons

The Answer

Sam's Supermarket was served with the plaintiff's complaint. Within the specified time limit, the paralegal drafts the defendant's answer to the plaintiff's complaint, has the attorney approve and sign it, and files it with the court. The components of an answer are similar to those of a complaint. The answer begins with the same caption as the complaint and ends with a subscription. The text of the answer is initiated by an introductory statement followed by the defendant's allegations.

Within the allegations the defendant either admits or denies the allegations set forth in the plaintiff's complaint. All allegations that are not specifically denied are deemed admitted. Therefore, the paralegal must make sure that the answer contains a specific admission or denial for every allegation, and the paralegal should include an allegation such as the following: "All other allegations of the plaintiff's complaint that are not specifically admitted are denied." The text should also include any affirmative defenses a defendant wishes to make under the specific heading of affirmative defenses. The paralegal ends the text with a clause that requests that the case be dismissed and the plaintiff recover nothing and that the costs of defending the claim be awarded the defendant.

After the subscription, the paralegal should prepare a certificate of mailing or certificate of service to be signed by whomever mails the answer to the other parties. This certificate functions as a verification of service of the document by mail or hand delivery. Any document that is not personally served upon another party must contain a certificate of service.

The defendant may also include within the answer a third party complaint. The allegations of this complaint come after the answer's affirmative defenses and bring another party into the action. The sample answer in Figures 5, 6 and 7 is an example of a combined answer and third party complaint. In this example, Sam's Supermarket alleges that the manufacturer of the vinyl floor tile is negligent in this action. Figures 8 and 9 provide the manufacturer's answer to the third party complaint.

DISTRICT COURT, CITY AND COUNTY OF DENVER, STATE OF COLORADO
Case No. 93CV1002 Division No. 10

ANSWER AND THIRD PARTY COMPLAINT

ROBERT SCOTT,

Plaintiff,

v.

SAM'S SUPERMARKET, INC.,

Defendant and
Third Party Plaintiff,

v.

COMMERCIAL TILE COMPANY, INC,

Third Party Defendant.

The defendant, and third party plaintiff, Sam's Supermarket, Inc., by and through its counsel, Jacob Armstrong, for its Answer and Third Party Complaint states and alleges as follows:

ANSWER

1. Defendant is without knowledge or information sufficient to form a belief as to the truth of the allegation contained in paragraph 1 of the Complaint, and, therefore, denies this allegation.

2. Defendant admits the allegation contained in paragraph 2 of the plaintiff's Complaint.

3. Defendant denies the allegations contained in paragraphs 3, 4, 5, 6, 7, 8, 9, 10, and 11 of the plaintiff's Complaint.

4. All other allegations of the plaintiff's Complaint that are not specifically admitted are denied.

Figure 5: Sample Answer

AFFIRMATIVE DEFENSES

5. The Complaint fails to state a claim upon which relief can be granted.

6. The plaintiff's own negligence contributed to or caused his injuries.

THIRD PARTY COMPLAINT

1. Third party defendant, Commercial Tile Company, Inc., is incorporated to do business in Colorado, with its principal place of business located at 1400 Washington Avenue, Denver, Colorado 80201, and third party defendant's registered agent is Darris Hoch who can be served with process at the same address.

2. On October 12, 199_, Sam's Supermarket, Inc., purchased vinyl floor tile from Commercial Tile Company, Inc., for installation at the supermarket located at 150 North Alameda.

3. In deciding to purchase the vinyl floor tile, Sam's Supermarket, Inc., relied on written and oral warranties and representations that the vinyl floor tile, which was manufactured by Commercial Tile Company, Inc., was "skid proof" and "safe even when wet."

4. On October 12, 199_, Sam's Supermarket, Inc., paid $22,000.00 to Commercial Tile Company, Inc., for the purchase and installation of the vinyl floor tile, which was subsequently installed on October 19, 199_.

5. On December 27, 199_, Robert Scott, the plaintiff in this action, allegedly slipped and fell on tile sold and installed by Commercial Tile Company, Inc.

6. Sam's Supermarket, Inc., has been served with a Complaint for damages allegedly incurred by Robert Scott, and a copy of this Complaint is attached hereto as exhibit "A".

7. This process should have been served upon Commercial Tile Company, Inc., for its negligence and strict liability in selling and installing defective floor tile.

8. Any damages claimed by the plaintiff are a direct and proximate result of the negligence of Commercial Tile Company, Inc., and should any damages be assessed against Sam's Supermarket, Inc., Sam's Supermarket, Inc., is entitled to judgment against Commercial Tile Company, Inc., in that same amount.

2

Figure 6: Sample Answer - Page 2

WHEREFORE, the third party plaintiff prays that the plaintiff recover nothing by reason of his Complaint, that the plaintiff's Complaint be dismissed, and that the third party plaintiff receive judgment from third party defendant for all sums that may be adjudged against the defendant in favor of the plaintiff.

Defendant's Address:
150 North Alameda
Denver, Colorado 80213

DATED:

____
Jacob Armstrong, Registration #1444
Attorney for Defendant and
Third Party Plaintiff
430 Macmillan Circle, Suite A
Denver, Colorado 80222
(303) 799-2222

CERTIFICATE OF SERVICE

I certify that a true and correct copy of the foregoing Answer and Third Party Complaint was served this ____ day of ____________, 199_, by placing them in the United States mail, first class postage prepaid, addressed as follows:

Mary Cortez, J.D.
511 South Grape
Denver, Colorado 80203

Heidi Hamlin, J.D.
11th Floor
The Eagle Spring Building
101 West Willow Road
Denver, Colorado 80202

____

3

Figure 7: Sample Answer - Page 3

DISTRICT COURT, CITY AND COUNTY OF DENVER, STATE OF COLORADO

Case No. 93CV1002 Division No. 10

ANSWER OF THIRD PARTY DEFENDANT

ROBERT SCOTT,
Plaintiff,

v.

SAM'S SUPERMARKET, INC.,
Defendant and
Third Party Plaintiff,

v.

COMMERCIAL TILE COMPANY, INC.,
Third Party Defendant.

The third party defendant, Commercial Tile Company, Inc., by and through its counsel, Heidi Hamlin, responds to the Third Party Complaint as follows:

1. The third party defendant admits the allegations of paragraphs 1, 2 and 4 of the Third Party Complaint.

2. The third party defendant denies the allegations of paragraphs 7 and 8 of the Third Party Complaint.

3. The third party defendant is without sufficient information to admit or deny the allegations of paragraphs 3, 5 and 6 of the Third Party Complaint and, therefore denies these allegations.

4. The third party defendant denies all other allegations in the Third Party Complaint that are not specifically admitted.

AFFIRMATIVE DEFENSES

5. The third party defendant affirmatively alleges that the third party plaintiff has failed to state a cause of action upon which relief can be granted.

Figure 8: Sample Answer to a Third Party Complaint

6. The third party defendant affirmatively alleges that the acts or omissions of third persons other than this responding third party defendant proximately caused or contributed to the events leading up to and the occurrence by which the plaintiff allegedly sustained injuries.

7. The third party defendant affirmatively alleges that the third party plaintiff's subsequent care and modification of the vinyl floor tiles were the proximate causes of the plaintiff's alleged injuries.

WHEREFORE, the third party defendant prays that the plaintiff recover nothing as a result of his Complaint, that the Complaint and the Third Party Complaint be dismissed, and that the third party defendant be awarded costs and fees incident to its defense of this action.

Third Party Defendant's Address:
1400 Washington Avenue
Denver, Colorado 80201

DATED:

____

Heidi Hamlin, Registration #2039
Attorney for Third Party Defendant
11th Floor
The Eagle Spring Building
101 West Willow Road
Denver, Colorado 80202
(303) 243-3333

CERTIFICATE OF MAILING

I certify that a true and correct copy of the foregoing Answer of Third Party Defendant was served this ____ day of _________, 199_, by placing this pleading in the United States mail, first class postage prepaid, addressed as follows:

Jacob Armstrong, J.D.
430 Macmillan Circle
Suite A
Denver, Colorado 80222

Mary Cortez, J.D.
511 South Grape
Denver, Colorado 80203

____

2

Figure 9: Sample Answer to a Third Party Complaint - Page 2

The Memorandum of Law

The legal memorandum is among the most commonly used written tools of the paralegal profession. Through legal memoranda, paralegals convey information to clients and witnesses, analyze complex legal problems, and present the client's case to others. Legal memoranda may be internal or external and are prepared initially for the supervising attorney's perusal. Internal memos are directed to the supervising attorney or other members of the law office staff; external memos are directed outside of the law office to the opposing counsel, the court, or both. The major difference between an internal memo and an external memo is that while internal memos portray both sides of a client's case, favorable and unfavorable, in an attempt to anticipate all legal problems, external memos, such as trial briefs or memoranda in support of motions, convey only the favorable points of a client's case.

The Components of a Legal Memorandum

All legal memoranda should include the following elements:

1. A caption or heading. The caption includes information indicating to whom the memo is addressed, the name of the writer, the date the memo was written, the case name and number if available, and a brief explanation of what the memo is about.

2. The assignment. This is a one sentence statement of the purpose of the memo.

3. The facts. This section briefly outlines the relevant facts of the case.

4. The issues. The issues section lists the important questions of law and presents the issues as questions to be answered in the analysis. Issues are often provided by the attorney; however, the paralegal may have to formulate his or her own issues and submit them to the supervising attorney for revision or approval.

5. The analysis. Analysis is the process of answering each issue through a careful and thorough application of the law to the facts of the client's case. This is the most important part of the memo.

6. The conclusion. The conclusion summarizes the answers to the questions posed by the issues. The conclusion should be based on the legal analysis and should not contain any information that has not been discussed in the analysis section.

7. The recommendations. Based on the conclusion, this section proposes what steps should be taken on behalf of the client. This section is usually included only in internal memoranda.

The Process of Legal Analysis.

Legal analysis is the means of providing an answer to an issue through careful application of the points of law of applicable statutes and previous cases to the specific facts surrounding the client's case. Legal analysis should always involve applying a relatively unchanging body of law to the client's facts. Paralegals must apply law to facts because law changes far less frequently than do facts. A thorough analysis of an issue requires four steps.

__Step 1.__ The paralegal should introduce the analysis by restating the issue to be analyzed and then listing the elements of the pertinent legal authority. Analysis of a previous case requires a very brief, two to three sentence explanation of its relevant facts and issues. Analysis of a statute requires isolating its most important elements.

__Step 2.__ The paralegal then isolates the court's decision in the precedent case.

__Step 3.__ The paralegal carefully applies the precedent authority to the facts of the client's case. By comparing and contrasting the facts and issues of the precedent case with the facts and issues of the client's case, the paralegal determines whether the precedent case's decision applies to the client's case. In analyzing the important elements of a statute, the paralegal shows how the client's case applies to the legislative intent of the statute.

__Step 4.__ Based on the application of the legal authority to the facts and issues of the client's case, the paralegal presents a conclusion within the analysis section that provides an answer to the analyzed issue. This conclusion may be derived from an analysis of several different cases and statutes or from an analysis of just one case or statute.

In presenting support for an answer to an issue, the paralegal should concentrate on legal authority, such as cases and statutes, rather than on feelings or unfounded opinions. Conclusions should be firmly based on a thorough analysis of the law.

If the supervising attorney provides specific cases and statutes to analyze, the paralegal should discuss all of the authority provided. Internal memos of law should include an analysis of legal authority that may be detrimental to the client's case to assist the attorney in anticipating the case of the opposing party.

The sample interoffice memorandum of law in Figures 10-14 is written by the paralegal to her supervising attorney advising him on the possible success of filing a motion for summary judgment in the Robert Scott case. The information in this memo is used later to write the memorandum of law in support of the motion for summary judgment (see Figures 17-19).

INTEROFFICE MEMORANDUM

TO: Jacob Armstrong, J.D.

FROM: Tina Garcia, Paralegal

DATE: January __, 19__

RE: Motion for Summary Judgment, *Robert Scott v. Sam's Supermarket, Inc.*

OFFICE CLIENT: Sam's Supermarket, Inc.

OFFICE FILE NUMBER: CV 11196

DOCKET NUMBER: 93CV1002

STATEMENT OF ASSIGNMENT: Mr. Armstrong has asked me to research the primary authority supporting a motion for summary judgment in favor of Sam's Supermarket, Inc., and to assist in deciding whether this motion should be filed against the plaintiff.

FACTS: On December 27, 199_, the plaintiff, Robert Scott, a single, fifty-year-old store clerk, was shopping at our client's grocery store. While in the potato section of the produce aisle of the store, he allegedly slipped and fell on a portion of the floor which he states was wet.

Our client had purchased new tile from Commercial Tile Company, Inc., which they installed in the produce section on October 19, 199_. This tile was represented to be slip free and was designed for usage on floors that accumulate moisture. Our client has stated that the safety representations from Commercial Tile Company, Inc., constituted the primary reason for the purchase and installation of the tile. Based upon our investigation and research, we filed a third party complaint against Commercial Tile Company, Inc.

In response to interrogatories and deposition questions, plaintiff admitted that he had seen the sign which our client had placed next to the wet surface a "few seconds" before his apparent slip and fall. The sign, which read "Caution - Wet Floors" on each of its two sides, was freestanding on four metal tubular legs, and measured 14" by 14" square on each side. The background color of the sign was yellow, and the lettering was black. Each letter was 4" high and 1.5" wide. The sign is in our possession and will be introduced as an exhibit if this case goes to trial. Plaintiff also stated that he had been shopping at Sam's approximately every other week for the prior year and that he had seen this same sign in the produce aisle on a "few other" occasions.

Figure 10: Sample Interoffice Memorandum of Law

Within approximately two minutes of the plaintiff's fall, the produce department manager, Sandra Stevens, aided Mr. Scott. In her deposition, she stated that she did not witness the fall nor, to her knowledge, did anyone else witness the plaintiff's fall. She asked Mr. Scott to remain still because he told her that his leg and hip were aching. She then went to the courtesy counter and briefly informed the store manager, Michael Brokawski, of the occurrence. Ms. Turner called for an ambulance. Ms. Stevens returned to comfort Mr. Scott.

The ambulance arrived within ten minutes of the occurrence and transported Mr. Scott to the nearest hospital, which was St. Luke's Hospital. Mr. Scott was treated for a broken left hip, had a pin placed in his hip, and was released with the aid of crutches seven days after his admission. A copy of the complete ambulance and hospital records is in our client's file.

This interoffice memorandum will examine the propriety of a summary judgment motion and the possible defenses which might be raised by plaintiff to the motion. The critical fact that is not disputed is that the plaintiff saw the warning sign prior to his alleged slip and fall.

ISSUES:

1. Is our client's Motion for Summary Judgment likely to be granted?
2. What possible defenses to our client's Motion for Summary Judgment might the plaintiff allege?

BRIEF ANSWERS:

1. Yes. Although courts construe summary judgment to be a drastic remedy, summary judgment is proper as long as the court is convinced that no genuine issue of material fact exists in dispute between the parties, and in this case the plaintiff's discovery responses confirm that the material facts are not in dispute.

2. In opposing the summary judgment motion, the plaintiff might argue that he should be given the opportunity to amend his complaint to bring in additional causes of action and, perhaps, parties.

ANALYSIS:

1. Is our client's Motion for Summary Judgment likely to be granted?

Our client's Motion for Summary Judgment is likely to be granted since the plaintiff has admitted that he saw the warning sign prior to his alleged slip and fall. The relevant case law for the purposes of this motion is outlined in the case of *Drake v. Lerner's Shops of Colorado, Inc.*, 145 Colo. 1, 4, 357 P.2d 624, 626 (1960) where the Colorado Supreme Court stated:

2

Figure 11: Sample Interoffice Memorandum of Law - Page 2

> In order to establish a *prima facie* case of negligence, plaintiff's evidence must establish the existence on the premises of an unreasonable risk of harm to her as an invitee. The mere existence of risk is not sufficient. Some degree of risk is present in our every activity and if existence of hazard alone were the standard it would mean that the happening of an accident would be sufficient to raise the presumption of negligence and the landowner would be an insurer of the safety of his patrons. Such is not the law. The condition created by the conduct or activity of the landowner must pose an appreciable risk of harm. The defendant's conduct must threaten harm.

In *Drake*, the plaintiff testified that she walked out of a clothing store, failed to observe a warning sign, and failed to observe a five inch drop-off to the sidewalk which caused her fall and subsequent injuries. In upholding a directed verdict for the defendant, the court stated that "[c]onsidering the evidence in a light most favorable to the plaintiff, it cannot be said that the condition about which she complains was such to create an appreciable risk of harm. A step down five inches is not a hazard, which of itself suggests likelihood of harm . . . ." *Id.* at 5, 357 P.2d at 626.

In our client's case, the plaintiff admitted that he shopped at Sam's Supermarket every other week, and had seen the "Caution - Wet Floors" sign in the produce aisle on a few occasions prior to his alleged slip and fall. Furthermore, he admitted to having seen the sign immediately prior to his slip and fall and was thus aware of the potential harm. Under *Drake* alone, the court would be bound to grant our client's summary judgment motion.

In support of the summary judgment motion, our client can also argue that no presumption of negligence can arise on the part of a proprietor of a store from the mere fact that a customer is injured while lawfully on the premises. *Home Public Market v. New Rock*, 111 Colo. 428, 142 P.2d 272 (1947). This same proposition was recognized in *Geringer v. Wildhorn Ranch, Inc.*, 706 F. Supp. 1442, 1446 (D.Colo. 1988), where the federal trial court held that the Colorado premises liability law "does not establish a feudal realm of absolute protection from liability for simple negligence based only on a defendant's status as landowner." The plaintiff must establish the existence of an unreasonable risk of harm in the business premises to recover, and this is not possible in our client's case since the plaintiff had prior knowledge of the wet floor based upon previous shopping experiences and observation of the caution sign prior to his alleged slip and fall. Our client took reasonable and standard precautions in protecting business invitees from harm.

3

Figure 12: Sample Interoffice Memorandum of Law - Page 3

The Colorado courts have consistently recognized that storekeepers are not insurers of the safety of business invitees. In a set of facts congruous to our client's, the court in *Shutt v. Kaufman's Inc.*, 165 Colo. 175, 180, 438 P.2d 501, 503 (1968) stated that "although a storekeeper must exercise reasonable care for the safety of the business visitor, he is not an insurer of the safety of such visitor; thus the mere happening of an accident raises no presumption of negligence. . . ." According to *Shutt*, there can be no presumption of negligence especially considering plaintiff's knowledge of the wet floor.

Finally, as recognized in *Hennesy v. Tina Marie Homes, Inc.*, 153 Colo. 572, 388 P.2d 758 (1963), there can be no liability by the owner of premises from risks that are known to the injured plaintiff as well as to the defendant owner. Because Mr. Scott was aware of the risk of walking on the wet floor, there can be no liability on the part of Sam's Supermarket, Inc., and the motion for summary judgment should be granted.

2. What possible defenses to our client's Motion for Summary Judgment might plaintiff allege?

The plaintiff may rely on the argument that courts have consistently held that summary judgment is a drastic remedy to be granted only where the evidentiary and legal prerequisites have been clearly established. See, e.g., *Fountain v. Filson*, 336 U.S. 681, 69 S.Ct. 754, 93 L.Ed. 971 (1949); *Gleason v. Guzman*, 623 P.2d 378 (Colo. 1981); *McKinley Construction Co. v. Dozier*, 175 Colo. 397, 487 P.2d 1335 (1971); *Primrock v. Hamilton*, 168 Colo. 524, 452 P.2d 375 (1969). The plaintiff may also allege that a motion for summary judgment should not be sustained unless it appears that pleadings are such that no amendment could be made. *McLaughlin v. Niles, Co.*, 88 Colo. 202, 294 P.2d 954 (1930).

The plaintiff may argue that the court should grant him the opportunity to amend his complaint to allege strict products liability against the floor tile manufacturer or to otherwise plead new facts that might preclude the granting of a summary judgment motion.

Finally, the plaintiff can always rely on the argument that pleadings are to be liberally construed, and that all doubts are to be resolved in favor of the pleader as recognized in C.R.C.P. Rule 8(f) and cases such as *Lyons v. Hoffman*, 31 Colo. App. 306, 502 P.2d 980 (1972).

Despite the policy for the liberal construction of pleadings and trial on the merits of a case, courts will grant summary judgment motions if it is apparent that the material facts underlying the plaintiff's cause of action are not in dispute. Summary judgment is one method of easing the burden on the court's congested trial docket, and would be appropriate in our client's case since we have performed well in obtaining critical admissions from the plaintiff to pivotal facts which, according to *Drake v. Lerner's Shops of Colorado Inc.*, *supra*, permit the court to grant summary judgment in our favor.

4

Figure 13: Sample Interoffice Memorandum of Law - Page 4

CONCLUSION:

Because there appear to be no material facts in dispute in this matter and the law appears to support a ruling in favor of our client, the granting of our Motion for Summary Judgment is likely. Although the plaintiff may request to amend his complaint to include new facts, there seems to be little doubt that the material facts of this case are agreed upon by both parties.

RECOMMENDATIONS:

Our client should be consulted and informed of our intent to file a Motion for Summary Judgment. Immediately prior to filing the motion, each of the authorities set forth in this memorandum should be shepardized and updated on WESTLAW. Please inform me if there is any further research on this case that you would like me to do.

5

Figure 14: Sample Interoffice Memorandum of Law - Page 5

The Motion

The format of a motion is similar to that of a pleading. As with all documents filed with the court, the motion begins with a caption. The text of the motion is comprised of an introductory statement, a list of reasons why the court should grant the motion, and a request that the court grant the motion. Like answers, motions must contain a certificate of service. Figures 15 and 16 provide a sample of a motion for summary judgment.

As stated earlier, paralegals should also prepare a notice to set hearing on the motion, a memorandum of law or brief in support of the motion, and a proposed order to accompany the motion. All of these documents are headed with the caption of the case, ended with a subscription, and completed with a certificate of service.

The Notice to Set Hearing and the Notice of Hearing

The notice to set hearing is directed to the opposing parties and states the time and place for the setting of the hearing on a motion. Once the hearing has been set, the movant prepares a notice of hearing on motion, which is similar in form to the notice to set hearing on motion. Figures 20 and 21 demonstrate a notice to set hearing.

The Memorandum of Law in Support of the Motion

The memorandum of law in support of the motion presents the points of law in support of the motion. It states the purpose of the motion, the burden of proof, and the reasons that the movant is entitled to have the motion granted. Each of these points is substantiated with an analysis of the applicable law as it relates to the facts of the case. A sample memorandum of law in support of the motion is shown in Figures 17-19.

The Order

The movant submits a prepared order in hopes that the Court will rule in favor of the movant's motion. The text of the order states that the motion has been granted and provides a signature line for the Court. Figures 22 and 23 display a sample order.

DISTRICT COURT, CITY AND COUNTY OF DENVER, STATE OF COLORADO
Case No. 93CV1002, Division No. 10

MOTION FOR SUMMARY JUDGMENT

ROBERT SCOTT,

Plaintiff,

v.

SAM'S SUPERMARKET, INC.,

Defendant and Third Party Plaintiff,

v.

COMMERCIAL TILE COMPANY, INC.,

Third Party Defendant.

The defendant, Sam's Supermarket, Inc., by its attorney, Jacob Armstrong, moves for summary judgment against Plaintiff and Third Party Defendant, pursuant to the Colorado Rules of Civil Procedure, Rule 56, and as grounds for this motion, states as follows:

1. The pleadings, exhibits and affidavits on file show that there is no genuine issue as to any material fact and the moving party is entitled to a judgment as a matter of law.

2. The plaintiff slipped and fell on recently cleaned tile in the defendant's store, and a conspicuous "Caution - Wet Floors" sign was positioned beside this tile.

3. Based upon defendant's answers to discovery, it is undisputed that the existence of the "Caution - Wet Floors" sign was known and apparent to the plaintiff prior to and at the time of the incident.

4. As a matter of law there can be no liability by the owner/occupier of a premises for injuries to others from conditions that are obvious and known to the plaintiff. *Drake v. Lerner's Shops of Colorado Inc.,* 145 Colo. 1, 357 P.2d 624 (1960).

Figure 15: Sample Motion for Summary Judgment

WHEREFORE, pursuant to Rule 56, the defendant requests that this court grant its Motion for Summary Judgment in this action.

Respectfully submitted,

____
Jacob Armstrong #1111
Attorney for Defendant and
Third Party Plaintiff
430 Macmillan Circle, Suite A
Denver, Colorado 80222
(303) 799-2222

CERTIFICATE OF SERVICE

I certify that a true and correct copy of the defendant's Motion for Summary Judgment was served this ____ day of ________, 199_, by placing it in the United States mail, first class postage prepaid, addressed as follows:

Mary Cortez
511 South Grape
Denver, Colorado 80203

Heidi Hamlin
11th Floor
The Eagle Springs Building
101 West Willow Road
Denver, Colorado 80202

____

2

Figure 16: Sample Motion for Summary Judgment - Page 2

DISTRICT COURT, CITY AND COUNTY OF DENVER, STATE OF COLORADO
Case No. 93CV1002, Courtroom No. 10

MEMORANDUM OF LAW IN SUPPORT OF DEFENDANT'S MOTION FOR SUMMARY JUDGMENT

ROBERT SCOTT,

Plaintiff,

v.

SAM'S SUPERMARKET, INC.,

Defendant and Third Party Plaintiff,

v.

COMMERCIAL TILE COMPANY, INC.,

Third Party Defendant.

The defendant, Sam's Supermarket, Inc., by and through its attorney, Jacob Armstrong, submits the following Memorandum of Law in Support of Motion for Summary Judgment pursuant to Rule 56 of the Colorado Rules of Civil Procedure.

FACTUAL BACKGROUND

On December 27, 1997, the plaintiff was shopping for groceries in the defendant's store when he allegedly slipped and fell on the floor in the produce aisle. In responses to discovery, plaintiff has admitted that prior to his slip and fall, he saw the warning sign which was located adjacent to the portion of the floor where he fell.

PURPOSE OF RULE

Rule 56 is designed to avoid unnecessary trials and delay as the Supreme Court of Colorado has stated in *Lenell v. Walter A. Heller Co.*, 165 Colo. 463, 439 P.2d 989 (1968). The rule allowing summary judgment is designed to pierce through the allegations of fact in a pleading and to avoid an unnecessary trial where the matter submitted in support of a

Figure 17: Sample Memorandum of Law in Support of Motion for Summary Judgment

motion for summary judgment shows that there is no genuine issue as to any material fact and that the moving party is entitled to a judgment as a matter of law under section c of the rule.

BURDEN OF PROOF

The moving party has the burden of proof for a summary judgment motion according to the authority in *Abrahamsen v. Mountain States Telephone*, 177 Colo. 422, 494 P.2d 1287 (1972). Once a moving party makes a convincing showing that genuine issues of material fact are lacking, Rule 56 requires that the opposing party adequately demonstrate by relevant and specific facts that a real controversy exists as recognized in *Ginter v. Palmer*, 196 Colo. 203, 585 P.2d 583 (1978). The argument of counsel alone cannot create a factual issue according to *Ginter, id.*

APPLICATION OF RULE 56 TO SLIP AND FALL CASES

UNDER COLORADO LAW THE DEFENDANT IS ENTITLED
TO A SUMMARY JUDGMENT

The Colorado Supreme Court in *Drake v. Lerner's Shops of Colorado, Inc.*, 145 Colo. 1, 4, 357 P.2d 624, 626 (1960), addressed the issue of summary judgment relief in a case involving almost identical facts. The Supreme Court stated that:

> In order to establish a *prima facie* case of negligence, plaintiff's evidence must establish existence on the premises of an unreasonable risk of harm to her as an invitee. The mere existence of risk is not sufficient. Some degree of risk is present in our every activity and if existence of hazard alone were the standard it would mean that the happening of an accident would be sufficient to raise the presumption of negligence and the landowner would be an insurer of the safety of his patrons. Such is not the law. The condition created by the conduct or activity of the landowner must pose an appreciable risk of harm. The defendant's conduct must threaten harm.

Similarly, in *Hennesy v. Tina Marie Homes, Inc.*, 153 Colo. 572, 388 P.2d 758 (1963), the Supreme Court recognized that as a matter of law, there can be no liability by the owner or occupier of premises for injuries to others from conditions that are obvious and known to the plaintiff. Plaintiff, Robert Scott, has admitted throughout discovery that he was aware of the "Caution - Wet Floors" sign, and accordingly there can be no liability on defendant's part.

2

Figure 18: Sample Memorandum of Law in Support of Motion for Summary Judgment - Page 2

Thus, plaintiff has failed to present a *prima facie* case of negligence and this Court must grant defendant's Motion for Summary Judgment. Furthermore, the issues of the existence of negligence and contributory negligence are questions of law, properly to be resolved by this Court only. See, for example, *Ridenour v. Diffee*, 133 Colo. 467, 297 P.2d 280 (1956); *Clark v. Joslin Dry Goods Co.*, 128 Colo. 317, 262 P.2d 546 (1953); and, *City of Grand Junction v. Lashmett*, 126 Colo. 256, 247 P.2d 909 (1952).

CONCLUSION

It is therefore submitted that in accordance with the undisputed material facts and the relevant Colorado law, the defendant, Sam's Supermarket, Inc., is entitled to summary judgment pursuant to Rule 56 of the Colorado Rules of Civil Procedure.

Respectfully submitted,

____

Jacob Armstrong #1111
Attorney for Defendant and
Third Party Plaintiff
Suite A
430 Macmillan Circle
Denver, Colorado 80222
(303) 799-2222

CERTIFICATE OF SERVICE

I certify that a true and correct copy of the foregoing Memorandum of Law in Support of Defendant's Motion for Summary Judgment was served this ____ day of ___________, 199_, by placing it in the United States mail, postage prepaid, addressed as follows:

Mary Cortez	Heidi Hamlin
Attorney for Plaintiff	11th Floor
511 South Grape	The Eagle Springs Building
Denver, Colorado 80203	101 West Willow Road
	Denver, Colorado 80202

____

3

Figure 19: Sample Memorandum of Law in Support of Motion for Summary Judgment - Page 3

DISTRICT COURT, CITY AND COUNTY OF DENVER, STATE OF COLORADO
Case No. 93CV1002, Division No. 10

NOTICE TO SET HEARING ON DEFENDANT'S MOTION FOR SUMMARY JUDGMENT

ROBERT SCOTT,

Plaintiff,

v.

SAM'S SUPERMARKET, INC.,

Defendant and Third Party Plaintiff,

v.

COMMERCIAL TILE COMPANY, INC.

Third Party Defendant.

TO: Mary Cortez
Attorney for Plaintiff
511 South Grape
Denver, Colorado 80203

Heidi Hamlin
Attorney for Third Party Defendant
11th Floor
101 West Willow Road
The Eagle Springs Building
Denver, Colorado 80202

YOU ARE HEREBY NOTIFIED that the undersigned for the defendant will appear in Division 10 at the Judicial Building in Denver, Colorado, located at 1437 Bannock Street, on the _____ day of ________, 199_, at _:__ _.m. and request the assignment clerk of said court to set a time, date and place for a hearing on the Defendant's Motion for Summary Judgment in the above-entitled action, where and at which time you may be present as you are so advised.

Figure 20: Sample Notice to Set Hearing

Respectfully submitted,

____

Jacob Armstrong #1111
Attorney for Defendant and Third
Party Plaintiff
Suite A
430 Macmillan Circle
Denver, Colorado 80222
(303) 799-2222

CERTIFICATE OF SERVICE

I hereby certify that I have mailed, postage prepaid in the U.S. mail, a copy of the foregoing Notice to Set Hearing on Defendant's Motion for Summary Judgment to the following counsel of record this _____ day of _________________, 199_:

Mary Cortez
Attorney for Plaintiff
511 South Grape
Denver, Colorado 80203

Heidi Hamlin
Attorney for Third Party Defendant
11th Floor
The Eagle Springs Building
101 West Willow Road
Denver, Colorado 80202

____

2

Figure 21: Sample Notice to Set Hearing - Page 2

DISTRICT COURT, CITY AND COUNTY OF DENVER, STATE OF COLORADO
CASE NO. 93CV1002 Courtroom No. 10

ORDER

ROBERT SCOTT,

Plaintiff,

v.

SAM'S SUPERMARKET, INC.

Defendant and Third Party Plaintiff,

v.

COMMERCIAL TILE COMPANY, INC.

Third Party Defendant.

This matter comes before the Court upon defendant's Motion for Summary Judgment and Memorandum of Law in Support thereof, and after considering all pleadings, affidavits, oral argument, and answers to discovery, the Court hereby grants defendant's Motion for Summary Judgment.

DONE BY THE COURT this ______day of _______, 199_.

BY THE COURT:

____

District Judge

Figure 22: Sample Order

CERTIFICATE OF SERVICE

I certify that a true and correct copy of the foregoing Order was served this ____ day of __________, 199_, by placing it in the United States mail, postage prepaid, addressed as follows:

Mary Cortez
Attorney for Plaintiff
511 South Grape
Denver, Colorado 80203

Jacob Armstrong
Attorney for the Defendant
430 Macmillan, Suite A
Denver, CO 80222

Heidi Hamlin
Attorney for Third Party Defendant
11th Floor
The Eagle Springs Building
101 West Willow Road
Denver, Colorado 80202

____

2

Figure 23: Sample Order - Page 2

Discovery

Each party may engage in discovery by drafting interrogatories, request for admissions, request for mental or physical examinations, and request for production of documents or conducting a deposition. Usually, a party will begin the discovery process with the written forms of discovery, which are less expensive than depositions.

Written Discovery

Written discovery documents begin with the caption of the case. The text includes an introductory statement that provides the time limit that the other party has in which to answer the questions, provide admissions, produce documents, or submit to an examination. The text then continues with a list of interrogatories, statements to be admitted, or items to be produced that are relevant to the issues of the case. Usually these lists are quite lengthy, requiring the other party to spend a great amount of time and effort to fulfill the conditions of the discovery. These documents end with a subscription and a certificate of service. The discovery samples in Figures 24-29 are from a California medical malpractice action.

Interrogatories, request for admissions, request for mental or physical examinations, and request for production of documents may be sent as separate documents or they may be combined in one series of documents. To demonstrate the format of different states, the sample discovery on the subsequent pages is arranged according to California form. The caption is structured differently, the text is double-spaced, and each of the lines in the document is numbered for convenient reference.

Depositions

Depositions usually take place after the parties have responded to written discovery. The deponent may be a party or a witness to the action. The deponent is served with a subpoena and a notice of deposition (similar in form to a notice to set), and the notice of deposition is sent to all of the parties in the action. Through the use of a subpoena *duces tecum*, the deponent may be required to bring specified items with him or her to the deposition. Depositions usually take place in the attorney's conference room where the deponent is sworn in by a certified or registered shorthand reporter. Any objections to questions made by counsel during the deposition are preserved for a judge's review, and the oral testimony is transcribed for use in the court trial. A sample of a transcribed deposition is set forth in Figures 30-38.

The paralegal may be asked to digest the transcribed deposition. In the form of an interoffice memorandum of law, the paralegal summarizes the deposition for the supervising attorney. The form of the digest is determined by the supervising attorney. For instance, the attorney may desire that a 500 page deposition be synthesized into a five page summary, or the attorney may want the paralegal to summarize only certain issues discussed in the deposition.

(Please note that California documents typically are printed on numbered paper.)

Leroy Tate
Tate & Associates
14 South Hill Street
Los Angeles, California 90010
(310) 999-8999

IN THE SUPERIOR COURT OF THE STATE OF CALIFORNIA

FOR THE COUNTY OF LOS ANGELES

ANDREW SMITH, a minor child, by and through his next best friends, OWEN SMITH, father, and GLORIA SMITH, mother, and OWEN SMITH and GLORIA SMITH, individually, Plaintiffs,	CASE NO.
v.	PLAINTIFFS' FIRST SET OF INTERROGATORIES
PEAKS HEALTH INSURANCE, LTD., a limited partnership, MEL P. IRWIN, M.D., MARILYN EVANS, M.D., JIM KANAS, M.D., MEMORIAL HOSPITAL, and unknown and unnamed physicians and employees of defendants, Defendants.	

COME NOW the above-named Plaintiffs, by and through their attorney of record, Mary Smith, and pursuant to Code of Civil Procedure, § 2030, request Defendant, MEMORIAL HOSPITAL, to respond to the following interrogatories within thirty (30) days of service of these interrogatories.

1

Figure 24: Sample Interrogatories

1. State the name of the person answering these interrogatories.

2. State the name and address of the custodian of records for Defendant MEMORIAL HOSPITAL.

3. How many years have Defendants KANAS and IRWIN been on the staff of MEMORIAL HOSPITAL?

4. Etc.

DATED: ___________ day of ____________, 199_.

BY:______________

Leroy Tate
Tate and Associates
14 South Hill Street
Los Angeles, CA 90010
(310) 999-8999

CERTIFICATE OF MAILING

I hereby certify that I have mailed, postage prepaid in the U.S. mail, a copy of the foregoing Plaintiffs' First Set of Interrogatories to the following counsel of record this ______ day of _________________, 199_:

Willie Hide
Spencer, Cole and Hide
1443 Wilshire Boulevard
Los Angeles, California 90011

____

2

Figure 25: Sample Interrogatories - Page 2

Leroy Tate
Tate & Associates
14 South Hill Street
Los Angeles, California 90010
(310) 999-8999

IN THE SUPERIOR COURT OF THE STATE OF CALIFORNIA

FOR THE COUNTY OF LOS ANGELES

ANDREW SMITH, a minor child, by and through his next best friends, OWEN SMITH, father, and GLORIA SMITH, mother, and OWEN SMITH and GLORIA SMITH, individually, Plaintiffs, v. PEAKS HEALTH INSURANCE, LTD., a limited partnership, MEL P. IRWIN, M.D., MARILYN EVANS, M.D., JIM KANAS, M.D., MEMORIAL HOSPITAL, and unknown and unnamed physicians and employees of defendants, Defendants.	CASE NO. PLAINTIFFS' REQUEST FOR ADMISSIONS (FIRST SET)

COME NOW the above-named plaintiffs, by and through their attorney of record, Leroy Tate, and pursuant to Code of Civil Procedure, § 2033, request Defendant MEMORIAL HOSPITAL to respond to the following requests for admission within thirty (30) days of service of these requests.

1

Figure 26: Sample Request for Admissions

1. Admit that Defendant Doctors KANAS, IRWIN, and EVANS share in the profits of Defendant MEMORIAL HOSPITAL.

2. Admit that there is an economic disincentive for doctors of MEMORIAL HOSPITAL to hospitalize their patients.

3. Admit that it is common practice to provide bonuses to doctors who refer the least number of patients to the emergency room of MEMORIAL HOSPITAL.

4. Etc.

NOTE: Defendant's failure to respond to these Requests for Admission may result in each of the requests' being deemed admitted.

DATED: _____________ day of_____________, 199_.

By:_____________________

Leroy Tate
Tate and Associates
14 South Hill Street
Los Angeles, CA 90010
(310) 999-8999

CERTIFICATE OF MAILING

I hereby certify that I have mailed, postage prepaid in the U.S. mail, a copy of the foregoing Plaintiffs' Request for Admissions to the following counsel of record this _____ day of _________________, 199_:

Willie Hide
Spencer, Cole and Hide
1443 Wilshire Boulevard
Los Angeles, California 90011

____

2

Figure 27: Sample Request for Admissions - Page 2

Leroy Tate
Tate & Associates
14 South Hill Street
Los Angeles, California 90010
(310) 999-8999

IN THE SUPERIOR COURT OF THE STATE OF CALIFORNIA

FOR THE COUNTY OF LOS ANGELES

ANDREW SMITH, a minor child, by and through his next best friends, OWEN SMITH, father, and GLORIA SMITH, mother, and OWEN SMITH and GLORIA SMITH, individually, Plaintiffs, v. PEAKS HEALTH INSURANCE, LTD., a limited partnership, MEL P. IRWIN, M.D., MARILYN EVANS, M.D., and JIM KANAS, M.D., MEMORIAL HOSPITAL, and unknown and unnamed physicians and employees of defendants, Defendants.	) CASE NO.) PLAINTIFFS') REQUEST FOR) PRODUCTION OF) DOCUMENTS) (FIRST SET)

The above-named plaintiffs, by and through their attorney of record, Leroy Tate, and pursuant to the Code of Civil Procedure, § 2031, request Defendant MEMORIAL HOSPITAL to produce the following documents at the office of Leroy Tate on or about 9:00 a.m. on the _________ of _________, 199_.

1

Figure 28: Sample Request for Production of Documents

1. Copies of Defendant MEMORIAL HOSPITAL's contracts with Defendant Doctors KANAS, IRWIN, and EVANS.

2. Copies of Defendant MEMORIAL HOSPITAL's terms of employment for Defendant Doctors KANAS, IRWIN, and EVANS.

3. A copy of Defendant MEMORIAL HOSPITAL's license to provide medical services in the state of California.

4. Etc.

DATED:__________ of ______________, 199_.

BY:________________
Leroy Tate
Tate and Associates
14 South Hill Street
Los Angeles, CA 90010
(310) 999-8999

CERTIFICATE OF MAILING

I hereby certify that I have mailed, postage prepaid in the U.S. mail, a copy of the foregoing Request for Production of Documents to the following counsel of record this _____ day of __________________, 199_:

Willie Hide
Spencer, Cole and Hide
1443 Wilshire Boulevard
Los Angeles, California 90011

____

2

Figure 29: Sample Request for Production of Documents - Page 2

Leroy Tate
Tate & Associates
14 South Hill Street
Los Angeles, California 90010
(310) 999-8999

IN THE SUPERIOR COURT OF THE STATE OF CALIFORNIA

FOR THE COUNTY OF LOS ANGELES

ANDREW SMITH, a minor child,	)	CASE NO.
by and through his next best friends,	)	
OWEN SMITH, father, and GLORIA SMITH, mother,	)	
and OWEN SMITH and GLORIA SMITH, individually,	)	
	)	
Plaintiffs,	)	DEPOSITION OF
v.	)	JAMES
	)	SYLVESTER
PEAKS HEALTH INSURANCE, LTD.,	)	STEINKE
a limited partnership,	)	
MEL P. IRWIN, M.D., MARILYN EVANS, M.D.,	)	MAY 23, 199_
JIM KANAS, M.D., MEMORIAL HOSPITAL,	)	
and unknown and unnamed physicians	)	
and employees of defendants.	)	
	)	
Defendants.	)	
	)	

APPEARANCES:

For the Plaintiffs:
Leroy Tate
Tate & Associates
14 South Hill Street
Los Angeles, California 90010
(310) 999-8999

Figure 30: Sample Transcribed Deposition

For the Defendants: Willie Hide
Spencer, Cole and Hide
1443 Wilshire Boulevard
Los Angeles, California 90011
(310) 765-8787

STIPULATIONS:

All parties, through their respective counsel, stipulate and agree that all objections, except to the form of the questions, will be reserved until the time of the trial.

BY MR. TATE:

Q: Would you please state your full name for the record?

A: James Sylvester Steinke.

Q: Where are you presently employed Dr. Steinke?

A: I am a pediatrician in a private practice located at 450 South Vermont Avenue in Los Angeles.

Q: How long have you been practicing pediatric medicine?

A: For eight years.

Q: Are you recognized as a plan physician for Peaks Health Insurance?

A: Yes.

Q: Could you please briefly list your educational background?

A: I received my undergraduate and medical degrees from U.C.L.A.

2

Figure 31: Sample Transcribed Deposition - Page 2

Q: Dr. Steinke, are you familiar with Andrew Smith?

A: Yes.

Q: How have you come to know Andrew?

A: I am his pediatrician and have treated him since he was one year old.

Q: Dr. Steinke could you please explain the current medical condition of the child, Andrew Smith?

A: Andrew needs around the clock care as a result of an episode of viral encephalitis. He needs an apnea monitor around the clock. We could not have sent him home from the hospital without it, the child would have had to go to a nursing facility. We talked about this and the question was, do you go to a nursing facility or do you go home with the family? And, the Smith's response was that they wanted to go home, because that's what they desired. And I thought the child would do better at home, and I felt that the monitor was very necessary in the initial few weeks after his illness. Now, four months later, I still feel that the monitor is essential.

Q: Does the child currently need oxygen equipment?

A: Yes, and suction equipment, too.

Q: Is Andrew on a special diet?

A: Yes, he requires a special formula.

Q: In your opinion, Dr. Steinke, is the monitor, oxygen equipment, suction equipment, and formula medically necessary?

3

Figure 32: Sample Transcribed Deposition - Page 3

A: Yes.

Q: Dr. Steinke, does Andrew require any special therapy?

A: Yes he does. Four months ago, I requested that the Smith's health insurance carrier provide occupational therapy and physical therapy once he was discharged from the hospital.

Q: To your knowledge, has either occupational or physical therapy been provided to Andrew?

A: No.

Q: Do you know why Peaks Health has not provided Andrew with occupational and physical therapy?

BY MR. HIDE:

A: Objection. Dr. Steinke is not in a position to know why therapy has not been provided to Andrew, and even if he did know, his answer would constitute hearsay.

BY MR. TATE:

Q: Allow me to rephrase the question, Dr. Steinke. Have you seen any correspondence from Peaks Health in which they have denied therapy to Andrew?

A: Yes. I have read a letter which is apparently from Peaks addressed to Mr. and Mrs. Smith, wherein Peaks has stated that it would not pay for therapy since it was not a covered benefit under their health insurance policy. Ms. Smith provided a copy of this letter to me.

4

Figure 33: Sample Transcribed Deposition - Page 4

Q: Dr. Steinke, did you bring a copy of that letter with you today?

A: Yes, here it is.

(Deposition exhibit number 1 is marked for identification at this time.)

Q: Dr. Steinke, what else does this letter state?

A: In the letter, Peaks Health Insurance denies all further obligation to pay for Andrew's apnea monitor, therapy, suction equipment, oxygen supplies and formula, since, and I quote, "the policy only covers durable goods, equipment, and supplies which are deemed to be medically necessary by the Peaks Health Medical Director."

Q: Dr. Steinke, in your opinion, is the therapy, monitor, suction, oxygen, and formula for Andrew a medical necessity?

A: Yes.

Q: Please refer next to page three of the Smith's contract of insurance with Peaks Health, which I am handing to you now, under the heading of "Home Health Services." Under article eleven it reads that "home health services are limited to services of registered nurses and home health aides on a part-time or intermittent basis as prescribed or directed by a health plan physician and are provided without charge." As you have stated, the therapy, formula, monitor, suction and oxygen equipment were prescribed by you. Do you believe that these items are included under that definition of home health services?

DR. STEINKE: Yes I do.

5

Figure 34: Sample Transcribed Deposition - Page 5

(Deposition exhibit number 2 is marked for identification)

Q: Has anyone at Peaks Health Insurance informed you that pursuant to their health insurance contract with the Smiths, home health aides does not include therapy, formula, monitors, suction, and oxygen?

A: No.

Q: Do you know who is currently paying for Andrew's therapy, formula, monitor, suction, and oxygen?

A: I have seen copies of the bills which are apparently being sent directly to the Smiths, but I do not know if anyone is paying for those items.

Q: Dr. Steinke, in your opinion, for how long will the apnea monitor, suction, oxygen, formula and therapy be a medical necessity for Andrew?

A: The therapy, formula, and oxygen, indefinitely. He is progressing to the point that, hopefully, the suction and apnea monitor will no longer be necessary, say, in six months.

Q: Dr. Steinke, in your opinion as primary treating physician for Andrew Smith, can Andrew survive without the apnea monitor, suction, oxygen, formula and therapy?

A: No.

BY MR. TATE:

A: Thank you, Dr. Steinke, I have no further questions at this time.

6

Figure 35: Sample Transcribed Deposition - Page 6

BY MR. HIDE:

Q: For the record, Dr. Steinke, how many other patients have you treated with viral encephalitis?

A: Perhaps two others. This is a rare illness.

Q: Referring to exhibit number 2, do you suppose that home health aides could refer to a person?

A: Like a nursing aide? Yes, that could be one interpretation.

Q: In your opinion, is Ms. Smith capable of providing either occupational or physical therapy for Andrew?

A: No, not without significant formal education and training.

Q: Peaks Health Insurance Company's interpretation of the insurance policy is that home health services are very narrowly defined to include nurses and home health aides period, and that it is not additionally defined to include any sort of equipment or supplies such as the apnea monitor, oxygen, suction, therapy and special formula. Do you believe that could be a reasonable interpretation?

A: No. The monitor, oxygen, suction, therapy and formula are necessary for the child to survive at home, and would have been available at the hospital.

Q: But even if those items are medically necessary, they are still not covered benefits. Do you understand the difference between covered benefits and medical necessity?

7

Figure 36: Sample Transcribed Deposition - Page 7

A: That's what this litigation is about.

Q: Has Andrew exhibited improvement in his medical condition?

A: Yes, there has been a slow, but gradual improvement.

Q: When do you anticipate that he will become self-sufficient?

A: He may never be able to live without care.

BY MR. HIDE:

Q: Thank you, I have no further questions at this time.

(The deposition concluded at 12:55 p.m. on May 23, 199_.)

I, James Sylvester Steinke, do hereby certify that I have read the foregoing transcript and that the same and accompanying correction sheets, if any, constitute a true and complete record of my testimony.

____
Deponent

Subscribed and sworn to before this _______day of ______, 199_.

My commission expires__________________

____
Notary Public

Address: __________________

8

Figure 37: Sample Transcribed Deposition - Page 8

STATE OF CALIFORNIA)

) SS. REPORTER'S CERTIFICATE

COUNTY OF LOS ANGELES)

I, Kathy Brokaw, do hereby certify that I am a Certified Shorthand Reporter and Notary Public within the State of California and that previous to the commencement of the examination, the deponent was duly sworn by me to testify to the truth.

I further testify that this deposition was taken in stenotypy by me at the time and place herein set forth and was thereafter reduced to typewritten form and that the foregoing constitutes a true and correct transcript.

I further testify that I am not related to, employed by, nor of counsel for any of the parties or attorneys herein, nor otherwise interested in the result of the within action.

In witness whereof, I have affixed my signature and seal this _____ day of _
_______, 199_.

My commission expires ________________

____

Kathy Brokaw
P.O. Box 4455
Los Angeles, CA 90017

Figure 38: Sample Reporter's Certificate

JURY INSTRUCTION NO. 1

The complaint is a mere accusation against the defendant, and it is not in itself any evidence of the liability of the defendant, and no juror should permit himself or herself to be influenced to any extent, however slight, against the defendant because or on account of the filing of the complaint.

JURY INSTRUCTION NO. 2

(1) The burden of proof is upon Plaintiff to establish his case by a preponderance of the evidence.

(2) The burden of proof is upon Defendant to establish an affirmative defense by a preponderance of the evidence.

(3) By "burden of proof" is meant that the obligation rests on the party or parties who assert a proposition to establish the same by a preponderance of the evidence presented in this case, regardless of which party may have produced such evidence.

(4) By "preponderance of the evidence" is meant that evidence which is most convincing and satisfying in the controversy between the parties, regardless of which party may have produced such evidence.

1

Figure 39: Sample Jury Instructions

(5) If a party fails to meet his burden of proof or if the evidence weighs so evenly that you are unable to say that there is a preponderance on either side, you must resolve the question against the party who has the burden of proof and in favor of the opposing party.

JURY INSTRUCTION NO. 3

The evidence in the case consists of the sworn testimony of all the witnesses, all exhibits which have been received into evidence, all facts which have been admitted or agreed to, all facts and events which have been judicially noticed and all presumptions stated in these instructions.

In determining the facts, you must consider only the evidence received at the trial. Evidence offered at the trial and rejected or stricken by the court must not be considered. Statements, remarks, arguments, and objections of counsel and remarks of the court not directed to you are not evidence.

You are to consider only the evidence in the case and reasonable inferences from that evidence. An inference is a deduction or a conclusion which reason and common sense lead the jury to draw from facts which have been proved.

2

Figure 40: Sample Jury Instructions - Page 2

When the attorneys on both sides stipulate or agree as to the existence of a fact, or a fact has been admitted, the jury must regard that fact as proved. If the agreement is that a witness would testify in a certain manner, all that the jury is required to believe is that the witness would testify.

When the court declares that it has taken judicial notice of some fact or event, the jury must accept that fact or event as proved.

JURY INSTRUCTION NO. 4

Evidence may be either direct or circumstantial. Circumstantial evidence is the proof of facts or circumstances from which the existence or nonexistence of other facts may reasonably be inferred. All other evidence is direct evidence. The law makes no distinction between the effect of direct evidence and circumstantial evidence.

JURY INSTRUCTION NO. 5

These jury instructions are a part of the court record. You are not permitted to write any notes on these jury instructions or to deface them in any way. The original instructions and the exhibits are to be returned to the court at the conclusion of your deliberations.

3

Figure 41: Sample Jury Instructions - Page 3

The bailiff will now escort you to the jury room. Upon reaching the jury room, you are to select one of your members to be the foreman or forewoman of the jury. Your foreman or forewoman will preside over your deliberations. Your foreman or forewoman and all of the other members of the jury must sign whatever verdict you reach. Your verdict must be unanimous.

When you have agreed upon your verdict, your foreman or forewoman should notify the bailiff that you have agreed upon a verdict, but the verdict should not be revealed to the bailiff. The foreman or forewoman shall keep the verdict forms, these instructions, and the exhibits until otherwise instructed by the court.

These jury instructions were read and given to the jury by the court on this ______day of _______, 199_.

By the court:_______________________
The Honorable Judge Patty Bristol

4

Figure 42: Sample Jury Instructions - Page 4

DISTRICT COURT, CITY AND COUNTY OF DENVER, STATE OF COLORADO
Case No. 93CV1002 Division No. 10

SPECIAL VERDICT FORM A

ROBERT SCOTT,

Plaintiff,

v.

SAM'S SUPERMARKET, INC.

Defendant and Third Party Plaintiff,

v.

COMMERCIAL TILE COMPANY, INC.,
Third Party Defendant.

We, the jury, present our answers to questions submitted by the Court, to which we have unanimously agreed:

QUESTION NO.1: Did the plaintiff incur injuries and losses?

ANSWER NO.1:________

QUESTION NO. 2: Was the defendant's negligence, if any, the proximate cause of the injuries or losses suffered by the plaintiff?

ANSWER NO. 2:________

QUESTION NO. 3: State the amount of damages, if any, incurred by plaintiff and caused by the conduct of the defendant. (State the amount or "none")

ANSWER NO. 3:________

By the jury: ____________________ ____________________
____________________ ____________________
____________________ ____________________

Figure 43: Sample Special Verdict Form

Trial Documents

If a case goes to trial, it is usually the paralegal's responsibility to prepare a trial notebook. The trial notebook contains the information that the attorney needs to successfully conduct the client's case during trial. The contents of the trial notebook vary but usually include copies of pleadings and motions, witness lists, deposition digests, a copy of the trial brief, which outlines the arguments of the client's case, and jury instructions.

Jury Instructions

Although the judge is responsible for presenting the jury with instructions that explain the legal principles over which it should deliberate, attorneys are allowed to suggest jury instructions to the judge. The paralegal is often responsible for preparing the suggested jury instructions. Many offices have sets of instructions for each type of case they try. From these sets the paralegal chooses those that apply to the case on trial. The jury instructions should be numbered and double-spaced. Figures 39-42 show some possible jury instructions.

Special Verdict Form

Sometimes a jury will be asked to complete a special verdict form. This form contains questions to which the jury must provide answers in rendering its verdict. The form begins with the case caption, presents several questions, and ends with the signatures of all of the jury members. A sample special verdict form is shown in Figure 43.

The preceding figures are sample documents. Paralegals should always review their state's document format requirements.

CONCLUSION

Preparing proper letters, memoranda of law, pleadings, motions, discovery, and other documents is an essential skill that paralegals must apply to promote the orderly progression of a case. Paralegals also contribute to the progression of a case by obtaining crucial evidence through investigation and interviewing. The next chapter discusses the rules of evidence and the skills of investigation and interviewing.

CHAPTER 4: EVIDENCE, INVESTIGATION, AND INTERVIEWING FOR PARALEGALS

The outcome of a client's case hinges on the attorney's ability to access the relevant evidence to support the client's position. The paralegal is instrumental in uncovering evidence. There are basically two forms of evidence: tangible evidence, such as photos and documents, and testimonial evidence, such as witness testimony. Investigation techniques allow paralegals to uncover relevant physical evidence and interviewing techniques provide paralegals with important witness testimonies. Before paralegals embark on investigation or interviewing, however, they need to understand the rules of evidence.

THE RULES OF EVIDENCE

Just as there are state and federal rules governing civil procedure, there are state and federal rules governing evidence. The following discussion highlights the Federal Rules of Evidence, or F. R. E. Most state rules of evidence parallel the federal rules.

The F. R. E. establishes guidelines for determining the admissibility of evidence. These rules ensure that anything introduced in court as evidence does not prejudice the case in any manner. The most common test for the admissibility of any piece of evidence is to balance the probative, or possible, value of the evidence against the possible prejudice that may be introduced by that evidence. If the prejudice outweighs the probative value, the evidence will usually be disallowed. In short, the primary test for evidence is relevancy: logical relevancy and legal relevancy.

The following is a partial list and explanation of the important Federal Rules of Evidence. Evidence is essentially admissible in court if it is logically and legally relevant, not privileged, reliable (as with the testimony of witnesses), based on a reasonable opinion, in accordance with the rules of hearsay, and authentic. The general rule of evidence law is that competent and relevant evidence is admissible unless it falls under an exclusionary rule like hearsay and opinion evidence.

General Provisions

F.R.E. 103 - Rulings On Evidence.

Error may not be predicated upon a ruling which admits or excludes evidence unless a substantial right of the party is affected.

Any objection to the admission of a piece of evidence must be timely and specific. An objection should be made at the first reasonable opportunity and must state specific grounds. The opposing counsel may provide an offer of proof as to why the objection should be withdrawn and the evidence should be admissible.

Relevancy

Basically, to be admissible evidence should be logical, that is relevant to the issue, and legal, that is the value of the evidence outweighs its prejudicial impact.

F.R.E. 401 - Definition of "Relevant Evidence"

"Relevant evidence" means evidence having any tendency to make the existence of any fact that is of consequence to the determination of the action more probable or less probable than it would be without the evidence.

Generally greater weight is attached to direct evidence since the weigher of the facts finds it more credible than circumstantial evidence. Direct evidence provides direct support for an issue; circumstantial evidence requires that one make an inference about the evidence in order for it to support an issue. For instance, eyewitness testimony that a defendant's car hit the plaintiff's car and drove away is direct evidence of the defendant's responsibility, while paint marks found in the dents in the plaintiff's car that match the color of the defendant's car are circumstantial evidence that the defendant hit the plaintiff's car.

F.R.E. 402 - Relevant Evidence Generally Admissible; Irrelevant Evidence Inadmissible

Generally, relevant evidence is admissible and irrelevant evidence is not admissible. If challenged, the party presenting the evidence must prove its relevancy.

F.R.E. 403 - Exclusion of Relevant Evidence on Grounds of Prejudice, Confusion or Waste of Time

Relevant evidence may be excluded if it is prejudicial or misleading, it confuses the issues, or it causes an undue delay or wastes time.

F.R.E. 404 - Character Evidence Not Admissible to Prove Conduct; Exceptions; other Crimes.

Generally, character evidence is not admissible unless it is designed to show habitual tendencies. Character evidence is usually allowed for the purpose of impeaching the credibility of witnesses.

Privilege

Privileged communications are not admissible evidence in court. Under Article V of F.R.E., determining what information is privileged is left up to the state rules. Most states recognize the following privileged communications: legally married couples, attorneys and their clients, clergy and their penitents, and physicians and psychotherapists and their patients. These privileges are in place to protect the sanctity and security of these communications and the underlying relationships.

Competency to Testify

A witness is competent to testify if the witness (1) understands the obligation to tell the truth, (2) has the ability to communicate, and (3) has knowledge of the matter that he or she will testify about.

F.R.E. 602 - Lack of Personal Knowledge

A witness may not testify to a matter unless evidence is introduced to show that the witness has personal knowledge about the matter.

F.R.E. 607 - Impeachment

The credibility of a witness may be attacked by any party, including the party calling the witness.

Reasonableness of Opinion

For an opinion to be admissible, the witness must be reasonably qualified to form the opinion.

F.R.E. 701 - Lay witnesses may testify to their opinions only if the opinions are rationally based on the perception of the witness and are helpful to a clear understanding to the witness' testimony.

F.R.E. 702 - Expert witnesses may testify as to their opinions if they are qualified by knowledge, skill, experience, training, or education to speak on the relevant issues.

Hearsay

The hearsay rules regard the admissibility of statements, either oral or written, made outside of the courtroom.

F.R.E. 801 (c) - Definitions

"Hearsay" is a statement, other than one made by the declarant while testifying at the trial or hearing, offered in evidence to prove the truth of the matter asserted.

One of the most difficult concepts in the rules of evidence is that of hearsay and its exceptions. Hearsay is made up of the following elements:

1. In-court testimony,
2. of an out of court statement,
3. made by someone other than the witness,
4. offered to establish the truth of matters asserted in court.

A statement that meets the preceding four requirements is inadmissible as evidence unless it can be deemed admissible under one of the exceptions to hearsay. The exceptions to the hearsay rule are divided into two categories: exceptions despite the availability of the declarant as a witness and exceptions if the declarant of the statement is unavailable as a witness. Paralegals should note that there are also non-hearsay categories under F.R.E. 801(d). Categories of non-hearsay include a prior statement by a witness and an admission by a party-opponent.

F.R.E. 803 - Hearsay Exceptions; Availability of Declarant Immaterial

The following statements are admissible whether or not the declarant of those statements is available as a witness:

(1) *Present sense impressions.*

The declarant makes a descriptive or explanatory statement about his or her own sensory impressions during or immediately after an event. For example, an airplane struggles to get in the air at take-off. There is a twenty story building 1000 feet from the end of the runway. Upon seeing the plane struggle to take off, the declarant exclaims, "That plane is not going to make it!"

(2) *Excited utterance or spontaneous declaration.*

The declarant makes the statement during a state of extreme anxiety or excitement. For example, upon seeing a major explosion in the World Trade Center, the declarant shouts, "Those terrorists are at it again!"

(3) *Then existing mental, emotional, or physical condition.*

The declarant makes a statement concerning his or her mental, emotional, or physical condition (regarding issues such as intent, motive, mental feeling, pain, and physical conditions). Statements regarding a memory of or a belief about a condition are not included in this exception. Statements about how the declarant feels are admissible; statements about why the declarant thinks he or she feels that way are not admissible. For example, at a private party where alcohol is being served, the declarant states, "I am feeling very dizzy; I think I'm going to pass out." This statement would be admissible to show the declarant's mental and physical condition and might be used to show the declarant's lack of ability to consent in a rape prosecution.

(4) *Statements for purposes of medical diagnosis or treatment.*

A declarant makes a statement about his or her present condition for purposes of medical diagnosis or treatment; included are statements about past or present pain or the inception of the cause of the condition requiring medical treatment. For example, the declarant tells his physician that he has had severe pain in his neck ever since an automobile accident.

(5) *Recorded recollection.*

If a witness once had knowledge of a matter but now has an insufficient recollection, that witness may refresh his or her recollection with a memorandum or record made about the matter when it was fresh in the witness' memory. The information may be read into the court record but may not be included as an evidence exhibit unless it is offered by an adverse party. For example, a list of stolen items prepared by a homeowner immediately after her home was burglarized may be read into evidence at a trial occurring several years later to establish the value of stolen items taken in the burglary when the homeowner has difficulty recalling all the items taken.

(6) *Records of regularly conducted activity.*

Any form of record kept in the course of regular business activities that contains acts, events, conditions, opinions, or diagnoses may be admitted through witness testimony. Hospital records, school records, tax records, business records, and military records may be admitted under this exception.

(7) *Absence of entry in records kept in accordance with the provisions of paragraph (6).*

The absence of an entry in the records is admissible to show whether something did or did not occur. For example, a hospital patient's chart normally shows the drugs the patient has received, the amount of the drug given, and the time administered. If the charts do not show that a drug was administered, the absence of its entry in the charts is admissible to show that the patient never received the drug.

(8) *Public records and reports.*

Public records, except for police surveillance reports, are admissible. Admissibility is subject to the trust-worthiness of the sources of information.

(9) *Records of vital statistics.*

Records of birth, fetal death, death, or marriage are admissible if the records were filed within the confines of the law.

(10) *Absence of public record or entry.*

Absence of records in paragraphs 8 and 9 can be proven if official certification is provided showing that a diligent search failed to disclose the record.

(11) *Records of religious organizations.*

Statements of birth, marriage, divorce, death, legitimacy, ancestry, relationship, and other facts of personal and familial history are admissible if these records are regularly kept by a religious organization.

(12) *Marriage, baptismal, and similar certificates.*

Statements of facts contained in such certificates are admissible.

(13) *Family records.*

Statements contained in family records concerning the facts of personal and familial history are admissible.

(14) *Records of documents affecting an interest in property.*

Records that establish an interest in a piece of property are admissible if they are recorded according to statute in the appropriate public office.

(15) *Statements in documents affecting an interest in property.*

Statements included in such documents are admissible if they are relevant to the purpose of the document and more recent information is consistent with the statements.

(16) *Statements in ancient documents.*

Statements contained in authenticated documents over twenty years old are admissible.

(17) *Market reports, commercial publications.*

Reports that are considered to be reliable and are regularly used in the business world can be admitted.

(18) *Learned treatises.*

Expert witnesses can incorporate into their testimonies statements contained in treatises, periodicals, or pamphlets if these sources are considered to be reliable authorities. These may be used to impeach the credibility of an expert witness.

(19) *Reputation concerning personal or family history.*

Statements regarding facts of personal or family history made by one's family or personal associates are admissible.

(20) *Reputation concerning boundaries or general history.*

Statements made prior to the controversy concerning the reputed boundaries or customary use of land in a community or a community's reputed general history are admissible.

(21) *Reputation as to character.*

Statements regarding a person's reputed character within the community are admissible if character is at issue.

(22) *Judgment of previous conviction.*

Evidence of a prior felony conviction can be admissible if the evidence is necessary to prove any fact essential to sustain the judgment.

(23) *Judgment as to personal, family, or general history, or boundaries.*

Judgments providing such information are admissible if the information would also be provable by evidence of reputation.

(24) *Other exceptions.*

Other exceptions to the hearsay rule may be made if the court determines that the statement (a) is offered as evidence of a material fact, (b) is more probative on the point that any other evidence, and (c) best serves the general purposes of justice.

F.R.E. 804 - Hearsay Exceptions; Declarant Unavailable

The following exceptions to the hearsay rule apply if the declarant is unavailable to testify:

(1) *Former testimony.*

The declarant makes the statement as part of testimony given as a witness in a prior hearing or trial or testimony given in a deposition regarding the same event.

(2) *Statement under belief of impending death.*

The declarant makes a statement concerning the cause or circumstances of his or her impending death when he or she was under the immediate impression that his or her death was imminent.

(3) *Statement against interest.*

The declarant makes a statement that is so against his or her interest that a reasonable person would not make the statement unless it were true.

Authenticity

F.R.E. 901 - Requirement of Authentication or Identification

Each piece of evidence, including testimony, must be authenticated. Authentication involves confirming that the evidence is what it purports to be.

F.R.E. 1002 - Requirement of Original

Generally the original document, recording or photograph is required to prove the authenticity of its content. This requirement is known as the "best evidence rule;" the best evidence must be presented in its original form.

F.R.E. 1003 - Admissibility of Duplicates

A duplicate is admissible unless the authenticity of the original is questionable or the submission of a duplicate would be unfair, such as with documents whose duplicates could be easily altered.

As stated earlier, the preceding rules are federal. Paralegals should check their states' rules of evidence for any additions to the federal rules.

For Discussion Discuss how your state's rules of evidence differ from the federal rules of evidence. What rules does your state have that are not addressed in the federal rules?

INVESTIGATION

To assist in uncovering relevant evidence for their cases, many large law firms have their own investigators as members of their staffs, but in a small firm or for a less complex case, the paralegal may be the primary fact finder. Investigation provides information that assists the paralegal in preparing pleadings; it defines the type of questions the paralegal and attorney should present in interrogatories and at depositions; and it uncovers evidence that is used in settlement negotiations and in court to strengthen the client's case.

Papers and photographs are two of the most unimpeachable sources of information that the paralegal can find. Papers include any documents that support the client's version of the facts and may include letters, contracts, and public records. Photographs may be pictures of the scene of the event in dispute, or they may be pictures of evidence that is not easily presented in court, such as a damaged car. Because their contents are virtually indisputable, original documents and photographs are easily admissible in court. Investigation for relevant evidence requires four steps: obtaining the evidence, marking it, protecting it, and organizing it.

Obtaining Evidence

The first, and often hardest, step is getting the evidence. Every investigative project has an objective, and it is critical for paralegals to succinctly understand why their employers are asking them to gather certain facts. Paralegals must listen closely and take notes while their supervisors are assigning tasks. It never hurts to obtain too much detail regarding assignments; therefore paralegals should never hesitate to ask questions pertaining to the projects that they are being assigned.

When gathering facts, many paralegals begin by imitating the style of an investigative role model. After a few weeks of fact gathering and investigation, however, each paralegal should develop a unique style of his or her own. This uniqueness is predicated upon the processes which work best for that individual. Trial and error assist in determining those methods which work most effectively in developing each paralegal's fact gathering style.

Issue Spotting

One way to pinpoint the focus of an investigation is to spot the relevant issues of law and fact in a particular case. The issue is the legal controversy that litigation is attempting to resolve. There may be more than one issue in a case, in fact most cases involve several issues. Issues are usually presented as questions. Finding the information necessary to answer these questions is the main goal of investigation. For instance, in the slip and fall case of Robert Scott as outlined in chapter 3, the following are relevant issues: (1) Was Sam's Supermarket negligent in the maintenance of its floor? (2) If Sam's Supermarket was negligent, was this negligence the proximate cause of Robert Scott's fall and subsequent injuries? (3) Was Robert Scott contributorily negligent? (4) Was Commercial Tile Company strictly liable for manufacturing and installing defective floor tile? The paralegal would then attempt to uncover and verify through investigation the facts necessary to provide answers for each of these questions.

Checklists

Based on the relevant issues of a case, paralegals should create and rely on checklists to begin the fact gathering process. A checklist is merely a sequential listing of questions that must by answered and duties that must be accomplished in order to fully complete an investigative project. For instance, if an investigative project is to determine whether process was properly served upon the party named in the summons and complaint, the following checklist of questions would form the basis of the fact gathering process:

1. Was the process sufficient on its face?
2. Was the proper defendant named in the process?
3. Was the named defendant served with the process?
4. Was the person who served the process over 18 years of age?
5. Was the process server a party to the action?
6. Were there any documents other than the complaint served with the summons? If so, what were these documents?
7. Were there any witnesses to the service of process?
8. Was the return of service properly executed?
9. Was the properly executed return of service returned to the correct court?

Once a paralegal creates several checklists, he or she can compile them into workbooks for the office's future use. As paralegals become successful fact gatherers, they should create new chapters of checklists in their workbooks that correspond to each area of inquiry.

A great source of sample checklists is the *American Jurisprudence Proof of Facts* (P.O.F.) series, which details the necessary facts that should be garnered for virtually any investigative project. This series of formbooks can be found in law school libraries and most county courthouse law libraries. Paralegals should begin their research in the topical index at the end of the P.O.F. series. Reference to this series will also demonstrate how to prepare checklists.

When creating checklists the paralegal should keep in mind that fact gathering is an evolutionary process. Even the most structured plans of attack may end up as only a guideline for the investigation. The plan designated by the checklist, when implemented with diligence, may uncover unanticipated facts. It should not be discouraging for a paralegal to merely "stumble" upon pertinent information.

Sources of Information

Working from the checklist, the paralegal then seeks to obtain the information necessary to answer the questions. The sources of public information are vast. To locate general information about individuals, many paralegals begin with the phone book.

Phone directories Paralegals usually begin investigative fact gathering with the white and yellow pages of the appropriate telephone directory. Telephone directories and telephone calls may turn up a large amount of information.

Public libraries and telephone companies are the best sources of telephone directories for geographic localities outside the paralegal's immediate area, and, if a law office performs an extensive amount of work in a particular foreign locality, it should purchase the telephone directories from the telephone companies in that area. Directory assistance must also be consulted to update and verify the information obtained from the directories.

Other excellent directories are the criss-cross directories which contain the names, addresses, and phone numbers of individuals who live in or businesses that operate in many metropolitan areas of the United States. The primary publishers of these tomes, Cole and Polk, arrange listings of people and businesses by city and county. These directories even list the occupations of the persons listed within them and contain the names of owners of telephone numbers sometimes even if those numbers are unlisted. Thus, with a criss-cross

directory, paralegals can frequently find the phone numbers of persons who do not appear in local telephone directories.

Analysis of Court Documents Other sources of information are court documents filed in the case. Paralegals may begin the search for information by consulting the case pleadings. From the plaintiff's complaint, a paralegal for the defense attorney may acquire information regarding the location of the incident, who was involved in the incident, the damages claimed, and salient details about the plaintiff's lifestyle, family, and job. This information is used to determine whether the defendant should fight the claim in court. Depending on what the paralegal finds in the investigation, the lawsuit either progresses or the defendant negotiates a settlement of the claim. A paralegal for the plaintiff's attorney may use information from the defendant's answer to begin the investigation of the plaintiff's claim.

Discovery documents, such as interrogatories, request for admissions, request for production of documents, and deposition digests, are also excellent sources of information for paralegals. However, discovery is rarely filed with the court. Motions and affidavits more commonly assist in fact gathering since they are filed with the court.

Records Hospital, school, court, motor vehicle, and military records are excellent informational tools. These records contain information that even eyewitnesses have difficulty refuting, and they are usually admissible in court as evidence. For instance, a paralegal for the defendant's attorney in a personal injury case will undoubtedly retrieve the records from the hospital at which the plaintiff stayed. These records indicate the types of injuries the plaintiff suffered, the treatment the plaintiff received, and the cost of the treatment, information that is of vital importance if the suit goes to trial.

Much of the information that paralegals need to find can be located in public records. The key to accessing the records is knowing where to go. Paralegals must become familiar with sources of public records. For example, they must know what records are kept by the county clerk, the local school district, and the tax assessor's office. If the paralegal does not know where information may be found, he or she should not hesitate to pick up a phone book, and begin making calls to governmental agencies. Tables 3 and 4 summarize the sources for records and the kinds of information the records contain.

Once paralegals locate the appropriate records, they must be polite to the office personnel who are helping them access the information. If paralegals are impatient or abrupt with the records staff, they will usually make it difficult for the paralegal to collect any information at all. If politeness does not achieve the desired result, paralegals may announce themselves as paralegals and mention the attorney or law firm they represent. Most public employees are fairly willing to accommodate attorneys and law firms with which they are familiar, so it does not hurt to name-drop.

Paralegals must choose their words carefully when asking for certain information. If paralegals are well prepared and know precisely for what information they are looking, their requests will more likely produce a fruitful result. When asking for information, paralegals should be very concise and precise about what they are requesting. Instead of asking for Mr. Robert Scott's hospital records, they should ask for specific information. Requesting Mr. Robert Scott's hospital records from the admittance date of December 27, 199_, to a release date of January 8, 199_, enhances the chances that the record's clerk will pull the correct file. Imprecise requests waste the paralegal's time and the time of the person from whom the paralegal is requesting information.

Conversations with Knowledgeable People Every paralegal comes across a situation for which no obvious answer is available. The paralegal may then need to consult sources other than witnesses or parties to the action. Some people in the community have a vast amount of knowledge and are usually

willing to share the information with someone who appears interested in obtaining the information from them. These people include courthouse employees, city hall employees, reporters, experienced legal investigators, and even local gossips.

Obtaining information from disinterested sources may require a little social skill. Valuable information is usually provided by people who know and trust the paralegal. Therefore, the paralegal should take time to establish a professional relationship with people who are good sources of information and are familiar with the legal process. Sometimes helpful insight into the character of a judge may be gained from a person who makes a hobby of observing trials. Paralegals should be aware of all potential informational sources in their investigative endeavors.

Other Sources In addition to the list of sources in Tables 3 and 4, the paralegal can gain information from many state and federal sources. Every licensing and regulatory agency is a potential source of information, and there is a wealth of information in various state offices. Table 2 lists the state and federal agencies that may provide possible informational leads.

Although some federal sources of information may not be open to the public, if the individual the paralegal is investigating has engaged in any business or activity that is taxed, regulated, or licensed by the federal government, there may be information available.

Individuals usually obtain their social security numbers in the state where they were born or raised. Therefore, knowing an individual's social security number can provide helpful information about that person's origins. A paralegal can discover in which state an individual's social security number was issued by noting the social security number's first three digits. Table 5 lists the first three digits of most social security numbers and their probable corresponding places of issuance.

State Offices and Agencies	Federal Offices and Agencies
Secretary of State Department of Agriculture Department of Industrial Relations Department of Natural Resources Other administrative agencies may be found by consulting the government listings in the telephone directory	Armed Forces U.S. Customs Bureau United States Secret Service Internal Revenue Service Alcohol Tax and Firearms Unit Division of Investigations: Interior Department Agriculture Department Veterans Administration Federal Bureau of Investigation Securities and Exchange Commission Department of Transportation Social Security Administration

Table 2: State and Federal Offices and Agencies

SOURCES OF INFORMATION	
Source	**Type of Information**
Police Department Incident or Offense Reports	Statements of the facts of an incident and the names, birthdates, addresses, and telephone numbers of the participants
Arrest Records	Name, address, birthdate, physical description, social security number, and fingerprints of the accused
Traffic Accident Reports	The location and time of the accident, the names of the driver and the passengers and their addresses and birthdates, the driver's license numbers, and the automobile registration number
Arrest Warrants	The name and birthdate of the accused, the charge, and the case number
Telephone Company Records	An individual's full name, address, telephone number, length of phone service, record of toll calls, and number of extensions
Post Office	An individual's full name, address and box number, and any forwarding addresses
Credit Card Companies	An individual's employment and credit references and information regarding the types of charges an individual makes
County Assessor's Office	Dimensions and taxable income on real property and information about property improvements
Health Department Records	The names and maiden names of a child's parents, their occupations and ages, and the name of the child's physician
Public School Records	Past and present records of students and possibly their photographs
Professional Trade, Association, and Union Records	List of members' names and their addresses and telephone numbers
Banks and Other Financial Institutions	An individual's full name, address, occupation, sources of income, expenditures, personal and business references, net worth, and handwriting samples
State and Federal Licensing Agencies, such as the State Bar Association, State Board of Medical Examiners, and the Real Estate Commission	An individual's educational and professional background and experience, such as whether the individual is bonded or has liability insurance
Moving Companies	An individual's forwarding address

Table 3: Sources of Information

SOURCES OF INFORMATION	
Source	**Type of Information**
Bureau of Vital Statistics	
Birth Certificates	An individual's full name, birthdate, place of birth, time of birth, and parents' names
Death Certificates	The name, birthdate, last known address, and cause of death of the deceased
County Clerk's Office	
Marriage License Records	An individual's marital information, birthdate, signature, and last known address
Divorce Records	An individual's marriage date and location, separation date and location, children's ages, community property, signature, and place of employment
Civil Files	Name changes, property liens and property descriptions, and the types of civil cases in which an individual is involved
Criminal Files	Transcripts of preliminary hearings, probation officer reports, subpoenas issued in a case, and names of attorneys who are involved in the case
Election Commission	A registered voter's full name, address, occupation, political affiliation, spouse's name, and most recent location of voter registration
Credit Reporting Agencies	An individual's full name, address, birthdate, occupation, present and former addresses, credit rating, marital status, information regarding whether he owns or rents his home, who his personal and professional references are, what banks and financial institutions he uses, and what the names of his relatives may be
Immigration and Naturalization Service	The full name, address, occupation, age, physical description, marital status, signature, photograph, and date and manner of entry of an alien
Federal Aviation Administration	Aircraft ownership information
Coast Guard	Ship and boat ownership and docking information
Lloyd's Registered Yacht	Ship, boat, and yacht ownership information
Division of Motor Vehicles	An individual's full name, address, physical description, birthdate, vehicle information, operator's license number, photograph, and signature
Public Service and Other Utility Companies	An individual's name, address, and prior addresses and information regarding who is responsible for paying an individual's bill

Table 4: Sources of Information - Page 2

First Three Digits of SSN	Place of Issuance	First Three Digits of SSN	Place of Issuance
001-003	New Hampshire	440-448	Oklahoma
004-007	Maine	449-467	Texas
008-009	Vermont	468-477	Minnesota
010-034	Massachusetts	478-485	Iowa
035-039	Rhode Island	486-500	Missouri
040-049	Connecticut	501-502	North Dakota
050-134	New York	503-504	South Dakota
135-158	New Jersey	505-508	Nebraska
159-211	Pennsylvania	509-515	Kansas
212-220	Maryland	516-517	Montana
221-222	Delaware	518-519	Idaho
223-231	Virginia	520	Wyoming
232-236	West Virginia	521-524	Colorado
232,237-246	North Carolina	525,585	New Mexico
247-251	South Carolina	526-527	Arizona
252-260	Georgia	528-529	Utah
261-267, 589	Florida	530	Nevada
268-302	Ohio	531-539	Washington
303-317	Indiana	540-544	Oregon
318-361	Illinois	545-573	California
362-386	Michigan	574	Alaska
387-399	Wisconsin	575-576	Hawaii
400-407	Kentucky	577-579	Dist. of Columbia
408-415	Tennessee	580	Virgin Islands
416-424	Alabama	580-584	Puerto Rico
425-428,587	Mississippi	586	Guam
429-432	Arkansas	586	American Samoa
433-439	Louisiana	586	Philippine Islands
		700-729	Railroad Retirement Board

Table 5: Place of Issuance for Social Security Numbers

Marking Evidence

Once tangible evidence is obtained and verified, it should be carefully marked. Paralegals should designate the evidence with their initials, date the evidence, and record the evidence in a journal. This record assures that the evidence will be identifiable and guards against the evidence's being deemed inadmissible. Paralegals should also include in their investigation journals the names, addresses, and phone numbers of witnesses and others with important information about the case. Good records lead to credible and admissible evidence.

Protecting Evidence

Evidence should be protected. Certain types of physical evidence must be placed in protective containers or plastic bags. These containers should be carefully marked and sealed. Proper protection prevents evidence from being damaged or destroyed and rebuts charges that the evidence is incomplete or has been altered. To ensure that the evidence is not tampered with and that the chain of custody is unbroken, physical evidence should be kept in a locked container and handled under the supervision of the same paralegal at all times. The paralegal that handles the evidence may be called upon to testify at trial as to the handling and custody of the evidence.

Organizing Evidence

The final step is to organize the evidence so that it establishes the chain of events of the client's case. A good story line that is supported by evidence will be more persuasive than will a story that does not relate logically to the presented evidence. If the evidence does not directly relate to the client's story, the paralegal must provide a logical explanation for the incongruity. A paralegal's primary consideration is to organize the evidence in accordance with the supervising attorney's instructions. If the supervisor leaves organizing the evidence to the paralegal's discretion, the paralegal should organize the evidence to conform to the attorney's strategy of the case.

There are three ways to organize evidence. The paralegal may organize the evidence chronologically, by version, or by inconsistency.

Chronological Organization

The evidence should first be ordered chronologically. In arranging evidence chronologically, the paralegal links each piece of data to the others in the order that the related action occurred. Chronological ordering of evidence is helpful in promoting the accuracy of the client's version of the story.

Organization by Versions

Organization by version is used in cases where there are significant discrepancies in the evidence. This arrangement allows the attorney to see the strengths and weaknesses in the case. It also allows the attorney to see any factual gaps in the case that need further investigation or clarification. In organizing the evidence by version, the paralegal must examine the different versions of what happened and prepare an outline or chart. The chart should include the differing version and the evidence that tends to support or refute those versions.

Organization by Inconsistency

Once evidence has been ordered chronologically and by version, the paralegal may note inconsistencies in the information. These inconsistencies can then be organized into checklists in preparation for further investigation. In organizing evidence by checklists, the paralegal may prepare a chart of the crucial events in the case and a list of all the inconsistencies in the evidence as to that event. This will highlight for the attorney the weaknesses and gaps in the evidence so that further investigation may be done.

Investigation continues throughout the litigation process. The paralegal prepares investigation checklists for one issue, diligently draws upon the sources of information to answer the questions on the checklist, and prepares the products of the investigation so that they will be valuable to the client's case. Often investigation of one issue will uncover new issues and new checklists to be answered through further investigation.

Most of the discussion in this section has focused on obtaining tangible evidence in support of the client's case. The next section concentrates on the skill of interviewing as a means of obtaining the relevant facts of a case and gaining testimonial evidence for use at trial.

For Discussion Discuss what sources of information would be most beneficial for a family law practice, a corporate law practice, a personal injury law practice, a bankruptcy law practice, and a real estate law practice.

INTERVIEWING

Perhaps the most valuable sources of information are derived from interviews with clients and witnesses. Paralegals are usually best suited for conducting interviews because the client may find them to be less intimidating than their supervising attorneys. The paralegal may be more sensitive and more approachable than the attorney, and therefore, may be able to gain more information from the client or the witness being interviewed. The interviews that paralegals conduct usually serve one of two purposes: to gain information from a client or witness or to prepare the client or witness to give testimony. The first, and perhaps most important, interview is the initial client interview.

The Initial Client Interview

The primary goal of the initial client interview is to gather enough information to determine whether the client has a valid case and to start a proper investigation of the case if it is valid. To conduct a successful interview, the paralegal must be properly prepared. Paralegals often provide the first and most lasting impression of their law firms, so they must be professional and competent. In order to assuage any misgivings of the client, the paralegal must know how to set the stage for the interview, control the discussion within it, and provide a proper conclusion.

The Setting for the Interview

Setting the stage for the interview not only entails locating the proper office or room, but it also entails the positioning within the office or room of the people involved in the interview. The room must be comfortable and free of clutter, and the decor of the room must not detract from the matter at hand. A bad choice for an interview would be a law library or reception area. A good choice would be a conference room, a general meeting room, or the paralegal's own office. Once the location of the interview is settled, the paralegal should consider the arrangement of the people in the room.

There are three basic seating arrangements that can be used in interviews: face to face across a desk, face to face at an angle on the corner of a desk, or side by side. Sitting face to face across a desk is the most formal arrangement. This may be fine for a meeting with corporate executives about company litigation, but other clients may find this situation to be intimidating and formal. Sitting face to face at the corner of a desk or table is more personable and still retains a professional atmosphere. This position allows the paralegal to share documents very easily with the interviewee. This arrangement also works well to provide support in emotional or traumatic situations while still attempting to maintain a professional posture. Eliminating the desk or the table creates a more personal atmosphere. Sitting side by side at a table is especially effective when there are numerous documents that the paralegal and the interviewee need to view or refer to. This arrangement provides limited eye contact; however, the client may feel more involved in the interview and, therefore, may be able to provide more information.

The setting of an interview in many cases depends upon the personality of the client, the type of legal work being done, and whether the client is familiar with the person conducting the interview. The initial client interview should probably be conducted in a formal setting, and subsequent interviews should be more informal and personal. If the nature of the legal work is more personal, such as a divorce proceeding, personal injury case, or criminal defense, the client will probably prefer a more informal an d personal setting. If the work performed is of a business nature, such as real estate, securities, or commercial transactions, the client will usually prefer a more formal, professional, and business-like setting. Eventually, a paralegal will almost instinctively determine the best location and seating arrangement for an interview. However, the experience comes with practice. After conducting a few interviews, the paralegal will be able to focus almost entirely on preparing for the content of the interview rather than its setting.

The Content of the Interview

The content of the interview may be broken into four stages: background, pre-event, event, and post-event. The paralegal initiates the interview with background questions about the client and the cause of action.

Background Stage The paralegal raises questions to discover the client's biographical data as well as information about the client that is pertinent to the case. The paralegal should prepare a checklist of questions before the interview. The *American Jurisprudence Proof of Facts* is an excellent source for appropriate checklists. In a case involving a drunk driving charge, the paralegal may ask about the client's driving record for insight into the client's driving background.

Pre-event Stage The pre-event stage of questioning asks the client to explain the event upon which the cause of action is based. Questions should be phrased to determine what circumstances occurred immediately before the event. Asking questions about the chain of events that led up to the incident assists in organizing and establishing the order of events. The paralegal should ask questions such as the following: What did you do when you woke up that morning? What did you do throughout the day? What were you doing one hour before the event?

Event Stage The initial interview should focus on the event stage. This may be the most emotional part of the interview for the client, so the paralegal must be prepared to handle the anger, sadness, or fear that may accompany the client's recollection of the event. The paralegal must also pay close attention to the details that the client relates while recreating the event. Often seemingly insignificant details are actually crucial to the success of the case.

Post-event Stage The paralegal then asks questions relating to the incidents that occurred immediately after the event up to the time of the interview. This information includes the amount of damages and the extent of the pain and suffering.

The success of any interview is contingent upon the client's ability to impart the necessary information. One means of persuading the client to talk is to have the client explain the stages in story fashion. If possible, the client should be encouraged to recount the events in chronological order. The paralegal should avoid interrupting the client during the account; and at the end of the client's story, the paralegal should try to summarize the chain of events as related by the client and repeat it to the client. The client can then clarify any misconceptions the paralegal may have.

Near the end of the initial interview, the paralegal should ask the client about any know weaknesses in the case, any discrepancies in the evidence, and any other previously undisclosed sources of evidence that might corroborate or refute the client's version of the facts. Clients are sometimes hesitant to discuss the weaknesses of their cases and may hide damaging evidence. Asking clients to place themselves in the positions of their opponents is a successful technique used to overcome this hesitancy. Clients may be asked what they think their opponents will argue and what evidence their opponents may use to support the arguments. If the paralegal phrases these questions as hypotheticals, the client is better able to view the case from an objective perspective. This information gives the paralegal better insight in the other case and may prevent any surprises that could arise as the case progresses.

When ending the initial interview, the paralegal should determine whether the client has any additional questions about the case or the fee arrangement. The client should be informed to discuss the case with no one and encouraged to contact the paralegal or attorney if he or she should remember something else or has any other questions.

The Witness Interview

Before they proceed to interview a witness, paralegals must determine whether the witness is represented by an attorney. If the witness is represented by an attorney, the paralegal must comply with the rules of ethics regarding communication with those represented by counsel and refrain from asking further questions. The paralegal must obtain the consent of the witness' attorney to continue the interview. To prevent a later allegation of lack of consent, the consent should be provided in writing.

Once they have received written consent, paralegals should conduct witness interviews much the same way as they do client interviews. The major difference between the two is that paralegals go into the witness interview with a more definite idea of what information they hope to gain. Paralegals, therefore, will usually have a set of prepared questions for the witness. As paralegals conduct the witness interview, they should note whether the witness would provide effective testimony in the event of a trial.

The Interview to Prepare the Client or Witness for Trial or Depositions

The client and witnesses should be thoroughly prepared to answer questions in depositions or at trial. A checklist similar to the following should be used in interviewing and preparing the client or witness for questioning by the opposing party.

I. Explanation of the purpose of the questioning, including the following:

   A. The process
   B. The proceedings
   C. The opposition's perspective
   D. How the answers will be used
   E. The surroundings
   F. Who will be present
   G. The timing of the questions and breaks

II. Explanation of the importance of listening to questions before responding:

   A. Think about what is being asked.
   B. Focus on the information being sought.
   C. Concentrate on the question before responding.
   D. Understand the intent of the question, and form a complete answer before speaking.

III. Explanation of how to answer a question:

   A. Do not think and speak at the same time.
   B. Complete the answer mentally before speaking.

C. Do not answer questions that are not fully understood. It is not the obligation of the person being questioned to understand unclear questions. It is the obligation of the examiners to make themselves clear.
D. Answer only the question asked. Do not provide answers to unasked questions, do not volunteer information, and make sure the answer is accurate and thorough.
E. Never argue with the examiner.
F. If you are anxious, nervous, tired, fatigued, upset or angry, take a break.
G. Choose words that accurately describe what is being said.
H. Stick to your guns; do not let the examiner put words in your mouth.
I. If answering a series of questions, make sure you agree with all the questions before you say "yes". If you disagree with any part of the question and agree with the rest, say so.
J. The cardinal principle is to never volunteer information.

IV. Explanation of the following:

A. "I do not remember", is the same thing as "I do not recall"; however, "I do not know", does not mean "I do not remember"; be accurate in using these terms.
B. If you are asked laundry list questions that ask for all, everything, anything, let the examiner know the extent of what you can recall at the time you are answering the question; you may recall something later so "leave the door open".
C. If you have no knowledge or information on something, say so; if you can give an estimate or approximation, do so, but make sure the examiner knows it is an estimation or an approximation.
D. If you do give an estimate or an approximation, or a lay opinion in another area, be prepared to back it up and reveal why you said the statement and how you can support it.
E. Do not mistake the truth. If you make a mistake, correct it immediately.
F. Do not exaggerate or unduly magnify or minimize any answer. Be exact even if you qualify it.

The preparation interview should cover all of the points on the preceding checklist and prepare the client or witness to answer all kinds of questions. To avoid unpleasant surprises, the paralegal should attempt to anticipate the questions that the opposition will ask and give the clients or witnesses a mock questioning so that they will already have formed many of their answers before the trial or deposition.

For Discussion Discuss the ways you would approach the following interviews:

1. an intial client interview with a woman who wishes to divorce her husband because he is abusive,
2. an interview with a witness who may have information that would help your office's client's case involving an automobile accident, and
3. an interview with a witness who has valuable information about your office's client's discrimination case against the client's former employer, but does not wish to testify because he was the clients former co-worker and fears that his negative testimony may hurt his position at work.

CONCLUSION

In addition to performing the skills of investigation and interviewing the paralegal is required to write memos and briefs about his or her information. The following chapter provides the paralegal with information that is important in developing a clear and concise writing style.

CHAPTER 5: WRITING STYLE FOR THE PARALEGAL

Effective written communication is an essential skill for the paralegal. Whether asked to compose a letter, draft a document, or write a memo, the paralegal must develop a writing style that is grammatically correct and easily understood. Developing a good writing style requires practice, study, and a determination to avoid imitating the language and structure of the majority of legal writing.

Unfortunately legal documents are notorious for being confusing and long-winded. Therefore they are not the best examples of good writing. Somewhere legal writers have gained the impression that big words and long sentences communicate importance and authority; in reality these long words and sentences obscure the writer's message and confuse the reader. They lack force and place a burden on the reader to decipher the writer's meaning. If a reader has to work to understand every sentence, chances are that reader will stop reading. The best way to assure effective communication is to employ proper grammar.

GRAMMAR: THE FOUNDATION OF A GOOD WRITING STYLE

Nothing provokes more moans and groans than the prospect of studying grammar. The mere mention of the word produces bad memories of diagraming sentences and memorizing complex rules; and although most people had hoped to leave the subject in the high school classroom, a precise understanding of grammar is essential for anyone who wishes to write well. Fortunately, the rules of grammar are really quite logical.

The Eight Parts of Speech

Effective communication begins with constructing effective sentences. Sentences are comprised of words, and each word within the sentence has a function. These functions are called the parts of speech. There are eight parts of speech in the English language: verbs, nouns, pronouns, adjectives, adverbs, conjunctions, prepositions, and interjections.

Verbs

The verb is the most important component of the sentence. The only part of speech that is capable of being a one-word sentence is the verb, and no sentence is complete without a verb. Verbs express the action carried out by or the condition of someone or something. It is important to keep in mind that there are essentially three categories of verbs. A verb can either be an action verb, the verb "to be", or a linking verb.

Action Verbs Action verbs express the activities of their subjects: *agree, run, support, write, extrapolate, submit, persevere.* They describe what the subject is doing. Action verbs can be either **transitive** or **intransitive**. A transitive verb requires that its action be received: *The court supported the motion*. The action of an intransitive verb cannot be received by nouns: *The appellate court agreed with the trial court's decision. Support* is a transitive verb because one must *support something* or *someone*. *Agree* is an intransitive verb because one does not *agree something* or *someone*; one agrees *with* someone or something. Therefore, transitive verbs are verbs capable of being immediately followed by nouns, and intransitive verbs are verbs incapable of being immediately followed by nouns.

The Verb "To Be" The verb "to be" (am, is, are, was, were, been, and being) is like an equal sign. It equates the subject with the remainder of the predicate, which may be either a noun or an adjective. For example, *Sarah is a paralegal* means *Sarah = a paralegal*, and *She is efficient* means *She = efficient*.

Linking verbs Linking verbs function much like the verb "to be". They join (or link) the sentence's subject to an adjective that describes the condition of the subject. Linking verbs are never followed by adverbs. Common linking verbs are *feel, seem, appear, look, taste* and *smell.*

Nouns

The noun is defined as a person, place, or thing, and it functions within the sentence in different ways. As demonstrated in the following sentences, the **subject**(1) plays the principal role in the sentence; the **direct object**(2) receives the action of the verb; the **indirect object**(3) receives the direct object; the **object of a preposition**(4) and the **object in a verbal phrase**(5) serve as the receivers of the preposition or verbal; **appositives**(6) clarify other nouns; and **predicate nominatives**(7) follow the verb "to be" and complement the subject.

> *Being a candidate(5) with few secrets(4), Johnson(1), a republican(6), provided every reporter(3) the opportunity(2) for an interview(4). She(1) was an honest woman(7).*

Pronouns

Simply stated, pronouns rename nouns. They provide a means of avoiding the needless repetition of nouns within a sentence or paragraph. There are three types of pronouns: personal, indefinite, and relative.

Personal Pronouns Most paralegals are familiar with the personal pronouns. They rename specific nouns and have two forms. The subjective personal pronouns are *I, he, she, it, we,* and *they*; the objective personal pronouns are *me, him her, it, us* and *them.* Subjective forms are used when the pronouns function as subjects or predicate nominatives and objective forms when the pronouns function as objects. Collective nouns, such as group and jury, are common in legal writing. In most cases, these nouns are singular; therefore the pronoun *it* must be used to refer to them. *It* also refers to company names. *The jury has not reached its decision regarding the trucking company and its negligence.*

Indefinite Pronouns Indefinite pronouns refer to generalities rather than specifics. Some common examples are *everyone, somebody, anything, each, one, none,* and *no one*. It is important to remember that all indefinite pronouns are singular, and that means that they require singular verbs. *None of the cases is settled.*

Relative Pronouns A third type of pronoun is the **relative** pronoun. Relative pronouns like *that, which* and *who* link adjective clauses to the nouns they describe. *Who* refers to persons, *which* refers to animals and things, and *that* may refer to both persons and things. *She is a lawyer* ***who*** *is accustomed to winning. The cases* ***that*** *she handles are usually settled for large sums of money,* ***which*** *makes her a very rich attorney*. Note that the pronoun *that* introduces a restrictive clause, and *which* introduces a nonrestrictive clause. Both types of clauses will be discussed later in this chapter.

Adjectives

Adjectives clarify nouns and other adjectives. They provide clearer descriptions of the words they define and therefore should be chosen carefully. One precisely chosen adjective can do the work of several indeterminate ones. *The demeanor of the* ***stern*** *judge cast a* ***somber*** *mood on the courtroom. Stern* defines the kind of judge, and *somber* describes the kind of mood. Without the adjectives the sentence would be devoid of description. *The demeanor of the judge cast a mood on the courtroom.*

Adverbs

Like adjectives, adverbs are clarifiers. Their primary function is to define verbs, but they also define adjectives and other adverbs. Many adverbs are formed by adding *-ly* to adjectives, but adverbs include all words and groups of words that answer the questions where, when, how, and why in a sentence. *The jury discussed the case* ***outside***. *Outside* reveals where the jury discussed the case. *Everyone expects that it will make a decision* ***tomorrow***. *Tomorrow* describes when it is expected to decide. *The jury has discussed each issue* ***carefully***. *Carefully* defines how the jury has discussed. *They deliberate* ***to reach a decision***. *To reach a decision* is a adverbial phrase explaining why they deliberate.

Conjunctions and Prepositions

The parts of speech discussed up to now have made up the main elements of the sentence. Conjunctions and prepositions link these elements together.

Conjunctions Conjunctions join together words, phrases, and clauses. The three types of conjunctions are **coordinating**, **correlative**, and **subordinating**. Most people are familiar with the seven coordinating conjunctions. They are *and, but, for, nor, or, so*, and *yet*. The three correlative conjunctions always appear in pairs: *either/or, neither/nor, not only/but also*. As the words coordinate and correlate mean similarity and equality, naturally the elements joined by coordinating and correlative conjunctions must be grammatically equal. This grammatical equality is the essence of parallel construction, which will be discussed later in this chapter. The third type of conjunction, subordinating, introduces dependent clauses and connects them to independent clauses. *Although, because, if, when,* and *while* are common examples of subordinating conjunctions.

Prepositions The preposition joins a noun to the sentence and shows how the noun relates to the sentence. A preposition cannot function within a sentence without a noun, and therefore the preposition will always be contained within a prepositional phrase. This phrase consists of the preposition and a noun, which is called the object of the preposition. *The man* ***in*** *the hat went* ***to*** *the lounge to sit down*. The preposition *in* relates its object, *hat*, to the noun *man*, and *to* relates *lounge* to the verb *went*. Note that the word *to* in *to sit down* is not a preposition but rather part of the infinite form of the verb *to sit*.

To list all prepositions would require pages, but several common examples are *about, above, for, over*, and *with*. Much of current legal writing glorifies **compound prepositions**, several prepositional phrases that work as one preposition. Compound prepositions, such as *at this point in time, with regard to,* and *by virtue of*, are weak and imprecise and should be stated in simpler, more definite terms. For instance, *at this point in time* may be shortened to *now*, *with regard to* shortened to *regarding*, and *by virtue of* to *by*.

Interjections

Generally, legal writing does not employ interjections, which are words that express emotion in the sentence. Rarely do legal documents or memos contain words like *wow, darn*, or *shucks* unless they are included in direct quotations. However, some four-letter interjections do make their way into settlement negotiations.

The Elements of a Sentence

As stated earlier, the eight parts of speech work together to form sentences, but the thrust of the sentence's information is actually conveyed by three main elements, the subject, the verb, and the element to which the verb links the subject. To locate the main idea of a sentence, one must focus on these three elements. All other information within the sentence is secondary in importance.

Subject, Verb, and Third Element

The subject is the main character of the sentence, the noun that is carrying out the action of the sentence or whose condition the sentence describes. Therefore, the pronouns *this*, *that*, or *there* should usually be avoided as subjects because they convey ambiguous information.

As stated previously, the verb holds a very important position within the sentence. Forceful writing includes an abundance of carefully chosen action verbs and employs sparingly the verb form *to be*.

Depending on the verb, the third important part of the sentence could be either a direct object, an adverb, an adjective, or a predicate nominative. Transitive verbs are completed by direct objects, intransitive verbs by adverbs, the verb *to be* by an adjective or a predicate nominative, and a linking verb by an adjective.

The type of subject will not vary, so the number of possible sentence structures is contingent on the sentence's main verb. Therefore, because there are four types of verbs, there are four essential sentence structures: (1)Subject + Transitive Verb + Direct Object, (2)Subject + Intransitive Verb + Adverb, (3)Subject + Verb *To Be* + Adjective or Predicate Nominative, and (4)Subject + Linking Verb + Adjective. Placing the bulk of the sentence's message within the three main elements will improve the clarity and impact of any written work.

Phrases and Clauses

Basically, the only possible additions to the three main elements of the sentence are more nouns, adverbs, and adjectives. These less important components of the sentence provide more information about the sentence's main message and appear as either single words, phrases, or clauses. Both phrases and clauses are groups of words that work together to form a single part of speech, such as an adverb or adjective, but clauses contain their own subjects and verbs; phrases do not. A good understanding of clauses is essential to a good understanding of sentence structure and punctuation.

Independent and Dependent Clauses Clauses are classified as either independent or dependent. Independent clauses are complete by themselves; no additional information is required. Dependent clauses express incomplete thoughts. Even though they contain subjects and verbs, they cannot stand alone as sentences without other information; they are sentence fragments. *When the jury reaches a decision, it will return to the courtroom.* The independent clause is *it will return to the courtroom.* No other information is required to complete this thought. *When the jury reaches a decision* leaves the reader wondering. The information is incomplete, and therefore the clause is dependent.

To form a complete sentence, a dependent clause must be attached to an independent clause. How the clauses are joined depends on how the dependent clause functions within the sentence. The dependent clause that functions as an adverb begins with a subordinating conjunction and answers the questions *how, when, where*, or *why*. *The client shot the man **because he was attacking her**.* *Because he was attacking her* is a dependent clause explaining *why* the client acted as she did. The adjective clause usually begins with a relative pronoun to provide more information about the noun that it modifies. *Frederick is an employer **who insists on perfection**.*

The clause *who insists on perfection* describes what type of employer Frederick is. Dependent clauses may also function as nouns. ***The client was oblivious to how much time had passed since the accident.*** The dependent clause in this sentence is the object of the preposition *to*.

<u>**Restrictive and Nonrestrictive Clauses**</u> Dependent clauses can be classified as either **restrictive** or **nonrestrictive**, and distinguishing between the two can sometimes be tricky. Essentially, a restrictive clause is one whose presence is vital to the meaning of the sentence whereas, although the nonrestrictive clause provides clarifying information, its presence is not mandatory for the sentence to make sense. *She never loses her cases that involve dog-bite victims.* The restrictive clause in this sentence, *that involve dog-bite victims*, provides essential information that pin points the particular type of cases she never loses. Out of the many types of cases she handles, she is always successful with those cases involving dog-bite victims. Compare to the following sentence: *She never loses her cases, which involve dog-bite victims.* The nonrestrictive clause, *which involve dog-bite victims*, makes a "by the way" statement; it provides additional information about what type of cases she handles. Apparently, as phrased in this sentence, her practice is limited to dog-bite victims and she never loses a case.

Note that the restrictive clause begins with the pronoun *that* and the nonrestrictive clause begins with the pronoun *which*. Also note that the restrictive clause does not require commas to set it apart from the rest of the sentence. The nonrestrictive clause must be separated with commas from the rest of the sentence.

Ambiguous writing often relies too heavily on the use of clauses. Limiting the amount of clauses in a sentence by replacing them with appropriate single words or phrases will improve sentence clarity. Likewise, the proper positioning of dependent clauses and other descriptive elements in a sentence emphasize and clarify the main message of the sentence. The positioning of the elements of the sentence is known as structuring the sentence.

For Discussion Discuss the following:

1. Identify the parts of speech (verb, noun, pronoun, adjective, adverb, conjunction, or preposition) of the following italicized words.

   The Postal Service *has*(1) a monopoly *on*(2) *first-class*(3) mail, *but*(4) *much*(5) of what *it*(6) *sends*(7) *first class*(8) could be transmitted *electronically*(9).

2. Determine which of the four sentence structures (1, 2, 3, or 4) is demonstrated by the following sentences.

   a. Jonathan seems sad today.
   b. The attorney thinks quickly during trial.
   c. Teresa offers advice to her clients.
   d. She is a good attorney.

SENTENCE STRUCTURE: POSITIONING THE SENTENCE'S ELEMENTS

Writers form their sentences using the four structures mentioned earlier in the discussion about the elements of a sentence. Sometimes the structures may be reversed to shift emphasis, but essentially all sentences are constructed as one of the four structures. To these basic structures are added descriptive elements. The well-constructed sentence conveys its message clearly and precisely; ambiguity occurs when the sentence's descriptive elements cloud the main message either because they are too numerous or because they are improperly positioned. Generally, a clear, concise sentence contains **one** main message and an average of 25 words. Obviously, some sentences will be longer than 25 words and some will be shorter, but legal writers should strive to convey a single message within 25 words.

Eliminating Wordiness

Legal writing is plagued by wordiness. The writers of statutes and many case opinions must hold to the philosophy that the longer the sentence the better. Anyone who has tried to decipher the points of long-winded statutes and case summaries will attest that this is not so. Once a sentence has conveyed its point, it is best to end it and begin a new sentence.

The first step in eliminating long-windedness is to merely end a sentence when it has made one point. Every bit of meaningful information does not have to be crammed into one sentence. Merely breaking long sentences into several shorter ones is often all that is needed to provide clarity. For instance the following seemingly unending sentence can be simplified by breaking it apart.

> *The jury in its careful deliberation lasting two days decided that the merits of the case stood with the plaintiff who was awarded $100,000.00 in damages because it found that the defendant, who had maintained a dangerous situation at her place of business because she had failed to place signs warning customers of a slippery floor, was negligent due to the fact that she should have anticipated that a floor that was unmarked could create potentially harmful circumstances for her patrons.*

The sentence actually contains two points: (1) what the jury decided and (2) why. The information could be better comprehended by separating it into two sentences.

> *After two days deliberation, the jury awarded the plaintiff $100,000.00 in damages. It found the defendant negligent because she should have anticipated that her failure to post warning signs on her business's slippery floor would create a dangerous situation for her patrons.*

In addition to separating the longer sentence into two shorter sentences, the second example also eliminates needless repetition and unnecessary words, phrases, and clauses. Eliminating wordiness is sometimes as easy as carefully choosing the precise word to convey one's thought. One distinctive word can take the place of several ambiguous ones, and a clearly made point need not be repeated. *The judge wrote an autobiography about his life*. By definition an autobiography accounts the author's life, therefore it is needlessly repetitive and distracting to add the phrase *about his life*.

Paralegals can avoid excess words by altering phrases and clauses. Some commonly used phrases can be reduced to a single word. *At this time* becomes *now*, *for the purposes of* means *for*, *with respect to* denotes *about*, and the list goes on. Long clauses can be exchanged for simple adjectives and nouns. *The man that manages the personnel department* can be simplified to *the personnel department manager*. Reducing the amount of phrases and clauses in a sentence allows the reader to more easily grasp its main idea.

Paralegals should be careful, however, when attempting to simplify their writing. Sometimes efforts to shorten sentence length result in a series of choppy, disjointed sentences that read more like a reading primer for the first grade than a legal document. A treatment for this broken style is to discover the common element of the shorter sentences and create a slightly longer sentence that incorporates the other elements. For instance, examine the following sentences. *The client had been injured in a car accident. The client was distraught. The attorney decided to talk to the client.* The main idea of each sentence is very clear, but they read as if the author has the hiccups. Because the sentences are short and have a common element, *client*, they can be combined into one more graceful sounding sentence. Paralegals should decide which sentence contains the most important idea, in this case the last one, then integrate the ideas of the other sentences. *The attorney decided to talk to the distraught client who had been injured in a car accident.*

Another method of smoothing out choppy writing is to use the less important of two sentences as an introduction for the more important sentence. *The jury awarded the plaintiff damages of $100,000.00. It based its decision on the testimony of the expert witness.* As far as the parties are concerned, the bottom line is the jury's award. Incidental to this information is the basis for the jury's award. Therefore the information could be more smoothly stated as follows: *Basing its decision on the testimony of the expert witness, the jury awarded the plaintiff damages of $100,000.00.* Paralegals should strive for a balance between clarity and style to prevent attempts to improve the flow of their writing from lapsing once again into cramming too many ideas into one sentence.

Positioning Modifiers

Modifiers are those elements of the sentence, be they words, phrases, or clauses, that provide more information about the main idea of the sentence. Mis-modification occurs when legal writers position adjectives and other modifiers so that they actually define an element other than the intended word. The best way to avoid mis-modification is to place the modifying adjective or adverb as closely as possible to the modified word. When a modifier is placed too far from the modified word, the results can be ludicrous. *The paralegal placed the schedule of depositions to be held in October on the top of the desk.* The sentence conjures up a picture of attorneys and their clients conducting October depositions while sitting on desk tops. *On the top of the desk*, an adverbial phrase that is intended to explain where the schedule was placed, is positioned so that it appears to describe where the depositions will take place. Positioning the phrase adjacent to the verb *placed* will clarify the meaning of the sentence. *The paralegal placed on the top of the desk the schedule of depositions to be held in October.*

Mis-modification is most noticeable when the modifier is a beginning participle phrase. A beginning participle phrase always refers to the subject of the sentence. *Running up to the courthouse, the door was held open for me by the mayor.* Taken literally, this sentence portrays the door as an entity capable of running up to the courthouse. The sentence must be rephrased to show that *I* was running up to the courthouse, not the door. A better sentence would be: *Running up to the courthouse, I was glad to see the mayor holding the door open for me.* The better sentence also changed the passive voice in the first sentence to active voice. Powerful writers construct a majority of their sentences in active voice rather than passive voice.

Using Active Voice

There is some debate over the active voice v. passive voice rule, but generally sentences written in active voice are clearer and more powerful than those written in passive voice. Passive voice is aptly named; it is passive. The main idea of a sentence written in passive voice is often obscured, and passive voice is wordier than active voice. It is more direct to say *Charles committed the crime* than it is to say *The crime was committed by Charles.* In the first sentence, written in active voice, the subject is the doer of the action expressed by the verb; the message is clear. In the second sentence, written in passive voice, the doer of the action is obscured and the message is weak.

Passive voice does have its advantages. There are some occasions where a writer may desire to downplay the doer of the action expressed by the verb or the doer of the action may be unimportant. *The dictionary was placed on the top shelf.* The emphasis in this sentence is not on *who* placed the dictionary but on *where* it was placed. Therefore, passive voice is sufficient to convey the idea.

Employing Parallel Structure

Another powerful writing tool is parallelism. A sentence just sounds better if it maintains parallel construction. Parallelism dictates that elements joined together by conjunctions should be grammatically alike. Compare the following sentences. *The students study to maintain good grade point averages, for increased knowledge, and because they enjoy the admiration of their peers.* Although this sentence is not flagrantly awful, it could be improved by using like grammatical forms for the elements that are linked by the conjunction *and*. *The students study to maintain good grade point averages, to increase their knowledge, and to inspire the admiration of their peers.* The sentence is better balanced because all of the elements joined by *and* are phrased as infinitives (to + verb).

Paralegals who pay careful attention to the way their sentences are structured will greatly improve the way their messages are received. Utilizing the sentence construction techniques mentioned above will result in more powerful writing.

For Discussion Examine the following sentences, point out the errors within them, and discuss ways to correct the errors.

1. Neither the attorneys nor their paralegals know why there is so little time to complete tasks.
2. The jury has stated that they will reach their verdict tomorrow.
3. The attorney, after working night and day on his closing arguments and after rephrasing them over and over again, decided that it might be best to consult his paralegal about the proper phrasing due to the fact that she had done most of the research and investigation for the case that he was trying to win for his client.
4. Using a precise research technique, many cases can be found that are relevant to the client's case.
5. The most common reasons for an attorney's willingness to use paralegals are that paralegals can be billed at a lower rate to the client, their use allows more time for the attorney to take on other cases, and the quality of their work.

PUNCTUATION AND MECHANICS: MASTERING THE RULES

Proper use of punctuation and mechanics is essential to good writing. The proper use of commas, semicolons, colons, dashes, and parentheses guides readers through a sentence and enhances their understanding. Mastering possessives, quotation marks, and capitalization polishes the writer's presentation.

Rules for Proper Punctuation

Punctuation follows definite rules that are easy to observe once one has a working knowledge of the basic grammatical concepts. Paralegals who familiarize themselves with the rules of punctuation will find them to be fairly logical.

Periods and Question Marks

Periods end declarative sentences and follow initials, as in *Ph.D.* and *D. H. Lawrence*, and abbreviations, like *id.* Periods are omitted for initials used in agency or organization names, such as *ACLU* and *YMCA*, and for commonly used shortened formations, like *ad* and *memo.*

Question marks end direct questions. *Which document has to be filed first?* Question marks should not be used with indirect questions. *He asked me which document had to be filed first.*

Commas

The most common mark of punctuation, other than the period, is the comma. The comma has many uses, but, as it is frequently misused, it should be applied sparingly and only when its placement is justified by one of the following conditions.

In a Series In a series of three or more expressions joined by one conjunction, it is customary to put a comma after each expression other than the last. *Mary, Bill, and Joan prepared the petitions, filed them with the court, and placed copies in the office files.*

When stating firm names, the last comma is omitted. *The defendant is represented by the firm of Howard, Thompson, George & Byrd.* Some employers prefer that the last comma be omitted in every series, so paralegals should follow the preferences of their supervisors.

Omitted Words A comma is used to replace words omitted from the sentence. *The Smith document was filed yesterday; the Jones document, today.* The comma replaces the words *was filed*.

Parenthetic Expressions Expressions that offer information that is not essential to the meaning of the sentence should be set off by commas. Sometimes it is difficult to determine whether an expression is parenthetic or not, but the following classifications should help.

Asides consist of words like *however, in my opinion*, and *for example* that are set apart from the rest of the sentence. *For example, the trial court in the White case, in my opinion, was biased toward the defendant.*

Appositives, as discussed previously, provide additional information about a noun that is not essential to the central idea of the sentence. *The attorney for the opposition, Ms. Brown, has scheduled a court date. Ms. Brown* merely provides the reader with the attorney's specific name. However if the name is expressed as a title, commas should not be used. *Attorney Brown requested a court date.*

Titles and distinctions that follow a name should be set off by commas. *Sarah Brown, J.D., is the attorney for the opposition. She represents Willey Trucking, Inc.*

Abbreviations such as *etc., e.g.*, and *i.e.* should be set off by commas. *Enclosed are the copies of court documents, letters, etc., that you requested.*

Dates and place names actually contain parenthetic information and should be punctuated accordingly. *Springfield, Illinois, is the venue for the trials, which are set to take place on April 11, 1994, and May 6, 1994.* If a date is written as *11 April 1994*, no commas are necessary.

Nonrestrictive clauses are by definition parenthetic. When a clause provides information that is not essential to the meaning of the sentence, it should be set apart from the rest of the sentence by commas. *The trial will take place in Morristown, where both the defendant and plaintiff reside.*

Separation of Clauses A comma separates two independent clauses when they are joined by a conjunction. The comma is placed before the conjunction. *Handling the case will require much organization, but the attorney has a competent paralegal to assist in preparing the case for trial.*

The comma also separates a beginning dependent clause from the independent clause. *Because his case is well prepared, the plaintiff will surely win.* A dependent clause should not be separated from the independent clause if the dependent clause follows the independent clause. *The plaintiff will surely win because his case is well prepared.*

Semicolons

The semicolon forms a break that is more definite than a comma but less final than a period. It is most commonly used to separate closely related independent clauses that are joined in one sentence without a conjunction or that are joined by a conjunctive adverb. *It is almost midnight; there is no possibility of digesting this deposition before tomorrow morning.* When the second clause begins with a conjunctive adverb, such as *accordingly, also, besides, consequently, furthermore, hence, however, indeed, likewise, moreover, nevertheless, otherwise, similarly, so, still, therefore,* and *thus*, the clauses must be separated by a semicolon. *We had best finish this memo tonight; otherwise, we will have to work on it during lunch tomorrow.* Note that a comma comes after the conjunctive adverb.

To reduce confusion semicolons are also used to separate an enumerated series or a series of expressions that are punctuated by commas. *The legal secretary's duties include (1) drafting and filing legal documents; (2) corresponding with clients and opposing counsel; and (3) organizing information within the office so that it is readily accessible. Forester, Black, Grady & Davis, Inc.; Thompson & Thompson, P.C.; and Fielding, Burgess & Lloyd are just three of the firms with which we correspond on a daily basis.*

Colons

Colons follow independent clauses and are used to introduce a lists of specifics, long appositives or explanations, or quotations that provide support for the preceding clause. The colon creates a more powerful impression than a comma and a more formal effect than a dash. Writers should avoid using a colon to separate a verb from the sentence's third element or a preposition from its object. *She will be finished when she completes three projects: the deposition digest, the letter to Johnson & Brown, and the memo to her immediate supervisor.* Note that it is incorrect to write the following: *She will be finished when she completes: the deposition digest, the letter to Johnson & Brown, and the memo to her immediate supervisor.*

Colons are also used after the salutation in a business letter, between the hour and minutes when indicating clock time, and between a main title and its subtitle.

Dear Mr. Thompson:

The book entitled Legal Research: A Guide to the Law Library *will be available today after 4:30 p.m.*

Dashes

Like colons, dashes introduce long appositives, but they are less formal and do not often appear in legal writing. More commonly they separate a beginning series from the corresponding clause. They are also used to indicate abrupt breaks in the continuity of the sentence but only when other marks of punctuation are inadequate. *Breakfast in bed, lunch by the pool, dinner by candlelight--such were the dreams of the overworked paralegal.*

Parentheses

Parentheses mark a stronger separation than do commas or dashes. They should be used sparingly within the context of sentences. *The format of the caption on the complaint (called a petition in some states) varies from state to state.*

As shown previously, parentheses are used to distinguish the numbers in an enumerated series. In legal documents they designate a numerical figure when it follows an amount that has been expressed in words. *The plaintiff requests damages in the amount of One Hundred Thousand Dollars ($100,000.00).* Parentheses are also used when transcribing legal testimony to designate the actions of the speakers.

MR. STEWART: Is this the document you signed? (hands Ms. Avery the contract)

The only punctuation marks that appear within parentheses are those that are essential to the parenthetical material. The rest of the sentence should be punctuated as it would be if the parenthetical information were not present.

Rules of Mechanics

In addition to the rules of punctuation there are several other rules in writing that require clarification. These rules govern the mechanics of writing, and they include how to form possessives, when to capitalize, when to italicize or underline, and how to properly quote other's material.

Forming Possessives

Many experienced writers have difficulty with possessives. The possessive form of a noun should be used when that noun is immediately followed by another noun that it possesses. According to *Elements of Style*, by Strunk and White, possessives are generally formed by adding *'s* to the end of a singular noun even if it ends in *s*.

Mrs. Wright's case
The jury's decision
Charles's opinion
Jack Jones's letter

If the possessive noun is plural and ends in *s* or it is singular but ends in *ss*, only an apostrophe is added.

The boys' bikes
The clients' wishes
The Joneses' front porch
The expert witness' testimony

When an appositive must be used with a possessive case, apply the possessive form to the noun that is closest to the thing possessed, usually the appositive. *The patient, Mr. Jones's, surgery lasted several hours.*

The possessive forms of proper pronouns are as follows: *my, his, her, your, its, our,* and *their* for pronouns preceding the noun and *mine, his, hers, yours, its, ours,* and *theirs* for possessive pronouns that occur at the end of a clause or that are used as a subject. ***Hers** is a very strange case; it is much stranger than **his**.* Note that none of the possessive pronouns contains an apostrophe. *It's* is a contraction of *it is*, and therefore rarely appears in legal writing. Possessive indefinite pronouns do contain apostrophes. ***Somebody's** dog has chewed my carpet.*

One last point about possessives, the possessive form of a noun should almost always be used before a gerund, a noun formed by a verb + *-ing*. *I am concerned about our client's presenting himself well at trial.*

Capitalizing Properly

Proper capitalization is a debatable issue. The standards for capitalization vary among authorities, so it is best to capitalize the same words consistently and follow the preferences of your employer. There are a few hard and fast rules, however, and most of them focus on capitalization as a designation of a proper noun. Essentially, if a noun is the proper name of an individual entity, it should be capitalized; if it names a generality, it should be lowercase.

Proper Names The name of a particular person, place, event, or thing should be capitalized. A person's name is capitalized, of course, as are the degrees and titles that accompany one's name: *Professor John Hill, Senator June Grey,* or *President Hammond.* But, professional titles that follow a name or stand alone should be lowercase. *John Hill, a professor of geology, will speak tonight. The senator and the president will attend.*

Legal Documents The official titles of specific acts, bills, codes, and laws should be capitalized: *First Amendment, Code of Civil Procedure, Securities Exchange Act.* General terms for legal documents are lowercase. *The prohibition amendment was repealed, but many codes and laws that are equally useless are still in effect.*

Numbers In a legal document a dollar amount should be written out and each word capitalized. *The accidents resulted in damages totaling Eight Thousand Nine Hundred Forty-Two Dollars ($8,942).* In all other cases the second number in a compound numeral should be lowercase. *He moved to 432 East Fifty-second Street.*

Courts and Judges Probably the most confusing capitalization rule for legal writers involves references to courts and judges. Generally if court or judge is included in the full title of a specific entity, it is capitalized; if it is a general term or stands alone, it is lowercase. *The most commonly recognized **court** of appeals is the **U.S. Supreme Court**. The case was heard by **Judge Fairway's court**. The **judge** will make her decision by the end of the week.* An exception to this rule occurs when *court* standing alone refers specifically to the presiding judge or officer. *The **Court's** decision was to sentence the defendant to three (3) years probation. Court* in this sentence refers specifically to the judge.

Terms of Government The words *government, administration, federal,* and *national* are capitalized only when they are included in titles: *the National Socialist party, The Federalist Papers, the Veteran's Administration, the federal government, a national pastime. City, state, county,* and *district* are capitalized when they are part of proper names: *Oregon State, Jersey City, Denver District Court, Bowie County.* They are lowercase when they stand alone: *the state of Georgia, the city of Detroit, the entire district, the largest county.* Full titles of boards, committees, departments, bureaus, and legislative bodies are capitalized, but general or incomplete designations are not. *The U.S. **Senate** approved a bill to provide more power to state **senates**.*

Enumerations The first word of enumerations that are introduced by a colon and include full sentences should be capitalized. *There are three reasons for the decision: (1) The new proposal is more cost-efficient. (2) It provides for an increase in production. (3) It allows us to use existing facilities.*

Directions Capitalize *east, west, north, and south* only when they name a section of the United States. *People who live in the Northeast tend to travel south to Florida for their vacations.*

Underlining or Italicizing

Legal writers should know three rules regarding underlining or italicizing. The two methods are interchangeable; however, italicizing is usually preferred over underlining if your office has the machinery capable of producing italics. Underline or italicize case names, book titles, and latin terms, such as *quid pro quo*, *respondeat superior*, etc.

> A case that involved the concept of *respondeat superior*, *Dach v. General Casualty Co.*, is located on page 170 of the *North Western Reporter*.

Quoting

The rules regarding the mechanics of quoted material in legal writing are presented in *A Uniform System of Citation*. When quoting information from case precedents, a paralegal should paraphrase lengthy statutes and points of law and should **never** quote case headnotes, prefatory statements, or an entire presentation of facts. (As with exact quotations, paraphrased material must be correctly cited.) Quoted material should be limited to especially important comments made by a key witness to an incident or a legal authority, but any copied material that is set forth exactly as it is presented in the original must be designated by quotation marks or indentation.

<u>Short Quotations</u> Generally, exact quotations that are shorter than 50 words are designated by quotation marks and included within the same paragraph as the introductory comments. A full-sentence quotation is separated from its introduction by a comma unless the introduction is an independent clause; in that case the mark of separation may be a colon. *The Court sentenced the defendant to life imprisonment stating, "All evidence reveals that the defendant is a habitual criminal incapable of being reformed." The following testimony of the defendant's sister best supports the judge's statement: "Lynn actually seemed proud of committing each crime."*

<u>Long Quotations</u> Quotations over 50 words are usually separated from the introductory comments, indented on both sides, and single-spaced. Quotation marks are eliminated as shown in the following example.

> *In reaching its decision, the Court stated the following:*
>
> > *The defendant did not permit the taxes to become delinquent. He was under no duty or obligation to pay the taxes. The default in payment of taxes was with the mortgagor, the predecessor in title of the plaintiff. There are no facts in this case which tend to establish a fraud, actual or constructive, nor any breach of duty on the part of the tenant . . . .*

<u>Altered Quotations</u> A writer must designate anything added to or deleted from an exact quotation. Words or letters added to a quotation for clarification are enclosed in brackets. *"We feel that it [the trial court's decision] should be upheld." The jury said, "[T]he defendant is guilty."* In the second example the jury's actual statement could have been, *"It is obvious that the defendant is guilty."* The *T* is added in brackets to show that is was actually lowercase in the original.

Eliminated words are indicated by ellipses. For example, four ellipses end each quotation that eliminates the end of the quoted material but ends the sentence. (The fourth ellipsis is the ending period of the sentence.) Words eliminated from the middle of a quotation are designated by three ellipses. *In reaching a decision, the jury considered "the defendant's clear assumption of risk . . . and his obvious negligence . . . ."* The original quotation could have been, *"We have decided thus because of the defendant's clear assumption of risk in deciding to take a bungee jump and his obvious negligence in not informing the attendants that he was ill."* There is a space between the ellipses and the words next to them.

If emphasis is added to any portion of a quotation, the words *emphasis added,* contained in parentheses, must follow the quoted material. The designation is placed after the ending quotation marks in a short quotation or after the period in a long one.

Punctuation All common marks of punctuation, such as periods, commas, semicolons, and question marks, are included **before** an ending quotation mark. Although it may not always seem logical, it looks better. *When she described the accused as a "lazy bum," she was not referring to his ability to hold a job.* The comma would get lost if it were placed after the ending quotation mark.

For Discussion Discuss corrections for the punctuation and mechanics errors in the following sentences:

1. The use of computers in the law office has resulted in increased office efficiency and most attorneys have accepted computers as essential to the workings of their offices.
2. The defendant, Mr. Johns is waiting in the outer office.
3. The jury wishes to have more time with which to make it's decision.
4. Mary Haines a Law Professor from Harvard university will make a presentation tomorrow.
5. The court requested that it be given more time to ponder Smith v. Jones.

ORGANIZATION: STRUCTURING THE FINISHED PRODUCT

The knowledge of grammar, punctuation, and mechanics is very important to good writing; equally important is careful organization of one's thoughts. All written matter should begin with a plan. The amount of planning required to produce a well-organized piece varies. Usually, longer documents require greater amounts of planning. Writing letters and short memos usually requires nothing more than jotting down a few notes; organizing briefs, formal memos, and many other legal documents requires creating a carefully constructed outline.

The Outline

Outlining begins with brainstorming. The paralegal should jot down all of the elements that seem to be important, compile them into major categories, and then provide more specific information about each category. It is not necessary to follow perfect outline form, but it is essential to note general categories of information and their specific elements. After the major categories of information have been defined, they should be ordered logically. Depending on the document, the information may be ordered chronologically, from general topics to specific, from least important to most important, etc., but all documents must have an underlying purpose, or main point, substantiating information, and a conclusion. Each bit of information must be essential to the purpose of the written work. As the paralegal completes the material, existing topics may be reordered, new ones added, or unimportant ones deleted as needed to advance his or her position.

The Paragraph

Working from the outline, the paralegal constructs paragraphs. Some elements may be discussed in a single paragraph while others may require several. When constructing paragraphs, the paralegal should include an introduction, a body, and a conclusion. Only the information essential to the point of the paragraph should be included and nothing else. The paralegal should introduce each paragraph to reveal its topic within the first few sentences and discuss the topic thoroughly providing examples if necessary. Persuasive paragraphs, such as are contained in briefs and some letters and memos, should always be concluded by clearly restating the purpose of the paragraph; the reader should have no doubt about the author's opinion. Restating the point of objective, informational paragraphs may be too redundant.

As discussed earlier, paralegals should also pay careful attention to sentence structure. Readers more willingly read paragraphs containing clear, well-constructed sentences, and are more likely to continue reading paragraphs that contain a variety of sentence structures. Readers are also more willing to read paragraphs that flow easily from one to another. The paralegal leads the reader from one idea to the next by implementing careful transition.

Transition may be accomplished in various ways, and the paralegal should include a variety of techniques. Words like *furthermore, also, for example, first, next, finally, however,* and *therefore* show the relationship that paragraphs have to one another. Referring to previous paragraphs by repeating key words and ideas or using words like *this, these, those,* and *that* ties together the thoughts of several paragraphs. *This, these, those* and *that* should not be used alone, however. *"This has been very confusing for all of us,"* is ambiguous; it is clearer to write: *"This breakdown in communication has been very confusing for all of us."* The paralegal can also provide transition by foretelling future topics by ending paragraphs with sentences like, *"Another feature of our office management system is automated billing."* The next paragraphs would then discuss automated billing.

Specific Documents

As discussed earlier, every written work has a purpose and every work has a reader. Focusing on who will read a document and why will make writing it much easier. Every document should introduce its intent to the reader, advance its purpose by carefully explaining each bit of necessary information, and conclude its explanation with a short summary of the main point.

The structure of court documents, such as pleadings and motions, follows specific rules. Their introduction consists of the caption and the statement of purpose. The purpose is then more specifically outlined in the document's text, which explains the elements of the case or the kind of information requested, depending on the type of document. Finally the purpose is summarized in the *ad damnum* clause. The text of a court document should contain all the elements necessary to achieve the desired result and nothing more. Its information should be clear and precise.

Letters should also contain introductions, bodies, and conclusions. The paralegal should begin each letter or memo by stating its purpose and noting any enclosures, follow with specific information and close with a short summary and a recap of any action that is required by the receiver of the communication.

Briefs and legal memos will be much easier to write if the writer organizes the information into the three parts. Introductory material includes the purpose of the document, a statement of the case, and a list of the relevant issues. The discussion of each of the issues by careful application of law to fact makes up the body of the argument, and the conclusion summarizes the answer to each issue. All three elements are essential for a complete organization and a persuasive presentation of the argument.

For Discussion Review some of the document samples in Chapter 3, and note which elements make up their introductions, bodies, and conclusions.

PROOFREADING: POLISHING THE FINISHED PRODUCT

A knowledge of the foundations of grammar and sentence structure paired with proper punctuation and careful planning will result in powerful writing. Good writers utilize one other important tool: proofreading. Often neglected because of time constraints or laziness, the process of proofreading can make a fair document good and a good document great. Ideally long works should be written in a series of drafts, but in law time is a precious commodity and numerous revisions are not practical. With the wide availability of word processors and word processing programs, though, proofreading has become a nearly painless process.

In rereading letters, court document, memos, and briefs for their final printing, the paralegal should play the part of the reader by looking at the document as if for the first time to make sure that its meaning is precise and its message clear. The paralegal should focus on the sentences, and read the three main elements of each sentence: the subject, verb, and third element. The paralegal should ask the following questions: (1) Is the message powerful? (2) Is it clouded by too many extraneous elements? (3) Is the sentence constructed and punctuated properly? (4) Do the adjectives and adverbs describe what they are intended to describe? If the answer is no to any of these questions, the paralegal should rework the sentence.

The paragraphs should then be examined by asking the following questions: (1) Does each paragraph contain one main topic? (2) Is the sentence structure varied? (3) Do the paragraphs flow together well? (4) Is the writing interesting? (5) Would a reader who is unfamiliar with the information understand what is written? If not, the paralegal should structure the paragraphs more carefully.

Next, the document should be checked for errors in spelling and typing. Spellcheck programs are excellent tools for the busy paralegal, but paralegals should not rely on them exclusively. Spellcheck programs will miss errors in forming plurals and verb tenses. After the document has been spellchecked, the paralegal should reread it to make sure nothing was missed. If the document's appearance is important (as is the case for most legal documents), the paralegal should have another person reread it. The author of a work is less likely to spot its errors than is a reader. Proofreading will get easier as one's writing style improves, and the practice of proofreading improves one's writing. Tables 6 & 7 list some of the more common proofreaders' marks.

Writing is a skill that improves with practice, and, with experience, the elements of good writing will come almost naturally. Clear sentence structure and precise organization become automatic. The paralegal should practice clear writing, avoid the ambiguity of most legal writing, and dazzle the legal community with unfamiliar clarity and impact.

For Discussion Discuss the attributes of a good proofreader.

CONCLUSION

Developing one's writing style is an ongoing process. Because paralegals are constantly engaged in written communication, they will have much opportunity to develop their writing skills. Much of paralegals' written work is performed to inform their supervising attorneys about information they have gained through legal research. The next chapter explores the various types of legal authority and provides an introduction to the manner in which paralegals access this authority.

Instruction	Mark in Margin	Mark in Type	Corrected Type
Delete	℘	the good word	the word
Insert indicated material	good	the ^ word	the good word
Let it stand	(stet)	the good word	the good word
Make capital	(cap)	the word	the Word
Make lower case	(lc)	The Word	the Word
Set in small capitals	(SC)	See word.	See WORD
Set in italic type	(ital)	The word is word	The word is *word*
Set in roman type	(rom)	the word	the word
Set in boldface type	(bf)	the entry word	the entry **word**
Set in lightface type	(lf)	the entry word	the entry word
Transpose	(tr)	the word good	the good word
Close up space	⁀	the wo rd	the word
Delete and close up space	℘	the woord	the word
Spell out	(sp)	2 words	two words
Insert: space	#	theword	the word
period	⊙	This is the word ^	This is the word
comma	^	words ^ words, words	words, words, words
hyphen	=/	word ^ for ^ word test	word-for-word test
colon	(:)	The following words ^	The following words:
semicolon	;	Scan the words ^ skim the words.	Scan the words; skim the words.
apostrophe	’	Johns words	John's words
quotation marks	“ / ”	the word word	the word "word"
parentheses	(/) /	The word ^ word ^ is in parentheses.	The word (word) is in parentheses.
brackets	[/] /	He read from the Word ^ the Bible ^.	He read from the Word [the Bible].
en dash	1/N	1964 ^ 1972	1964–1972
em dash	1/M / 1/M /	The dictionary ^ how often it is needed ^ belongs in every home	The dictionary—how often it is needed—belongs in every home
superior type	2	2 = 4	$2^2 = 4$
inferior type	2	HO	H_2O
asterisk	*	word	word*
dagger	†	a word ^	a word†
double dagger	‡	words and words ^	words and words‡
section symbol	§	^ Book Reviews	§Book Reviews
virgule	/	either ^ or	either/or

Table 6: Common Proofreaders' Marks

Instruction	Mark	Marked text	Corrected text
Start paragraph	¶	"Where is it?" ^"It's on the shelf."	"Where is it?" "It's on the shelf."
Run in	(run in)	The entry word is printed in boldface. The pronunciation follows	The entry word is printed in boldface. The pronunciation follows
Turn right side up	9	the word	the word
Move left	[	[the word	the word
Move right	]	the word	the word
Move up	⌐	the word	the word
Move down	⌙	the word	the word
Align	||	the word the word the word	the word the word the word
Straighten line	=	the word	the word
Wrong font	(wf)	the word	the word
Broken type	×	the word	the word

Table 7: Common Proofreaders' Marks, continued

CHAPTER 6: LEGAL AUTHORITY FOR PARALEGALS

Authority is anything the court may or must use in reaching its decision. There are two main categories of authority: primary and secondary. Primary sources of law include cases, statutes, and administrative regulations. Secondary sources include legal dictionaries, legal encyclopedias, annotated reporters, law reviews, treatises, and formbooks. Nonauthority includes all other materials that the court would not use in reaching its decision. Examples of nonauthority are Shepard's, digests, *A Uniform System of Citation*, and any authority that is not on point or is no longer valid because it has been overruled.

MANDATORY AUTHORITY

A further distinction can be made between mandatory and persuasive use of the authority. Only primary authority can be mandatory authority. Mandatory authority is anything a court must use in reaching its decision. Mandatory authority includes relevant statutes and rulings from a higher court. It is required that the lower court use these mandatory rulings in deciding its cases. For example, the Circuit Court of Appeals must use analogous United States Supreme Court cases to decide its own cases. The objective of legal research is to find as much mandatory, primary authority for a research problem as possible.

PERSUASIVE AUTHORITY

Persuasive authority may be used by the courts in deciding cases. Persuasive authority includes rulings from other courts, rulings from the same court, or nonbinding statutes from other jurisdictions. For instance, the New Mexico Supreme Court may consider an on point ruling from the Ohio Supreme Court, but the Ohio ruling would only be persuasive, not mandatory, authority. It is important to note that there is no mandatory case authority for the United States Supreme Court as its own rulings are the highest rulings in the United States. Although the United States Supreme Court is not bound by any of its prior decisions, these decisions constitute persuasive authority upon the Supreme Court. The Court may choose to either consider or disregard these rulings. The United States Constitution is the only mandatory authority for the United States Supreme Court. Paralegals must also remember that on point cases from the federal trial court and federal court of appeals are at most persuasive authority upon state supreme and appellate courts.

The major categories of authority are set forth in Table 8. The authorities listed under primary and secondary authority are assumed to be so only if the authority is on point, or analogous, to the facts and issues of the research problem.

For Discussion Discuss the general differences between primary and secondary authority. Name the characteristics of mandatory authority and the characteristics of persuasive authority.

CATEGORIES OF LEGAL AUTHORITY		
Primary	**Secondary**	**Nonauthority**
Any on point case from the following sources: United States Supreme Court United States Courts of Appeals United States District Courts State Supreme Courts State Appellate Courts Regional Reporters (such as *Pacific Reporter*, *Atlantic Reporter*, and *North Western Reporter*) Any on point law or statute from the following sources: United States Constitution United States Code State constitutions State statutes Court rules Municipal regulations	Any on point authority from the following sources: Legal dictionaries Legal encyclopedias (such as *American Jurisprudence 2d*, and *Corpus Juris Secundum)* Annotated Reporters (such as *American Law Reports*) Law reviews Treatises Formbooks	Shepard's Digests *A Uniform System of Citation* Any invalid, reversed, or otherwise overruled primary or secondary authority Synopsis of a case Headnotes of a case Table of Cases and other resources used as finding tools Any indices, such as the Descriptive Word Index Abstract of periodical articles

Table 8: Categories of Legal Authority

CONCLUSION

Once paralegals are familiar with the differences between mandatory and persuasive authority and know what constitutes primary and secondary authority and nonauthority, they may better focus on legal research. The next chapter provides techniques for approaching the challenging task of legal research.

CHAPTER 7: LEGAL RESEARCH FOR PARALEGALS

Conducting legal research may be the paralegal's most challenging and most rewarding responsibility. Through legal research the paralegal can find answers to virtually every legal issue, but legal research can be frustrating since it involves accessing an extensive amount of material that is constantly being accumulated and revised. Attorneys notoriously spend an inadequate amount of time in law libraries because they have been exposed to the rigors of legal research in law school and they are acutely cognizant of the demands that thorough legal research necessitates. When an attorney schedules research time in the law library, he or she is subconsciously aware that an hour project may easily become a three or four hour project before the attorney has thoroughly researched the issues. Therefore, because thorough legal research is so important and because paralegals are able to perform legal research, paralegals are called upon to spend the time in the law library that attorneys cannot afford to spend.

Paralegals must not be dogmatic in their approach to legal research. Open-mindedness and flexibility are critical to success in legal research because as paralegals spend more time researching a problem, more issues develop. Thus, single issue research problems are rare; and even though paralegals may think that they have only one issue to research, that issue may quickly multiply into numerous related issues as the research progresses.

At first, beginning a research problem will seem to be the major obstacle to thorough and efficient legal research. Neophyte paralegals are easily identifiable as those persons who are listlessly roaming the law library like zombies. This may be natural at first; however, as paralegals become acclimated to a law library, they will develop a legal research routine. With time, this routine will become so ingrained in their research styles that the question of where to begin researching will quickly become academic and legal research will become immensely enjoyable and challenging. Many paralegals find themselves thriving on the challenges presented by complex legal research problems. Tables 9, 10, and 11 provide an overview of the major sources of primary and secondary authority and nonauthority with which paralegals must be familiar to effectively perform legal research.

INTRODUCTION TO LEGAL RESEARCH

Although there is no universally accepted correct approach to thorough legal research, a simple approach that many paralegals, law students, and attorneys use involves the following five steps:

1. **Paralegals should begin the research process by consulting legal dictionaries, like *Black's Law Dictionary*, *Words and Phrases*, and *Ballentine's Legal Dictionary and Thesaurus*, and using common sense and brainstorming to derive as many terms pertaining to the legal research problem as possible. To more efficiently attack the research problem, paralegals should compile a comprehensive list of terms that appear to relate to the issues of the case, including synonyms, antonyms, and other relevant expressions.**

2. Second, the paralegal should determine what court jurisdiction is involved in the research problem. This requires determining whether the research problem involves the federal or state court system and what the specific level of court is within the federal or state system.

   a. If the problem is a state court matter, the paralegal should follow these steps:

      i. Obtain a better understanding of the nature of the case and obtain primary case and statutory leads by consulting the major legal encyclopedias: *Corpus Juris Secundum* and *American Jurisprudence, 2d*.

      ii. Then, obtain more leads in *American Law Reports*.

      iii. Next, find a digest topic, or topics, from West's "Outline of the Law," which is found at the beginning of each of West's digests. The topics will lead to applicable state, regional, and federal digests, which in turn direct the researcher to primary authority.

      iv. Locate as many on point state supreme court, appellate court, and federal court cases as possible. Remember that on point federal court cases may be difficult to find in researching a state court matter since federal court jurisdiction differs from state court jurisdiction.

      v. Finally, apply any pertinent provisions of the United States Constitution and the applicable state constitution and statutes to the facts.

   b. If the problem is a federal court matter, a paralegal should follow these steps:

      i. First, repeat steps 2(a)(i), 2(a)(ii), and 2(a)(iii), above.

      ii. Find and apply as many on point federal court cases as possible. Remember that the relevant federal court decisions that emanate from the United States District Courts and the United States Court of International Trade are found in the *Federal Supplement*; those that emanate from the United States Courts of Appeals are found in the *Federal Reporter*; and those that emanate from the United States Supreme Court are found in the *United States Reports*, the *Supreme Court Reporter*, and the *United States Supreme Court Reports, Lawyers' Edition*.

      iii. Finally, apply any pertinent provisions of the United States Constitution, United States Code, and applicable state constitution and statutes to the facts of the problem.

3. Last but not least, paralegals must shepardize each of the primary authorities that they have found to make certain that none of the authorities has been overruled or reversed. Shepardizing may also lead to additional authorities that may be on point. If paralegals have access to WESTLAW or LEXIS, they should consult these update services because they are usually more current than Shepard's.

Through utilizing this or a similar approach, paralegals will successfully meet the challenges of legal research. The principal concern with legal research then becomes not *where* to begin a project but *when* to end it. Once in a law library, paralegals will discover that they are so inundated with information and so intellectually stimulated by tracking down the answers to the research problem that they lose track of the time. Paralegals and their supervising attorneys should consider the following four factors in deciding when to end a research problem:

1. Authority on point. The object of any legal research problem is to find mandatory primary authority that is on point to the paralegal's research problem. Perhaps it will take two hours to find this applicable law or maybe it will take twenty, but once paralegals locate mandatory primary authority and properly shepardize it, the authority need only be integrated into the research memo and presented to the court and opposing party.

2. Deadline. A much more common determinant for ending a research project than finding analogous mandatory authority is working under a deadline. Most law offices function in crisis situations and are constantly under deadlines so that the amount of time necessary to thoroughly research an issue is rarely available. Unfortunately, because most law offices have heavy workloads, attorneys are known for waiting until the last minute to give research projects to the paralegals; the paralegals then need to do the best job possible in a limited amount of time and simply must end their research when time runs out.

3. Exhaustion of research resources. Each client is entitled to zealous, competent, and thorough representation. Paralegals and attorneys have ethical and financial incentives to perform the most thorough research possible in the quest for an answer to the research problem. Thoroughness necessitates exhausting all books in the law firm's library and then examining all research sources in the county law library, state supreme court law library, and local law school law library. If the law firm has WESTLAW or LEXIS, those must also be tapped. Obviously, in populous metropolitan areas, a thorough exhaustion of the resources takes considerably longer than in smaller cities.

4. Amount of retainer. The final factor of which paralegals and attorneys should be aware in researching an issue is the amount of retainer that the client has provided or is willing to provide to the firm. Upon receipt of a legal research project from a supervising attorney, paralegals should immediately ascertain if the supervising attorney has a suggested time limit for the research. Paralegals and attorneys must always perform thorough research; however, more research time will be spent on a client who has provided a large, or unlimited, retainer than on a client who has provided a smaller retainer.

For Discussion Discuss the steps you would take to research the following hypothetical case.

Daphne has consulted with your supervising attorney regarding her father, Samuel. Samuel was crossing the street when a cement truck hit him. Samuel suffered brain damage and has undergone six months of therapy to regain his previous mental capacity. Doctors suggest that Samuel will undergo years of therapy and may never regain normal mental capacity. Daphne has told you that the cement truck was driven by an employee of Hard as Rock Cement Mixers ("HRC"), who was driving from a job site to the company's headquarters. The driver failed to observe a sign that stated, "No Turn on Red," and made a right turn while the stoplight was red. As the driver was turning, he hit Samuel while Samuel was walking across the street despite a sign that stated, "Don't Walk." Daphne wants to know if she will prevail on behalf of her father in a suit against HRC and its driver.

Type of Primary Authority	Sources
Statutes: Federal (slip laws → statutes at large → codes)	official - *United States Code* (U.S.C.) unofficial - *United States Code Annotated* (U.S. C.A.) unofficial - *United States Code Service* (U.S. C.S.)
State (slip laws → session laws → statutes at large → codes)	state compilation of statutes
Administrative regulations	Chronological - *Federal Register* (Fed.Reg.) Codified - *Code of Federal Regulations* (C.F.R) Miscellaneous - *U.S. Code Congressional and Administrative News* (U.S.C.C.A.N.), which includes parts of U.S.C. and C.F.R. and provides legislative history
Case law: Federal United States Supreme Court	official - *United States Reports* (U.S.) unofficials - *U.S. Supreme Court Reporter* (S.Ct.) *U.S. Supreme Court Reports, Lawyer's Edition* (L.Ed) *U.S. Supreme Court Reports, Lawyer's Edition 2d* (L.Ed.2d) *United States Law Week* (U.S.L.W.) *United States Supreme Court Bulletin* (S.Ct.Bull.)
United States Courts of Appeals	*Federal Reporter* (F.) *Federal Reporter, Second Series* (F.2d)
United States District Courts	*Federal Supplement* (F.Supp)
State	Regional Reporters (each is currently a second series): *Atlantic Reporter* (A.2d), *North Eastern Reporter* (N.E.2d), *North Western Reporter* (N.W.2d), *Pacific Reporter* (P.2d), *South Eastern Reporter* (S.E.2d), *Southern Reporter* (So.2d), *South Western Reporter* (S.W.2d)
Specialty Reporters	*Federal Rules Decisions* (F.R.D.) (opinions of United States District Courts that involved the Federal Rules of Civil and Criminal Procedure) *Military Justice Reporter* (M.J.) *Bankruptcy Reporter* (Bankr.)

Table 9: Primary Sources of Authority

Type of Secondary Authority	Sources
Legal Dictionaries	*Ballentine's Legal Dictionary and Thesaurus* *Black's Law Dictionary* *Words and Phrases* Statsky's *Legal Thesaurus/Dictionary*
Legal Directories	*Martindale-Hubbell Legal Directory* Legal Directory on WESTLAW
Legal Encyclopedias	*American Jurisprudence 2d* (Am.Jur.2d) *Corpus Juris Secundum* (C.J.S.) *Florida Jurisprudence* and other state series
Legal Periodicals	*The Yale Law Journal* and numerous other law reviews
Other Legal Commentary	*American Law Reports* (A.L.R., 2d, 3d, 4th, 5th, Fed.) *Restatement of the Law* by the American Law Institute Hornbooks Treatises

Table 10: Secondary Sources of Authority

Type of Nonauthority	Sources
Indexes to Legal Periodicals	*Index to Legal Periodicals* (I.L.P.) *Current Law Index* (C.L.I.) *Legal Resource Index* (L.R.I.)
Digests: National level	The American Digest System *Century Digest* (1658-1896) *Decennial Digests* (10 year periods since 1897) *General Digests* (summaries of opinions since most recent Decennial)
Federal cases	*Federal Digest* (to 1939) *Modern Federal Practice Digest* (1939-1961) *Federal Practice Digest 2d* (1961 - 1975) *Federal Practice Digest 3d* (1975 - present)
Supreme Court Cases	*U.S. Supreme Court Digest* *U.S. Supreme Court Digest, L.Ed.*
Regional digests	*Atlantic Digest, North Western Digest, Pacific Digest*, and *South Eastern Digest* (no North Eastern, Southern or South Western Digest)
Specialty digests	West's *Bankruptcy Digest* West's *Military Justice Digest* *U.S. Claims Court Digest*

Table 11: Sources of Non-authority

IMPORTANT TOOLS FOR LEGAL RESEARCH

Once paralegals understand where to begin and end their legal research, they should become aware of the usefulness of the five most universally important research tools in a law library: legal encyclopedias, *American Law Reports* (A.L.R.), digests, Shepard's citations, and WESTLAW. These research tools comprise the heart of any law library and are exceptionally useful for performing background research on a topic, understanding a research topic, finding leads to primary authority, and validating the primary authority once it has been found.

Although there are not many shortcuts to legal research, prior to utilizing the previously mentioned legal research tools, paralegals should examine all available office form files and copies of previously prepared briefs on the same topic to obtain leads to primary authority. Additionally, experts on the topic to be researched should be consulted for leads to the proper primary authority. Often attorneys who have been successful litigating cases similar to the one being researched will accommodate a paralegal's request for copies of briefs and other documents that will expedite the paralegal's research. These experts should be reimbursed for copy charges and other reasonable expenses incident to providing this helpful information. Paralegals should also offer to send a copy of the resulting briefs to the attorney who has contributed his or her expertise. Through receiving leads and sample briefs from others who have been successful in similar litigation, paralegals will save their office's client a considerable amount of time and money. Rarely do attorneys refuse to provide information to other attorneys, but if they do refuse, the paralegal should contact the clerk of the court where the previous action was filed and request copies of the pertinent documents from the court.

After exhausting leads from within the law office and from other attorneys, paralegals must embark upon performing original research utilizing legal encyclopedias, A.L.R., digests, Shepard's, and WESTLAW. Recently, International Thomson Publishing ("ITP"), owner of Lawyers Cooperative Publishing and Bancroft-Whitney, purchased West Publishing Company. Thus, most law books are now published by ITP. The following discussion will assist the paralegal in understanding the types of information these sources provide and the method for accessing them.

Legal Encyclopedias

Through using legal encyclopedias, the researcher obtains a broad understanding of the legal issue to be researched and the relevant facts surrounding that issue. Legal encyclopedias are comprehensive and therefore helpful as starting points in legal research because they provide a background of information that calls attention to the important points of an issue.

The footnotes of legal encyclopedias reference primary authority, and updated primary authority can be found in the pocket part to each volume. Paralegals should first find the general topic in the encyclopedia and scan through the text until they uncover a specific topic that matches their research problem. They then should consult the footnotes to find the applicable cases and consult the current updated authorities in the pocket part.

Corpus Juris Secundum

Corpus Juris Secundum (C.J.S.) is arranged by titles that are combined into very broad categories and subsequently narrowed into more specific subdivisions. Within each title, the subdivisions are numbered by section. The sections within each title are organized in the following fashion:

1. definitions and general topic information,
2. individual elements and requirements, and then
3. procedural and evidentiary subtopics.

Topics in C.J.S. can be found either through the title outline or through the index. Near the front of each C.J.S. volume is a topic outline that includes all of the titles in the C.J.S. series. After finding a relevant topic in the outline, the researcher should access the particular volume that includes that title. From the title outline in that particular volume, the researcher can narrow the general title to a subtitle that is relevant to the research problem. At the beginning of each title section is an even more detailed outline from which the researcher can find more specific information about the researched issue.

Using the index is another way to research C.J.S. The index alphabetically lists titles, subtitles, and cross-references. The index approach is helpful if the paralegal already knows the vocabulary for the legal topic he or she is researching.

American Jurisprudence 2d

American Jurisprudence 2d (Am.Jur.2d) is organized similarly to C.J.S. However, Am.Jur.2d also provides two items that C.J.S. does not provide: (1) New Topic Service, which contains topics that have been added after publication of the topic volumes, and (2) Table of Statutes, Rules, and Regulations Cited, which enables the researcher to do further research on the topic if the researcher already knows the federal statute, regulation, or court rule that governs a particular situation and is found in its own volume.

The legal encyclopedia is an excellent secondary source from which paralegals can start their research. However, paralegals must research beyond the information discovered in legal encyclopedias to finish their research projects.

American Law Reports

Each volume of *American Law Reports* (A.L.R.) , except for the index volumes, contains case opinions and articles entitled "annotations." In general, an annotation is a collection of explanatory notes and commentary on a topic of law. The A.L.R. annotation technique has evolved from the selective case system of legal reporting in which only cases of general legal significance are reported. These cases are then analyzed, interpreted, and placed into a current legal context by the editors. Today, each A.L.R. annotation is preceded by a complete transcript of a recent appellate case, which is used to illustrate the annotated point of law. The annotations have become so informative and comprehensive that they have far eclipsed the importance of the illustrative cases that are reported.

A.L.R. has developed in six stages from 1919 to the present. The resulting six series, not to be confused with editions, mirror the rapid growth of American law and the development of increasingly advanced methods of legal research. A.L.R. 5th is the most recent series, and it, along with A.L.R. 4th, covers state topics but no federal topics. A.L.R. 3d presents both state and federal topics from 1965 to 1969, and only state topics from 1969 to 1980. A.L.R. Fed. presents only federal topics from 1969 to the present. The A.L.R. 2d series was published from 1948 through 1965, and the first series of A.L.R. was published from 1919 to 1948; both series offer federal and states cases and annotations.

Even though the first series of A.L.R. is more outdated than the A.L.R. 5th series, there is nothing inherently wrong in utilizing the case authority and annotations in the earlier series. Obviously, any authority must be updated and validated through Shepard's, WESTLAW, or LEXIS prior to being integrated into research memoranda, and with A.L.R., all annotations should be updated through the A.L.R. 3d, 4th, 5th, and Federal supplements, *A.L.R. 2d Later Case Service*, and *A.L.R. Blue Book of Supplemental Decisions*.

A.L.R. entries contain information written or edited by the A.L.R. staff, including a summary of the decision, headnotes, a listing of the appearances of counsel, several sample briefs of counsel, and the case opinion. As stated earlier, following the case opinion is the annotation, which collects and analyzes the law pertaining to the legal issue which is being annotated. Most annotations include the following:

1. Total Client Service Library references ("TCSL"),
2. a table of contents for the annotation,
3. an index to the annotation,
4. a table of jurisdictions represented in the annotation, and
5. the text of the annotation.

The "TCSL box" contains cross-references to other sections of books published by Lawyers Co-operative Publishing Company that relate to the topic that is annotated. The Total Client Service Library is similar to the

West topic and key number system which references other West publications. As stated earlier, West and Lawyers Co-operative Publishing Company have joined together under ITP.

To find specific topics in the A.L.R. books, paralegals should use the following three main research approaches:

1. by index; the Index to Annotations and the pocket parts lead to the specific legal category that relates to the issue being researched,
2. by digest; the digests lead to synopses of the cases included in A.L.R. by topic. The first and second series have their own digest, and the third, fourth, fifth, and federal A.L.R. have a unified digest.
3. by computer; computer databases like VERALEX 2 and LEXIS lead to the A.L.R. annotations.

After references are found, the Annotation History Table can be used to see if the annotations have been overruled or supplemented since the annotation was published.

Overall, A.L.R. is an excellent source for beginning virtually any legal research problem. Its major limitation is its lack of comprehensiveness since it does not discuss every area of law like encyclopedias and digests do. However, the topics of law that A.L.R. does annotate are contemporarily significant and are discussed in a very thorough manner with references to cases from every jurisdiction that has taken a position on the topic cited, making the series an indispensable research tool.

Digests

Digests are used to find relevant cases by topic. West Publishing Company is the primary publisher of digests, and its key number digests are indispensable to the legal profession. A key number is permanently assigned to a specific point of case law, and every point of case law has its respective key number. The West key number system is organized according to West's "Outline of the Law," which includes seven main divisions of the law and 414 subdivisions. Most research questions can be answered by finding references to the pertinent case law in the key number digests, and then examining the resulting primary authority. The West key number digests are among the most significant creations for accessing case law.

In order to use the West digests, paralegals should access the topic names and key numbers through one or more of the following means:

1. the Descriptive Word Index, which is usually located in the first volume of the set and refers to a topic name and a key number,
2. the Topic Outline, which is helpful if the paralegal is already familiar with the topic being researched because the outline further breaks down the listed topics so that the paralegal can conduct more precise research,
3. the key number system, which can be used to access a topic anywhere within the digest system because once a paralegal finds a key number that fits the topic, he or she can use it to transfer from one reporter to another, or from one digest to another, and
4. the Table of Cases, which is usually located in the last volume of the set and is helpful if the paralegal knows the name of an on point case, but does not know the citation for that case.

In most cases, the West key number system is the fastest, most universally accessible approach to researching any digest or reporter. Paralegals can use the key number system to find cases on the topics of their choice in any other jurisdiction included in the West digest system. All that is required is that a paralegal remember the topic and key number for reference when moving back and forth between jurisdictions.

The West digest system contains a number of different volumes available for research purposes. The West system digests federal court decisions, federal issues (in different specialized reporters), and regional decisions. The West system also includes state digests that cover all of the states except Utah, Nevada, and Delaware. North and South Dakota and Virginia and West Virginia are combined into single state digests.

Although digests cover all jurisdictions across the country, the paralegal should access the digest most specific to the research problem. For instance, if a paralegal is trying to find a rule of law in a particular state, that paralegal should focus on that particular state's digest before turning to the regional digests.

Shepard's Case Citators

Once paralegals have found an on point primary authority, they must make sure that the authority is still valid. Shepard's citations provide a method of checking the status of a case. A citator provides a list of references to sources that have cited the cases a paralegal has found. For instance, if the paralegal has found an on point case, *Land v. Hill*, 70 Wn.2d 80, 644 P.2d 43 (1961), the paralegal needs to find out whether this is still good case law. The paralegal looks up *Land v. Hill* in a Shepard's citator to find all the cases that have cited *Land v. Hill*, how those cases have treated it, and any history relationship between the cited case and the citing cases.

The treatment that other cases give *Land v. Hill* determines whether the law is still valid and usable. For example, if a court has disapproved of the decision in *Land v. Hill*, *Land* will be shown as overruled in Shepard's. Thus the citator not only provides citations to courts that have mentioned *Land v. Hill* in their opinions, but also provides abbreviations showing how those cases treated it. In the above example, an "o" would be next to the case that overruled *Land v. Hill* showing that *Land* was disapproved in that case. When paralegals look up cases in Shepard's to determine if they are still valid law or to find other cases that may have followed or otherwise approved of their cases' decisions, they are "shepardizing," or checking the current status of a case.

To use Shepard's, paralegals must first locate the appropriate citator. Because *Land v. Hill* was heard by a Washington Court, to shepardize it paralegals must find either the set of Shepard's covering *Pacific Reporter*, which would be *Shepard's Pacific Reporter Citations*, or they may look in the set covering Washington cases, *Shepard's Washington Citations*. There is a set of *Shepard's Citations* for nearly every existing reporter as well as several topical citators covering cases dealing with particular areas of law, such as labor law and tax law.

Once they have found the correct set of *Shepard's Citations*, paralegals need to consult the page that lists the volume and page number where the case that they are shepardizing may be located. In the appropriate volume on the specified page, they will find the list of cases that have cited the shepardized case. The first of the listed cases is the parallel citation, which is a cross-reference to another publication that sets forth the shepardized case and is shown in parentheses. For example, if paralegals were shepardizing *Land v. Hill* in the *Shepard's Pacific Reporter Citations*, the first of the listed citing references would be the parallel cite, shown as (70Wsh2d80).

After parallel citations, the column lists cases that have a history relationship to the shepardized case. These cases generally involve the same parties, the same facts, or the same litigation as the cited case. The history relationship is shown by history letters, which are abbreviations indicating what happened to the case on appeal. For instance, if the citing case states that it set aside *Land v. Hill*, *Land* will be shown to be "vacated" in Shepard's. History letters may also indicate other locations where the same case or a connected case has been reported.

Next, cases are listed that do not involve the same parties, facts, or litigation but have made reference to the cited case. These cases are arranged chronologically by jurisdiction from least current to most current. For example, the listing of citing references for *Land v. Hill* may separate the cases with a reference to Cir.4. This means that the cases listed after the Cir.4 are cases from the Fourth Circuit Court of Appeals. Many jurisdictions may be listed, and cases within each jurisdiction are arranged chronologically.

Several of the key abbreviations indicating history and treatment analyses are as follows:

- r = reversed; the case has been reversed on appeal.
- a = affirmed; the case has been affirmed on appeal.
- o = overruled; the case is no longer valid authority.
- q = questioned; the continuing validity of the case is questionable.
- c = criticized; another court disagrees with the case.
- L = limited; the case has been limited to its facts and will not be extended to other facts.

There are many other abbreviations shown in Shepard's. A complete listing may be found in the front of each volume of *Shepard's Citations*.

Shepard's also enables the paralegal to narrow shepardizing to those points of law that are most relevant to the research. The paralegal can save much time by shepardizing a particular headnote number. The small raised or superior numbers before the page number of the citing case are the cited case's headnote numbers that are discussed by the citing case.

Once paralegals have examined the case listings, they should check for additional citing references in any of the supplements to the particular citator they are using. Supplements are found in the gold or red pamphlet volumes or in white advance sheets. If paralegals are shepardizing a case decided in a state for which Shepard's publishes *Shepard's EXPRESS Citations*, they will need to check for citing references in that publication as well. *Shepard's EXPRESS Citations* provides the most current citing references to a case and summaries of many of the treatment and history analyses that discuss the nature and impact of the citing judge's comments.

As with any other type of reporter, digest, or citator, paralegals must check the most current publications to verify that their research is accurate and their legal authority is still valid. The best way for paralegals to determine whether they have all of the necessary volumes, supplements, and advance sheets is to read the front cover of the most current publication, which presents "WHAT YOUR LIBRARY SHOULD CONTAIN." "WHAT YOUR LIBRARY SHOULD CONTAIN" lists every publication that should be consulted to thoroughly shepardize authority, including *Shepard's EXPRESS Citations* in states for which it is published. Reading "WHAT YOUR LIBRARY SHOULD CONTAIN" is sometimes referred to as "reading the box."

As they use Shepard's citators, paralegals will become familiar with the format of the books and the table of abbreviations in the front of each volume and supplement. Shepard's also has an on-line service available on LEXIS and WESTLAW, but *Shepard's EXPRESS Citations* and certain topical and statutory information are not yet available on-line. By utilizing Shepard's correctly, paralegals can be sure that they have consulted all relevant authorities and that their research is thorough and current.

WESTLAW

Computers and the practice of law are becoming increasingly interdependent. Not less than thirty-five years ago, virtually all of legal research had to be conducted manually. Today, computerized legal research, such as WESTLAW, is becoming so popular that paralegals should have a fundamental understanding of the functions of legal research databases.

Virtually any research that can be done manually in a law library can also be performed on WESTLAW, and the legal research skills discussed in this book are indispensable to performing computerized legal research. WESTLAW, however, makes any manual task much less time-consuming through the speed of computers and the convenience of having all research sources in one location, the computer terminal.

Although it is expensive to access, computerized legal research offers great flexibility and convenience for paralegals who lack adequate law libraries. Research databases allow paralegals to access a law library through their computers, and WESTLAW, with unique access to the West topic and key number system, is the most effective research database on the market. New databases and features appear on WESTLAW almost daily. Among the new databases is DIALOG which provides a plethora of secondary sources, such as law review articles, which may be relevant to the paralegal's case or legal issue.

WESTLAW also provides assistance for job searches in law through the Directory of Legal Employers - National Association for Law Placement (NALP-DIR) database, which lists important law firm information. To answer questions and keep pace with the new additions to WESTLAW, the West reference attorneys are available at 1-800-688-6363, seven days a week.

For Discussion Discuss how you would use legal encyclopedias, digests, Shepard's case citators, and WESTLAW in your research of Samuel's case mentioned earlier.

CITATION FORMAT

Once paralegals have found on point authority for their research, they must know how to cite it properly when they discuss the authority in memoranda, briefs, and any document filed with the court. Citing statutes is fairly simple. The format for citing each state's statutes is presented on pages 170 - 228 of the sixteenth edition of *A Uniform System of Citation*. Federal statutes are cited as follows. In the official publication, *United States Code*, the title number is stated first, followed by U.S.C and the section number, and ending with the supplement information in parentheses, like this: 42 U.S.C. § 1983 (Supp.III 1979). Citation should not be made to the unofficials although *A Uniform System of Citation* does recognize these styles: 12 U.S.C.A. § 635F (West Supp. 1981) and 8 U.S.C.S. § 43 (Law. Co-op. 1980).

When citing a case correctly, paralegals provide the reader with the following information: the parties to the litigation, the court that decided the case, the year the case was decided, and the publications where the case can be found. A properly cited case allows the supervising attorney, opposing counsel, or judge who is reading the memo or brief to quickly access the cited material in the law library. As stated earlier, the most widely used citation manual is *A Uniform System of Citation*, which is also known as the Bluebook. Because the purpose of a citation is to allow the intended reader to find the cited authority in the law library as quickly as possible, the paralegal should always consult the Bluebook for proper citation format. If there is still doubt about the proper format for a citation, the paralegal should include enough information to answer the following questions: (1) Who are the parties involved? (2) What court decided the case? (3) In what year was the case decided? (4) In what publications can the case be found?

The following citation is complete:

***Konas v. Red Owl*, 158 Colo. 29, 404 P.2d 546 (1965).**

It states the parties involved in the action: *Konas v. Red Owl*. It states which court decided the case: Colo. It provides the year in which the case was decided: (1965). It shows in what publications the case can be found: 158 Colo. 29, 404 P.2d 546.

The case name should be underlined or italicized and separated from the publication information by a comma. The different publications are separated by commas and the date is placed within parentheses. Reference to a publication includes the following information: its volume number, the abbreviated publication name, and the page number. In the *Konas v. Red Owl* example, the case may be found in volume 158 of *Colorado Reports* on page 29 and in volume 404 of *Pacific Reporter* on page 546. Pages 165 - 218 of the Bluebook present format and abbreviations for federal and state citations. Table 12 provides more rules for citing cases.

Unless the case is decided in a state that has discontinued publishing its official reports, the citation should include references to two publications. This is called a parallel cite. When presenting parallel cites in a citation, paralegals should present the state (official) publication before they present the West regional (unofficial) publication. Cases decided in the federal trial court are only cited to the unofficial publication, *Federal Supplement* (F.Supp), and the federal court of appeals is only cited to *Federal Reporter, 2d* (F.2d). Cases from the United States Supreme Court should be cited first to the official, *United States Reports* (U.S.), then to West's unofficial publication, *Supreme Court Reporter* (S.Ct.), and finally to Lawyer's Co-operative's unofficial publication, *United States Supreme Court Reports, Lawyers' Edition, 2d* (L.Ed 2d). The Bluebook, however, suggests that citation to the official (U.S.) is all that is necessary.

More advanced citation format may include a prior history for the case that reflects the disposition in the lower court. This information gives the reader the procedural history of the case. For instance the citation, *Smith v. Wesson*, 422 P.2d 123 (Colo. 1987), *aff'd*, 444 U.S. 185 (1991), provides information regarding the case's state court decision and the subsequent federal court disposition. Refer to the Bluebook for more details on advanced citations.

For Discussion Discuss why proper citation is important.

CONCLUSION

This chapter has provided an overview of the manner in which paralegals conduct legal research. The next chapter discusses the important rules of ethics that the paralegal must take into consideration when dispensing legal services.

SOME RULES OF CITATION FORMAT	
Omit	**Include**
et al.	abbreviations (see *A Uniform System of Citation,* 16th edition, pp. 47 - 49)
parties' first names correct: *Barto v. William Smith, Inc.* incorrect: *John Barto v. William Smith, Inc.*	the full date of a very recent case or a slip opinion 55 U.S.L.W. 4420 (U.S. Dec. 4, 199_)
The when it is the first word of a party's name correct: Wheeling Company v. James incorrect: The Wheeling Company v. James	case name on appeal if it is different from the name of the case in the lower court *Great W. United Corp. v. Kidwell*, 577 F.2d 1256 (5th Cir. 1978) *rev'd sub nom. Leroy V. Great W. United Corp.*, 443 U.S. 173 (1979)
City of unless it begins a party's name Correct: *City of Atlanta v. Palmer* *Mayor of New York v. Nilsen* Incorrect: *Atlanta v. Palmer*	date on appeal if it is different from that of the lower court *Reality, Inc. v. Meese*, 678 F.2d 1271 (D.C.Cir. 1984), *cert. denied*, 442 U.S. 102 (1989)
Prepositional phrases of location not following *City*, unless the omission would leave only one word in the name of a party Correct: *Lewis v. Bd. of County Commissioners* Incorrect: *Lewis v. Bd. of County Commissioners of La Plata County*	subsequent history *United States v. Eller*, 114 F.Supp. 284 (W.D.Wisc.1951), *rev'd*, 208 F.2d 716 (4th Cir. 1953), *cert. denied*, 347 U.S. 934 (1954)
Inc., *Ltd.*, *etc.*, if the name also contains words such as *Co.*, *Bros.*, and *Ass'n* that clearly indicate that the party is a business firm Correct: *Beal Word Processing Co. v. Dischinger* *Hart v. Miami Herald, Inc.*	

Table 12: Some Rules Regarding Citation Format

CHAPTER 8: ETHICS FOR PARALEGALS

The behavior of attorneys is governed by the American Bar Association. The activities of paralegals, as representatives of their supervising attorneys, reflect directly on their attorneys. Therefore maintenance of ethical standards by all members of the legal staff is imperative. Ethical considerations should be a part of every activity and decision in the law office.

The American Bar Association has created a guideline of ethical standards, called the ABA's Model Rules of Professional Conduct, for those who are engaged in the practice of law. These rules are a recent revision of the ABA's Model Code of Professional Responsibility. This revision has retained the essence of the past rules but has modernized their language and expanded their application. For example, the nine canons listed at the end of the model rules originated in the Code of Professional Responsibility.

Paralegals and their supervising attorneys should follow these canons of ethical behavior. The following discussion lists the most important rules from the ethical guidelines and gives a brief discussion of a rule if it is not self-explanatory.

There is a difference between the first two rules and the remainder of the rules listed in this section. The first rule, DR 3-101(a), is a disciplinary rule. The category of disciplinary rules indicates the bare minimum of conduct that will be allowed by any practicing attorney. The second rule, EC 3-6, is one of the ethical considerations from the guidelines. These ethical considerations are representations of the objectives that each member of the bar should strive to achieve. The final set of rules is designated as a set of model rules. These model rules indicate the general considerations that each practicing attorney should follow.

If an attorney violates any of these rules, the American Bar Association imposes established sanctions. These sanctions include a warning "slap on the wrist" for minor infractions, public reprimand for moderate infractions, suspension for serious infractions, and disbarment for major infractions and extremely unethical activities. Therefore, attorneys and their staffs must take these rules seriously.

GUIDELINES FROM THE ABA RULES OF PROFESSIONAL CONDUCT

The following list of rules from the ABA Rules of Professional Conduct is not exhaustive. However, the list conveys those ethical considerations that apply most directly to the paralegal. Paralegals should observe the following Disciplinary Rule and Ethical Consideration.

DISCIPLINARY RULE 3-101 (a)

DR 3-101 (a) -- *A lawyer shall not aid a nonlawyer in the unauthorized practice of law.*

Because the paralegal is a nonlawyer, this disciplinary rule directly relates to the use of paralegals in the law office. Inherent in this rule are the following stipulations:

1. Paralegals must not represent themselves as attorneys.

2. Paralegals must not do the tasks that only attorneys can do. These include giving legal advice, arguing cases in court, and establishing legal fees. Many of these activities may be planned or prepared by the paralegal, but the attorney must control the actual application of the legal process.

3. Paralegals must work under the supervision of an attorney. Refer also to EC 3-6.

ETHICAL CONSIDERATION 3-6

EC 3-6 -- *A lawyer often delegates tasks to clerks, secretaries, and other law office personnel. Such delegation is proper if the lawyer maintains a direct relationship with his client, supervises the delegated work, and has complete professional responsibility for the work product. This delegation enables a lawyer to render legal services more economically and efficiently.*

MODEL RULES

Model Rule 1.1 -- *An attorney shall provide competent representation to a client.*

Competence is based on the ability to complete a legal task for a client. Attorneys and their staffs must perform adequate research for and give proper attention to each client's case.

Model Rule 1.2(d) -- *An attorney shall not counsel a client to engage in conduct the attorney knows is criminal or fraudulent.*

Model Rule 1.3 -- *An attorney shall act with reasonable diligence and promptness in representing a client.*

Model Rule 1.5(a) -- *An attorney's fee shall be reasonable.*

Considerations for setting reasonable fees include the amount of experience the attorney has, the complexity of the case, the location of the law practice, and the potential costs incident to the case.

Model Rule 1.6 -- *An attorney must not reveal information relating to the representation of a client unless (a) the client consents to the disclosure or (b) the attorney reasonably believes the disclosure is necessary to prevent a client from committing a criminal act that is likely to result in imminent death or substantial bodily harm.*

Paralegals must refrain from relating any information about a client's case to anyone, including family members, and should make every effort to insure that confidential information is safe from public view.

Model Rule 1.7 -- *An attorney shall not represent a client if the representation of that client will be directly adverse to another client, unless*

(i) the attorney reasonably believes the representation will not adversely affect the relationship with the other client, and

(ii) both clients consent after consultation about the risks of the multiple representation.

Generally attorneys should not get involved in any case where they may have a conflict of interest.

Model Rule 1.8(a) -- *An attorney shall not enter a business transaction with a client, unless*

(i) the terms of the business transaction are fair and reasonable to the client and are fully disclosed to the client in understandable language in writing, and

(ii) the client is given reasonable opportunity to seek advice on the transaction from another attorney who is not involved with the transaction or the parties, and

(iii) the client consents to the business transaction in writing.

Model Rule 1.15 -- *An attorney shall hold client property separate from the attorney's own property.*

This rule includes property such as payments from outside entities which are designated for the client, any refundable fees, or any court awards that the client is to receive. For instance, if an attorney is performing a collection service for the client, any payments that the client's debtors make to the attorney's office should be deposited in an account separate from the office's general account.

Model Rule 1.16(a) -- *An attorney must withdraw from a case: if continuing would result in a violation of ethical rules or other laws; if the client discharges the attorney; or if the attorney's physical or mental condition materially impairs his or her ability to represent the client.*

Model Rule 3.1 -- *An attorney must not bring a frivolous claim or assert a frivolous defense.*

It is unethical for an attorney to file a case that he or she does not think has a valid cause of action or to put forth a defense that is unwarranted. It is especially unethical for an attorney to file a case solely for the purpose of maliciously injuring the other party.

Model Rule 3.2 -- *An attorney must make reasonable efforts to expedite litigation.*

Model Rule 3.3(a) -- *An attorney shall not knowingly:*

(1) make a false statement of material fact or law to a tribunal,

(2) fail to disclose a material fact to a tribunal when disclosure is necessary to avoid assisting a client commit a criminal or fraudulent act,

(3) fail to tell a tribunal about laws or other authority directly against the position of the attorney's client if this law or authority is not disclosed by opposing counsel, or

(4) offer evidence that the attorney knows is false.

Model Rule 4.2 -- *In representing a client, an attorney shall not communicate with a party on the other side about the subject matter of the case if the attorney knows that the party is represented by another attorney. The latter attorney must consent to such a communication.*

Model Rule 4.3 -- *If the other side is not represented, an attorney must not give him or her the impression that the attorney is uninvolved. The attorney should not give this person advice other than the advice to obtain his or her own attorney.*

Model Rule 5.5(b) -- *An attorney shall not assist a nonattorney in the unauthorized practice of law.*

Model Rule 7.2 -- *An attorney may advertise services on radio, on TV, in the newspaper, or through other public media so long as the ad is neither false nor misleading and does not constitute improper in-person solicitation.*

Model Rule 7.3 -- *In person, an attorney may not solicit employment from a prospective client with whom the attorney has no family or prior professional relationship when a significant motive for doing so is the attorney's monetary gain.*

This rule is quite complex to apply. There is a fine line between advertising one's services and soliciting business. Advertising is distinguished by the fact that the attorney is contacting possible clients who may need legal services in the future. Improper solicitation usually requires that the attorney personally approach an individual who is in obvious need of legal services.

This rule also indicates the complexities of determining whether an action is unethical. The determining criteria are often quite subjective.

Model Rule 8.3 -- *Attorneys with knowledge that another attorney has committed a serious violation of the ethical rules must report this attorney to the appropriate disciplinary body.*

Model Rule 8.4 -- *An attorney must not engage in criminal or fraudulent conduct.*

CANONS OF THE ABA'S CODE OF PROFESSIONAL RESPONSIBILITY

As stated earlier, the preceding model rules were derived and expanded from the original Model Code of Professional Responsibility. The guidelines expressed in this code are the foundation of ethical standards for attorneys.

Canon 1 -- *A lawyer should assist in maintaining the integrity and competence of the legal profession.*

Canon 2 -- *A lawyer should assist the legal profession in fulfilling its duty to make legal counsel available.*

Canon 3 -- *A lawyer should assist in preventing the unauthorized practice of law.*

Canon 4 -- *A lawyer should preserve the confidences and secrets of a client.*

Canon 5 -- *A lawyer should exercise independent professional judgment on behalf of a client.*

Canon 6 -- *A lawyer should represent a client competently.*

Canon 7 -- *A lawyer should represent a client zealously within the bounds of the law.*

Canon 8 -- *A lawyer should assist in improving the legal system.*

Canon 9 -- *A lawyer should avoid even the appearance of professional impropriety.*

For Discussion Discuss the paralegal's role in law office ethics.

CONCLUSION

This chapter addressed the ethical considerations that paralegals, as representatives of their supervising attorneys, must keep in mind each day. Paralegals must always be aware that under the doctrine of *respondeat superior*, the actions of the paralegal are imputed to the supervising attorney. While some of the rules of professional conduct pertain exclusively to attorneys, the paralegal plays an important part in setting the ethical tone of the law office. The next chapter discusses the procedures that paralegals follow to efficiently manage the daily functions of the law office.

CHAPTER 9: LAW OFFICE MANAGEMENT FOR PARALEGALS

A paralegal's duties will often include managing and organizing the law office. In a small firm the paralegal may be responsible for the management of the entire office. In a larger firm it is more likely that the paralegal will be limited to organizing the schedule of his or her supervising attorney. Proper office management is crucial to the productivity of any law office; this chapter focuses on proper management of time, monthly billings, and files.

TIME MANAGEMENT

Time is the law firm's stock in trade, and the value of managing it cannot be overstated. Time management is rewarding and prevents tension and stress in a busy office. Through proper management of time, paralegals are able to anticipate deadlines, avoid last minute projects, and improve the attorney's billable hours. Good time management produces efficiency and profit; poor time management terminates legal careers.

Paralegals have an obligation to manage their own time and that of their attorneys. A good time management system is not complicated but requires an interactive use of simple devices, such as lists, calendars, and records. The best approach to time management is to perceive the law office as an integrated, interdependent unit.

The Calendar

Every law office must have a master calendar that is readily available to the attorney, legal secretary, and paralegal. All scheduling of court appearances, appointments, meetings, and other events must be made on that one calendar. Even the personal plans (vacations, personal days off) of the law office personnel should be blocked on the master calendar.

Redundant calendars, such as a firm calendar or attorney's traveling calendar, are useful and recommended but must be regularly cross-checked against the master calendar. When the paralegal transfers an entry to the redundant calendar, he or she places a dot or a check mark beside the entry on the master calendar. If the office maintains two supporting calendars, the paralegal places beside the entry a dot for one calendar and a check mark for the other. The lack of a proper mark on the master calendar indicates a void on the redundant system.

The Tickler System

Another indispensable tool to an attorney is a tickler system that automatically calls attention to something that must be done by a certain time. Any or all of the following three devices may be used to provide a reliable reminder system.

- Deadlines are entered on the office's master calendar, with an appropriate lead time. (In other words, if something is due on the 15th of the month, the reminder entry is placed on the 10th.)

- Deadlines are tracked through the use of a document control register. Every document that leaves or comes to the office receives a document control number. The paralegal regularly peruses the register for unfinished business and for approaching deadlines.

- Deadlines are noted through the use of a tickler file (also known as a suspense file), which consists of one folder for each of 31 days for the current month, one folder for each of 31 days for the next month, and one folder for each month of the year.

  The paralegal places in the file with sufficient lead time (5 or 10 days before the deadline) a duplicate copy of just the first page of every document leaving or coming into the office which requires a response or action. The paralegal must check the tickler file every morning upon coming into the office and enter the required actions on the personal work schedule or "to do" list. If the system is not checked regularly, the greatest amount of preliminary organization will be wasted and the system will fail.

The "To Do" List

Attorneys and paralegals tend to keep a file on their desks until a pending action has been completed. They keep the file out to avoid forgetting about what needs to be done, but the consequence is chaos; files lie on top, under, and behind the desk and things are still not accomplished on time. In theory, the best method is to handle paperwork only once. When paralegals start projects, they should finish them by working on one file at a time, putting it away, and then beginning the next project. However, in the real world, paralegals are interrupted by situations that take them away from the work at hand and often divert them to entirely different matters that demand immediate and sustained attention.

To successfully deal with the great amount of projects, paralegals should at the end of each day review the work in progress on their desks, make a notation of the project on their "to do" lists, and then put their files away. The paralegals' desks will be clear of clutter in the morning, and they will be able to focus on their agenda in a logical, prioritized manner. Putting files away will relieve the anxiety that clutter causes and allow the paralegals to work more efficiently.

Each individual worker in a law office should keep a separate "to do" list. This list may be as simple as a running list of projects that are entered only once and checked off as they are completed; it can be a handwritten "things to do today," which requires a daily review of pending work and priorities; or it can be a similar list kept in the computer. Different members of the staff may use different types of lists.

Recording Time

Time is the element in an attorney's inventory that has a direct dollar value, and it should be kept track of just as a jewelry store keeps track of its diamonds. A good time inventory system demands the same kind of simplicity as the agenda and deadline control systems previously discussed. In an integrated approach to time management, the tasks performed by paralegals have inventory values in the sense that the attorney can and should bill that work to the client. If, for example, the paralegal sets a hearing and prepares the notice, a service has been rendered to the client, who should be billed in an appropriate fashion.

There are a number of commercial systems available to keep track of time, some computerized and some manual. The procedure set forth here, however, requires no additional forms or computer control and meets a standard of simplicity. Both the paralegal and the attorney keep independent track of the time they spend on each task throughout the month. The attorney's time may be recorded on the attorney's calendar or on the "to do" list; the paralegal's time should be kept on his or her own "to do" list. The system also relies on the paralegal's keeping a carbon copy or computer record of all telephone messages.

On the designated cut off day in the billing period, which is usually monthly, the paralegal types a chronological list of the tasks performed, merges into it a list of the telephone messages, and submits it to the attorney. The attorney is responsible for comparing the paralegal's report with his or her own calendar. The billable tasks performed by the paralegal may then be added to the billing at the paralegal's hourly rate.

For Discussion Discuss the time management systems that would be most practical for small law offices. How would the systems differ in a large law firm? What time management skills do you employ in your daily life that apply to law office time management?

BILLING SYSTEMS

Accurate recording of time is the first vital phase in operating a profitable law office. The second vital step is to actually bill the clients for this time. The most efficient method for sending out bills on time is a simplified approach. Billing procedures vary widely depending upon the size and type of the practice and the number of accounts receivable it has. Some firms may have a department dedicated solely to billing; others may use an independent firm to prepare their billings. Small firms usually rely upon the paralegal to perform this task.

The answers to the following two questions will help determine the best procedures for a particular firm:

1. What amount of retainer does the firm usually charge?

   Although it still must provide an accurate accounting to the clients, a firm that receives large retainers that cover most of the case's expenses in advance has less of a need to send bills on a regular basis. That firm may opt for a system of sending a final, single statement to the client upon completion of a case.

   A firm that charges modest retainers usually finds itself with more accounts receivable. This firm will need to perform regular monthly billings to assure its receiving a regular cash flow.

2. What type of cases and clients does a firm attract?

   The firm that takes large cases that require a great deal of the attorney's time will naturally have fewer clients. It does not take a computer system or a significant amount of time to bill a few clients on a monthly basis, and the paralegal will usually set aside an hour or two each month to complete the entire billing.

> The typical general practice firm handling domestic law, traffic violations, bankruptcies, and small civil cases typically finds itself with a large number, even hundreds, of accounts receivable, which requires a larger investment of time and equipment. This type of practice usually puts many other demands on the paralegal's time, so it is critical for such a firm to establish a procedure that accomplishes monthly billings quickly and accurately without monopolizing the paralegal's time.

The procedure described in Figure 44 is one that can be used by a firm with more than one hundred active accounts receivable ranging from less than one hundred to several thousand dollars each. The procedure works with most of the widely used word processing programs, using the programs' math and macro capabilities.

For Discussion Discuss how computers have aided billing procedures for law offices.

Step	Performed by	Task
1	Attorney or Paralegal	prepares and reviews monthly time from hours posted on individual calendars.
2	Paralegal	posts hours to "HOURLOG" file, which automatically posts the hours to each client's ledger. (See Figure 45.)
3		reviews and "debugs" computerized client ledgers.
4		moves ledgers with accounts receivable to a temporary directory.
5		activates "billing" macro which (1) brings up the first ledger in the file, (2) produces a statement, (3) puts the statement produced on a temporary file to be printed later, (4) makes a memo of the statement on the ledger, (5) saves the ledger, and (6) brings up the next ledger, and repeats the process. This macro runs without further input of the paralegal and usually takes about 30 minutes to produce a complete billing.
6		prints the file with the monthly statements.
7	Attorney or Paralegal	reviews the completed statements (see Figure 46), sometimes making modifications, "writing off" certain amounts, or adding a handwritten personal note to the client.
8	Legal Secretary	folds and inserts each statement into a window envelope, with a #9 size or smaller return envelope.

Figure 44: Billing Procedure

EXAMPLE OF ONE CLIENT'S LEDGER USING THIS SYSTEM:

<

Ann S. Doe
12345 67th Avenue
Tacoma, WA 98416

@

2/25/93	Init Off Conf Cli; facts invest.	1.0	120.00		120.00
2/27/93	Statement				120.00
3-04-93	DISBURS FOR FILING FEE		88.00		208.00
3-11-93	DISBURS FOR SERVICE FEE		35.00		243.00
3/2/93	TConf Cli re legal separation	.7	84.00		327.00
3/4/93	OConf Cli; review pldngs, discuss moving out	1.1	132.00		459.00
3/9/93	TConfs Cli re husband's heart attack	.6	72.00		531.00
3/10/93	TConf Cli & OC re TRO & Power of Atty	.8	96.00		627.00
3/11/93	TConfs OC & Cli re Temporary Orders	.5	60.00		687.00
3/12/93	Set Hearing, prep notice; file fin aff	.6	72.00		759.00
3/13/93	TConf Cli re status	.3	36.00		795.00
3/14/93	TConf Cli re living arrangements	.3	36.00		831.00
3/16/93	TConfs Cli & Scott re restraining order	.6	72.00		903.00
3/17/93	TConfs w/client's sons	.6	72.00		975.00
3/19/93	ROA			150.00	825.00
3/23/93	TCons OC; Reschd 4-way; Disc. Temp Maint	.7	84.00		909.00
3/24/93	TConf Cli re 4-way	.4	48.00		957.00
3/26/93	TConf re T.O.	.4	48.00		1,005.00
4/01/93	Off Conf Cli re T.O.	.8	96.00		1,101.00
5/05/93	Motion/Order & Notice to Court	.5	60.00		1,161.00
5/07/93	TCons Scott & OC	.4	48.00		1,209.00
5/15/93	TConf Scott & OC re T.O.	.6	72.00		1,281.00
5/18/93	Prep Notice to Set	.3	36.00		1,317.00
5/19/93	Review of Materials re Chron Disease	.4	48.00		1,365.00
5/22/93	Review Clients Medical Records	.4	48.00		1,413.00
6/11/93	Statement				1,413.00

Figure 45: Sample Ledger

JACK LIDLE
ATTORNEY AT LAW
8910 South Evergreen
Olympia, WA 98502
(206) 956-1100

STATEMENT

Ann S. Doe
12345 67th Avenue
Tacoma, WA 98416

June 11, 1993
Balance Due this Statement: $ 1,413.00

ACCOUNT ACTIVITY

Date	Activity	Hrs	Charge	Credit	Balance
2/25/93	Init Off Conf Cli; facts invest.	1.0	120.00		120.00
2/27/93	Statement				120.00
3-04-93	DISBURS FOR FILING FEE		88.00		208.00
3-11-93	DISBURS FOR SERVICE FEE		35.00		243.00
3/2/93	TConf Cli re legal separation	.7	84.00		327.00
3/4/93	OConf Cli; review pldngs, discuss moving	1.1	132.00		459.00
3/9/93	TConfs Cli re husband's heart attack	.6	72.00		531.00
3/10/93	TConf Cli & OC re TRO & Power of Atty	.8	96.00		627.00
3/11/93	TConfs OC & Cli re Temporary Orders	.5	60.00		687.00
3/12/93	Set Hearing, prep notice; file fin aff	.6	72.00		759.00
3/13/93	TConf Cli re status	.3	36.00		795.00
3/14/93	TConf Cli re living arrangements	.3	36.00		831.00
3/16/93	TConfs Cli & Scott re restraining order	.6	72.00		903.00
3/17/93	TConfs w/client's sons	.6	72.00		975.00
3/19/93	ROA			150.00	825.00
3/23/93	TCons OC; Reschd 4-way; Disc. Temp Maint	.7	84.00		909.00
3/24/93	TConf Cli re 4-way	.4	48.00		957.00
3/26/93	TConf re T.O.	.4	48.00		1,005.00
4/01/93	Off Conf Cli re T.O.	.8	96.00		1,101.00
5/05/93	Motion/Order & Notice to Court	.5	60.00		1,161.00
5/07/93	TCons Scott & OC	.4	48.00		1,209.00
5/15/93	TConf Scott & OC re T.O.	.6	72.00		1,281.00
5/18/93	Prep Notice to Set	.3	36.00		1,317.00
5/19/93	Review of Materials re Chron Disease	.4	48.00		1,365.00
5/22/93	Review Clients Medical Records	.4	48.00		1,413.00
6/11/93	Statement				1,413.00

Figure 46: Sample Statement

FILE MANAGEMENT

Setting up and using a well organized filing system is crucial to good law office management. A filing system has one purpose: to make important papers instantly accessible. Generally, files are kept in alphabetical order by client; however, some firms use a numerical system which, while it requires a cross-reference index to clients, provides a way of aging cases chronologically and acts almost as a tickler system. Color coding of labels or folders is often used to distinguish types of cases, and file users often use colored dots or signals to identify whether the case is in the pretrial, trial, or post-trial stage.

The system of arranging papers within a file is most important to the file's later use. The simplest procedure is to place the papers in chronological order with the latest information on top. This system is very easy for the file clerk to set up, but as a file grows, the contents become less accessible. Therefore, many offices using this procedure keep a written log in the file as an index, which requires extra work for the file clerk but improves availability to specific documents.

A better system is to subdivide the folder into subject areas and thus eliminate the need for a log. This process requires that the clerk determine the proper position of the paper being filed but eliminates the requirement for the clerk to log the document. This system is also much more usable for the attorney. Such a file also serves the function of a trial notebook that the attorney can rely on during trial.

Subject areas in this kind of system vary greatly by the type of case. For instance, in a personal injury case they might consist of the following:

- Intake Information (client interview, facts investigation, photos, etc.)
- Initial Pleadings (the summons and complaint, and responsive pleadings)
- Discovery
- Depositions
- Notices
- Correspondence
- Notes

Subject areas in a domestic relations folder may include the following:

- Initial Pleadings (summons and petition, custody affidavit, response)
- Temporary Orders
- Discovery
- Financial Affidavits & Support Worksheets
- Property Division
- Notices
- Correspondence
- Notes

File folders are available which are already subdivided into 6 or 8 subject areas, each with its own clip. A popular alternative is to use 3-ring binders in place of file folders.

To conserve space in the work area and enhance ease of access, the main file cabinets in an office should be limited to containing cases in progress. Closed files should be maintained in proper order in a convenient location either at the office or in a separate storage facility. In most practices, the active file system remains a constant size, but the closed file system continues to grow over years. Therefore, it is highly recommended that offices that do not file active cases numerically do so for their closed files. Numerical filing allows one to box closed files and avoid the constant shuffling of files to accommodate newly closed ones.

There is no particular legal requirement to keep closed files indefinitely because the legal record is maintained by the court, but old files can be valuable as reference sources for new cases, and an old case may reopen, particularly in domestic relations cases. Sometimes a file must be recovered to provide information to the client. Therefore, it is the policy of most firms to keep case files indefinitely, especially if space permits.

To save space, many offices have a practice of reviewing closed files after a year and reducing them to only the most critical documents. The files of some types of cases are completely discarded after two or three years. Both of these actions are, however, low priorities in a small, busy office and not particularly cost effective. It is cheaper to rent space at a self storage facility and let the files grow.

For Discussion Discuss ways that paralegals can prevent files from becoming lost in the attorneys' and paralegals' offices.

CONCLUSION

The preceding chapters have examined the procedures, forms, and practices one needs to practice paralegalism. The next step is to implement this knowledge in the legal environment. The final chapter provides helpful information regarding the job search so that paralegals can make use of their newly acquired skills.

CHAPTER 10: JOB HUNTING TECHNIQUES FOR PARALEGALS

Nothing can replace hands-on experience for providing paralegal training. To gain this hands-on experience, the paralegal must find a job. The following chapter outlines sources for job leads and provides sample resumes and a sample freelance rate sheet.

THE JOB HUNT

The following section provides a listing of most of the sources for finding a paralegal position. When embarking on the job search, the paralegal must be creative; paralegal jobs are plentiful, but the paralegal must know where to look for them.

Traditional Sources

Although traditional sources should not be overlooked, the paralegal should not rely on them exclusively. Traditional sources include newspaper ads, placement services, and bar association referral services. Paralegal positions are rarely advertised in the newspaper, but it is a good idea to look for them there nonetheless. Placement services are good sources for positions; there are some agencies that specialize in the legal field and do not charge fees to the job hunter. Most state and local bar associations provide job referral services for paralegals and may include job listings in their newsletters.

Networking

Participating in paralegal associations and enrolling in paralegal courses are excellent ways to meet working paralegals who may know of job openings in their offices. Many paralegal positions are filled through word of mouth, so it is helpful to associate with people who are aware of available jobs.

The Telephone Book

The telephone book is one of the paralegal's best job sources. The paralegal should create a list of the phone numbers, addresses, and names of personnel managers for all local law firms, banks, insurance claims offices, and state and federal agencies. From this list the paralegal should make at least five to ten calls a day to inquire about openings and arrange for interviews. Once a firm has been contacted, the paralegal should mark the date of contact on the list and record its result. The key to this technique is patience and diligence; the time and effort involved will eventually pay off.

For Discussion Discuss what job hunt resources are available to paralegals in your area.

THE COVER LETTER AND THE RESUME

Often a prospective employer's first impression of the paralegal is based on that paralegal's cover letter and resume. Therefore, these two documents must have a professional appearance and be well-written and mistake free.

The Cover Letter

The cover letter serves two important functions: it presents a glimpse of the paralegal's qualities, and it serves as an example of the paralegal's business writing style. The cover letter introduces the paralegal to the prospective employer. It prefaces the resume and customizes it to the specific position offered by the employer. It should be long enough to present a clear picture of the paralegal's intentions but short enough to be read quickly.

The cover letter should be written with a specific position in mind. Therefore the letter should be directed to the person in charge of hiring for that position and definitely not "To Whom It May Concern." The content of the cover letter should tailor the information contained in the resume by highlighting the education and experiences that relate directly to the position. The paralegal should enthusiastically present the personality characteristics that he or she possesses that directly apply to the position and show how he or she is uniquely suited to the job.

In constructing the cover letter, the paralegal must keep in mind that the cover letter is an obvious representation of his or her writing style and professionalism. Therefore, the letter must contain properly spelled words and must be properly formatted and grammatically correct. The tone of the letter should reflect confidence and enthusiasm. To highlight this tone, the paralegal should end the letter by stating that he or she will call the employer in a few days to arrange for an interview. It is, of course, imperative that the paralegal actually call the employer as promised in the letter. An example of a cover letter is set forth in Figure 47.

The Resume

The paralegal should arrive at the job interview with a current resume if he or she has not submitted one previously. The resume should include the following: a career objective, work experience, special skills, education, honors and distinctions, and references. The career objective should be brief and specific; work experience and skills should be described using action verbs; and education and employment should be listed in reverse chronological order (most recent first). If the paralegal's work experience is limited, the resume should highlight the paralegal's related skills and education. (See Figures 48 and 49.) If the paralegal's education is limited, the resume should highlight experience. (See Figure 50.) If references are not listed on the resume, the paralegal should submit a separate sheet of paper listing at least two or three business and education references with addresses and telephone numbers.

Robin Jones
309 Cordoba Drive
El Paso, TX 78148
915) 789-1986

August 11, 199_

Ms. Mary Garza
Baker, Garza, and Johnson
1201 Main Street, Suite 700
El Paso, TX 78148

Dear Ms. Garza:

Mr. Norman Freeman, J.D., has informed me that you are seeking a paralegal to assist you with legal research, document drafting, client interviewing, and other duties related to personal injury litigation. I am confident that I possess the qualifications necessary to fill that position.

As outlined on the enclosed resume, I have recently completed the Paralegal Certificate Course offered by the University of Texas at El Paso through which I acquired the skills that a paralegal needs to efficiently assist an attorney during the litigation process. Because of my communications background I am especially proficient in legal writing, document drafting, and client relations. I welcome the challenge of legal research, and I am pleased with the results of my diligence in the law library. Samples of interoffice memoranda of law composed during the course demonstrate my research and writing abilities. Interacting with students at Beales Business College has given me a broad insight into the delicacies of relating to different personalities, experience which will translate well in my associations with your clients. I realize that success in law is dependent upon adhering to strict deadlines, and my experience as newspaper editor and adult education instructor has provided me with the discipline and organization essential to meeting deadlines.

I am eager to meet with you so that I may share my writing samples and discuss the possibility of assisting you. I will call your secretary on Monday to arrange an interview. Thank you for the time that you have spent in considering me for the paralegal position.

Very truly yours,

Robin Jones

Enclosure

Figure 47: Sample Cover Letter

Robin Jones
309 Cordoba Drive
El Paso, TX 78148
(915) 789-1986

CAREER OBJECTIVE:

To secure a position in a law office that utilizes my communication, research, and organizational skills.

EDUCATION:

07/94: University of Texas at El Paso, Paralegal Certificate Course

05/90: University of Arizona, Tucson, AZ
B.A. English, Top 1/3, GPA 3.5

COMMUNICATION SKILLS:

Taught writing and grammar skills to adults attending a two-year business program. Conducted community writing seminars on weekends and established a successful tutorial program and writing lab for a business school.

Edited and managed *The Speaker*, the University of Arizona's college newspaper, which was awarded first place in the 1989 and 1990 Press Association's college newspaper competition and first place in the National Collegiate Association's 1990 student newspaper competition.

Edited business correspondence for errors in vocabulary, spelling, diction, and usage.

RESEARCH SKILLS:

Researched the law as it related to the preparation of draft leases and other legal documents for an office management company.

ORGANIZATIONAL SKILLS:

Organized curricula for writing seminars. Set up and managed a writing lab for adults.

Managed all of the functions of an office management company. Proficient in typing (75 wpm), filing, word and data processing (WordPerfect and Microsoft Word, Lotus 123, and DBase).

Figure 48: Sample Resume Highlighting Skills

ROBIN JONES Page 2

EMPLOYMENT:

8/92 - present	Business Writing Instructor - Beales Business College, El Paso, TX
6/89- 7/92	Administrative Assistant - Office Management Company, Inc., El Paso, TX
9/87-5/89	Editor - *The Speaker*, University of Arizona student newspaper

DISTINCTIONS:

First Student Member of the Arizona Press Club, Phoenix, AZ
National Honor Society, University of Arizona, 1987, 1988, and 1989

REFERENCES:

SCOTT A. HATCH, J.D.
Director
UTEP Paralegal Certificate Course
22316 Sunset Drive
Golden, CO 80401
1-800-522-7737

LEIGH H. THOMAS
Dean of Beales Business College
1111 Main Street
El Paso, TX 78148
(915) 444-2222

JOSEPH C. ORTEGA
Office Management Company, Inc.
4125 Broadway
El Paso, TX 78115
(915) 666-4444

WRITING SAMPLES AND ADDITIONAL REFERENCES
AVAILABLE UPON REQUEST.

Figure 49: Sample Resume Highlighting Skills - Page 2

Dominique Gerrera
444 University Boulevard
Albuquerque, NM 87103
(505) 898-4991

Career Objective: To work as a paralegal in a law firm specializing in real property and contract law.

Employment:

1993-present **Legal Secretary**, Martinez, Johnson & Sullivan, Albuquerque, New Mexico

Drafted pleadings, motions, and discovery documents for a small law firm specializing in real property representation and breach of contract actions. Corresponded with clients; conducted client interviews; maintained office files; and managed client billing procedures.

1987-1993 **Receptionist**, David P. Hammond, J.D., Albuquerque, New Mexico

Maintained office files, managed client billings, corresponded with clients, and answered telephone calls for a general practice attorney.

1984-1986 **Real Estate Agent**, Neighborhood Real Estate Company, Bakersfield, California

Responsible for fifty percent of the total homes sold in a real estate office of four agents. Negotiated sales and lease agreements.

1981-1984 **Secretary**, Neighborhood Real Estate Company, Bakersfield, California

Corresponded with clients and performed all clerical duties for a busy real estate office, including data and word processing, typing, billing, filing, and phone answering.

Education:

June, 1997 Certificate of Completion, **University of New Mexico Paralegal Certificate Course**, Albuquerque, New Mexico
January, 1983-July, 1984 **Smith Business College**, Bakersfield, California, Courses in real estate, including real estate law
December 1980 Certificate of Completion, **Bakersfield Secretarial College, Secretary Seminar**, Bakersfield, California

Skills:

Proficient in WordPerfect 5.1, Lotus 123, and Harvard Graphics
Proficient in speaking and writing the Spanish language

References: Available upon request

Figure 50: Sample Resume Highlighting Employment

PARALEGAL SPECIALISTS, INC.

HOURLY RATE SHEET

INVESTIGATION:

Personal Injury and Traffic Accident Investigation	$25.00 plus $.30/ mile
Financial and Equity Investigation	$25.00 plus $.30/ mile
Skip-Tracing	$25.00 plus $.30/ mile
Surveillance	$25.00 plus $.30/ mile

CIVIL PROCESS SERVICE:

Local (within 15 miles of PSI's office)	$30.00
Distant (greater than 15 miles from PSI's office)	$40.00 plus $.30/mile

LEGAL RESEARCH AND WRITING:

Research of local, state or federal issues (including preparation of memoranda of law)	$30.00
Preparation of draft pleadings or forms for attorney perusal	$30.00
Preparation of draft discovery documents for attorney perusal	$30.00
Preparation of draft trial or appellate briefs for attorney perusal	$30.00

Fees for other projects will be negotiated on a case by case basis.

10% monthly discount to all firms providing at least thirty (30) hours of continuous monthly billings.

All billings from Paralegal Specialists., Inc., are payable upon receipt, and 12% interest is charged on all balances over 60 days delinquent.

Contact the experts in legal research, writing, and investigation:

PARALEGAL SPECIALISTS, INC.
123 Hill Street
Los Angeles, CA 90017
(310) 623-4555 FAX (310) 623-4545

Figure 51: Sample Rate Sheet

FREELANCE WORK AS A PARALEGAL

Many paralegals enjoy the freedom of self-employment. Instead of being employed by one legal entity, the freelance paralegal can contract his or her services with several different law firms or attorneys. The attorneys that contract with a paralegal benefit from the convenience of paralegal services without having to hire a new employee and pay the concomitant benefits. The paralegal as independent contractor benefits from the freedom of setting his or her own hours and, with the computer technology of WESTLAW and LEXIS, the ability to work from one's home or freelance office.

In deciding whether to work freelance or not, the paralegal has many considerations. Ethically, paralegals must have all work supervised by a licensed attorney; therefore all legal documents must be signed by an attorney. Paralegals are not allowed to give legal advice, so paying clients must be advised by an attorney. Paralegals may perform legal research, prepare draft documents, and conduct investigation and interviewing. Many freelance paralegals center their activities on these areas.

The freelance paralegal must also be willing to accept the financial responsibility of self-employment. As with any new business, the owner must have sufficient capital to set-up the business and keep it running until it has built up a large client base and steady accounts receivable. Freelance paralegals are responsible for their own health insurance and social security taxes, so careful bookkeeping is essential.

Once a paralegal has taken into consideration ethics and finances and is willing to accept the responsibility of self-employment, the paralegal must create a business plan. If the paralegal has worked in law firms or the court system, he or she already has contacts for potential clients. New and experienced paralegals should also take advantage of the job sources mentioned previously in this chapter to obtain a client base.

Before they approach a prospective client, freelance paralegals should have rate sheets explaining the types of services they provide and the hourly cost for each service. New businesses should start by charging a low hourly rate, such as $15.00 -$20.00, depending on the location of the business. As the business grows and becomes more experienced, the paralegal may charge as much as $45.00 in metropolitan areas. Figure 51 provides a sample rate sheet.

Freelance paralegals should also consider printing business cards and stationery to professionalize their images. The business cards and letterhead must clearly state that the paralegal is a paralegal and not an attorney.

For Discussion Discuss what skills and experiences are important for you to emphasize in your cover letter and resume.

CONCLUSION

Job hunting can be quite challenging, but persistence and careful planning will enhance a paralegal's chances for success. Paralegals are employed in many areas and with many entities. Law firms, government agencies, banks, insurance companies, and corporate legal divisions supply the most jobs for paralegals, but other businesses that require employees to have knowledge of the law, such as real estate and public utility companies, also employ paralegals. The procedures, forms, and practical exercises in this book will go far to prepare paralegals to work in virtually all capacities of the law. With practical experience, the paralegal will develop skills that will supply a lifetime of career satisfaction.

INDEX TO FIGURES

Index to Tables

General Index